"It is important to recognize that the mental health of children and youth is essential to their overall health. For youth with serious mental health challenges, that require residential intervention, this book provides outstanding information and resources about strategies that work. Reading this volume will help practitioners implement cutting-edge services, improve the ability to engage and empower youth and families, and lead to better outcomes and life trajectories."
—**David Satcher**, MD, PhD, Director, Satcher Health Leadership Institute and Poussaint-Satcher-Cosby Chair in Mental Health at Morehouse School of Medicine, Atlanta, Georgia, and 16th U.S. Surgeon General

"This practical 'how-to' guide is a must-own resource for anyone working with children, adolescents, and families who need intensive residential services. It provides the latest research and best practice examples on delivering effective interventions in residential settings in order to help high-need young people and their families achieve the goals of safety, permanency, and well-being."
—**Bryan Samuels**, Former Commissioner, Administration for Children and Families, and Executive Director, Chapin Hall at the University of Chicago, Illinois

"For too long, residential treatment has been viewed outside of the system of care. This book turns that view on its head and promotes best practices that are truly consistent with the values and principles of a system of care, especially the message of family-driven and youth-guided care. Any parent who has needed to place their child in residential care will welcome the values and practices that are advocated in this book."
—**Jane A. Walker**, Executive Director, Family Run Executive Director Leadership Association (FREDLA)

"This readable and practically-focused volume contains an impressive array of 'best practices' for improving and enhancing residential interventions for youth and their families. It offers numerous creative examples of how present-day residential programs are moving their services to align with systems of care principles. These promising exemplars underscore the critical need for rigorous, empirical research to establish high-quality, evidence-based residential practices."
—**James K. Whittaker**, PhD, Charles O. Cressey Endowed Professor Emeritus, The University of Washington, School of Social Work, Seattle, Washington

"This book provides residential programs across the country with the research and innovative practices needed to create partnerships with families, young people, and communities that lead to long-term positive outcomes. A required read for all CEOs, managers, and staff."
—**Richard "Richie" Altman**, Chief Executive Officer, Jewish Child Care Association, New York, New York

"This outstanding book shows how residential interventions can be an essential part of services and supports when delivered using the system of care values and principles. The innovations and best practices detailed in this volume will guide the field for years to come, and demonstrates how high-quality, youth- and family-driven services can improve outcomes."

—**Beth A. Stroul**, MEd, President, Management & Training Innovations, McLean, Virginia

"Quality residential treatment is a critical part of a home and community-based system of care. Children who have mental health challenges and experienced significant trauma need a healing environment and relationships that help them and their families to move forward and thrive. This book serves as a critical guide to all organizations who want to embrace proven values and best practices that help all children and families have the greatest opportunities to succeed."

—**Susan N. Dreyfus**, President and CEO of the Alliance for Children and Families and former Secretary of the Washington State Department of Social and Health Services

"This book recognizes the integral role residential interventions can and should have in a comprehensive system of care. I recommend this best practice guide as a critical resource for anyone wanting to improve residential services for children, youth, and their families."

—**Joy Midman**, Executive Director, National Association for Children's Behavioral Health, Washington, DC

"For years young people and champions of the residential field have looked for a way to actualize a method of including youth voice in treatment, with the ultimate goal of returning home. This book will help make that happen. It captures the field like no other product or training and gives the system champions the tools they need to succeed."

—**Martin Rafferty**, Executive Director, Youth MOVE. Oregon, Eugene, Oregon

"As leaders in designing policies and systems for the care of young people with behavioral and emotional challenges, the authors offer a practical and comprehensive guide to improving services and outcomes. They explain how residential interventions can be successful only when the youth and families are involved in care and there are adequate supports and services in the community. This book points the way to a brighter future for youth, families, care providers, and the communities they live in."

—**Linda Rosenberg**, MSW, President and CEO, National Council for Behavioral Health, Washington, DC

Residential Interventions for Children, Adolescents, and Families

Now more than ever there is a need to ensure that best practices are being used in residential programs. As the focus on costs and outcomes increases, residential programs must clearly demonstrate that the interventions provided are efficient and effective. Readers will learn how to:

- create strength-based, empowering, and healing environments;
- better engage and partner with children, adolescents, and families in meaningful ways;
- support those who have experienced trauma and loss, and prevent and eliminate the use of restraint and seclusion;
- respect and include cultural indices in practices;
- train, mentor, supervise, support, and empower staff about how to deliver promising and best practices, and evidence-informed and evidence-based interventions; and
- track long-term outcomes and create funding strategies to better support sustained positive outcomes.

This book encourages readers to think strategically about how agencies, communities, and systems can identify and implement actions that lead to positive change and work more collaboratively to improve the lives of children, adolescents, and their families who have experienced emotional and behavioral life challenges.

Gary M. Blau, PhD, is a clinical psychologist and chief of the Child, Adolescent, and Family Branch at the Substance Abuse and Mental Health Services Administration (SAMHSA). In this role, he provides national leadership for children's mental health and for creating systems of care across the United States.

Beth Caldwell, MS, is the director of the National Building Bridges Initiative and a faculty member for the National Center for Trauma-Informed Care and Alternatives to Restraint and Seclusion. She has provided consultation to residential, hospital, and community programs across the United States and internationally.

Robert E. Lieberman, MA, LPC, is the CEO of Kairos, a multiservice intensive mental health program for youth, young adults, and families, and public policy chair of the American Association of Children's Residential Centers. He trains and consults with children's residential, hospital, and community programs nationally.

Residential Interventions for Children, Adolescents, and Families

A Best Practice Guide

Edited by Gary M. Blau, Beth Caldwell, and Robert E. Lieberman

NEW YORK AND LONDON

First published 2014
by Routledge
711 Third Avenue, New York, NY 10017

and by Routledge
27 Church Road, Hove, East Sussex BN3 2FA

Routledge is an imprint of the Taylor & Francis Group, an informa business

Library of Congress Cataloging-in-Publication Data

Residential interventions for children, adolescents, and families : a best
    practice guide / [edited] by Gary M. Blau, Beth Caldwell, and Robert E. Lieberman.
        pages cm
    1. Child psychotherapy—Residential treatment.   2. Adolescent
psychotherapy—Residential treatment.   3. Mental health services.
I. Blau, Gary M.
    RJ504.5.R47   2015
    616.89'140835—dc23   2014003302

ISBN: 978-0-415-85455-9 (hbk)
ISBN: 978-0-415-85456-6 (pbk)
ISBN: 978-0-203-74349-2 (ebk)

Typeset in Minion
by Apex CoVantage, LLC

Contents

About the Editors

Gary M. Blau, PhD, is a licensed clinical psychologist and is currently the chief of the Child, Adolescent and Family Branch of the Center for Mental Health Services. In this role he provides national leadership for children's mental health and for creating systems of care across the country. Prior to this, Dr. Blau was the bureau chief of quality management and director of mental health at the Connecticut Department of Children and Families (DCF) and the director of clinical services at the Child and Family Agency of Southeastern Connecticut.

Dr. Blau has been selected for and appointed to numerous positions, including chairperson of the National Association of State Mental Health program director's division of children, youth and families, and clinical faculty at the Yale Child Study Center. He has also received many awards, including the prestigious Pro Humanitate Literary Award for literary works that best exemplify the intellectual integrity and moral courage required to transcend political and social barriers to promote best practice in the field of child welfare, the Governor's Service Award in Connecticut, the Phoebe Bennet Award for outstanding contribution to children's mental health in Connecticut, and the Making a Difference Award presented by Connecticut's Federation of Families for Children's Mental Health. He was also proud that upon the occasion of his leaving Connecticut, the governor proclaimed December 12, 2003, as "Dr. Gary Blau Day."

For his national work, Dr. Blau received the Outstanding Achievement Award presented by the National Association of Children's Behavioral Health, and was the recipient of the 2009 HHS Secretary's Award for Meritorious Service for his national leadership in children's mental health. In 2011, he was the first recipient of the Rock Star Award, presented by Youth MOVE National, Inc. for "being a true champion for the youth movement and advocate for youth voice." This award has now been named the Dr. Gary Blau Award and is given yearly to a mental health professional who has distinguished him- or herself as a voice for youth. He was also the 2013 recipient of the Substance Abuse and Mental Health Services Administration (SAMHSA) Administrator's Award for "unparalleled and innovative leadership in children's mental health."

Dr. Blau has authored more than 50 professional publications and has been the editor of six books. His most recent book, co-edited with Dr. Sylvia Fisher and Jeff Poirier, is *Improving Emotional and Behavioral Outcomes for LGBT Youth.* Other volumes include a book he co-edited with Dr. Phyllis Magrab, titled *The Leadership Equation: Strategies for Individuals Who Are Champions for Children, Youth and Families;* a book co-edited with Beth Stroul, titled *The System of Care Handbook: Transforming Mental Health Services for Children, Youth and Families;* and a book co-edited with Thomas Gullotta, titled *The Handbook of Childhood Behavioral Issues: Evidence Based Approaches to Prevention and Treatment.* Dr. Blau received his PhD from Auburn University (Auburn, Alabama) in 1988. He has been happily married since December of 1982 to his best friend, Gwenn Blau, and they are incredibly proud of their wonderful adult children, Jennifer and her husband, Riley, and Andrew and his partner, Kristina.

Beth Caldwell, MS, has been the principal consultant in Caldwell Management Associates since 1980, a group dedicated to supporting organizations who serve individuals with complex needs and their families. Ms. Caldwell focuses on helping organizations support the individuals they serve to achieve their hopes and dreams and to realize their full potentials. Examples of recent and/or continuing consultation contracts include the following:

- Since 2004, through a contract with the New York State Office of Mental Health, Ms. Caldwell has provided consultation and training to improve the use of best practices in out-of-home programs serving children and their families.
- Ms. Caldwell is a consultant and trainer for the New York City (NYC) Health and Hospitals Corporation. She has provided training and on-site reviews for NYC's 11 hospital behavioral health programs—including emergency and forensic services, and adult and child/adolescent units—which are focused on reducing coercive interventions and promoting recovery, resiliency and trauma-informed care.
- Since 2000, through a contract with the Massachusetts Department of Mental Health, Ms. Caldwell has provided consultation and training for a statewide initiative to develop strength-based and trauma-informed alternatives to the use of coercive interventions in child and family serving hospitals and intensive residential treatment programs.
- Ms. Caldwell is also a consultant and trainer for initiatives in New South Wales, Australia, and Ontario, Canada, to promote trauma-informed, family-driven, and youth-guided care, and to prevent the use of coercive interventions in hospital and residential programs.

In addition to her consultation activities, Ms. Caldwell has served as the director of the national Building Bridges Initiative (BBI), an initiative dedicated to helping child- and family-serving residential programs, and their community counterparts, incorporate best practices to achieve sustained positive outcomes. She has also served as a faculty member for the National Center for Trauma-Informed Care and Alternatives to Restraint and Seclusion (formerly the Office of Technical Assistance), under the National Association of State Mental Health Program Directors.

As an individual consultant and faculty member, Ms. Caldwell has provided training, consultation, and/or on-site reviews for programs in all 50 U.S. states and several countries on trauma-informed care, resiliency and recovery, family-driven and youth-guided care, and preventing the need for coercive interventions, specifically restraint and seclusion.

Well versed in the literature on effectiveness in the fields of mental health, substance abuse, child welfare, juvenile justice, and education, and using state-of-the-art training and consultation practices, Ms. Caldwell has been called upon frequently to provide technical assistance and to develop written documents related to topical issues. She has authored multiple publications and received both national and state recognition and awards for her tireless work to ensure that compassionate, respectful, and effective services are provided to individuals and families. She and her husband, Bob, are blessed with four adult children and their spouses, and have three adorable grandchildren, Sophia, Amara and Aidan.

Robert E. Lieberman, MA, LPC, is the chief executive officer of Kairos (formerly Southern Oregon Adolescent Study and Treatment Center [SOASTC]), an intensive-treatment services agency for children, youth, young adults, and their families with serious mental and behavioral disorders. Over the 36 years since its inception, he has helped the organization achieve statewide and national acclaim for its innovative work, quality, accountability, and leadership in implementing best practices.

Mr. Lieberman has been integrally involved in advancing public policy for children's mental health nationally as well as helping forge the regulatory and policy environment for children's mental health services in Oregon. He serves on several state and national advisory committees and task forces, including the following:

- National Building Bridges Initiative: Steering committee and co-chair of Outcomes Workgroup, Center for Mental Health Services, SAMHSA
- Public Policy Chair, American Association of Children's Residential Treatment Centers (AACRC); former president of that national organization
- Advisory committee, Think:Kids, Massachusetts General Hospital
- Oregon Children's System advisory committee, Addictions and Mental Health Division, Department of Human Services (co-chair from October 2005 through December 2012)
- Statewide Wraparound Initiative Advisory Committee, Department of Human Services (co-chair through 12/2012)
- Nonprofit Association of Oregon, board of directors

In the past, Mr. Lieberman served for 10 years on the Oregon Commission for Children and Families (gubernatorial appointment) and was also appointed by the governor to the Metrics Workgroup of the Oregon Health Plan Transformation and the Mental Health Alignment Workgroup. He has had national appointments to the Outcomes Roundtable for Children and Families of the

Center for Mental Health Services, SAMHSA; the Professional and Technical Advisory Committee of the Joint Commission; and the Child Welfare League of America Advisory Committee on Best Practices in Behavior Management (Restraint and Seclusion Initiative).

Mr. Lieberman has received many honors, including the Children's Mental Health Advocate of the Year (Oregon Council of Child and Adolescent Psychiatry); the Heart of Change award (YouthMOVE Oregon); the AACRC Life Fellow award; Oregon Mental Health Award of Excellence; Asante Spears Healthcare Award; and the Josephine County Asset Builder Award. He has published national papers and journal articles, and makes presentations at statewide and national conferences. Mr. Lieberman conducts trainings, consultations, and workshops with treatment centers, schools, college seminars, governmental entities, juvenile justice facilities, and parent groups. He is a certified trainer in Collaborative Problem Solving. Mr. Lieberman also operates his own practice as a professional counselor for youth and their families.

About the Contributors

Marvin Alexander, MSW, LCSW, is a founder and current board president of Youth MOVE National, Inc., a national organization devoted to uniting the voices and advocating for the causes of youth and young adults with lived experience in America's child and youth serving systems.

Sue Beck, MSW, prior to overseeing residential and community-based programs in New Hampshire and Massachusetts, focused on developing MPA's first Community Based Programs, Project Connect & Solid Foundations. Over the past 13 years, Sue has served youth and families in a variety of capacities. Sue is a graduate of the University of New Hampshire Graduate School of Social Work. Sue's true passion is in providing hands-on leadership; creating unique, strength-based youth and family-driven programs; navigating around any barriers to care; and finding solutions as well as being a change agent to better meet the needs of children, youth, and families.

Christopher Bellonci, MD, is a board-certified child/adolescent and adult psychiatrist, associate professor at Tufts University School of Medicine, and senior psychiatric consultant at Walker, in Massachusetts. Dr. Bellonci is president of the American Association of Children's Residential Centers. Dr. Bellonci provides consultation, lectures and technical assistance nationally on the subjects of child psychiatric practice, foster care, special education, residential treatment, and mental health best practices.

Samantha Broderick, LSW, is the provider/member communications manager at PerformCare New Jersey, an AmeriHealth Caritas Company, the administrative service organization for the NJ Children's System of Care. She has a focus on system-level outcome data and 15 years of experience in public serving systems for children, with a focus on transition-age youth and residential care.

Julie Collins is the director of standards for practice excellence at the Child Welfare League of America (CWLA) and oversees CWLA's standards of excellence for child welfare services. She provides training and technical assistance to public and private child-welfare-related agencies on best practices and system transformation.

Jim L. Dalton, PsyD, HSPP, CSAYC, is a licensed child psychologist and president and CEO of Damar Services, Inc. He is the author and chief investigator of an Indiana-based residential reform model, Integrated Services. Dalton is the founder of Indiana's training and credentialing body for professionals working with youth with sexual behavior problems (IN-AJSOP). He also serves as superintendent of Indiana's first public charter school for children with autism.

John Damon, PhD, is the chief executive officer for Mississippi Children's Home Services. He is the president of the National Association for Children's Behavioral Health in Washington, DC. Dr. Damon has served as the featured presenter at many state, regional, and national conferences and has published in multiple peer-reviewed journals.

Maryann Davis, PhD, is an internationally recognized expert on services and policies for transition-age youth and young adults with serious mental health conditions. Her research emphasizes the development of evidence-based interventions for this population that facilitate mental health treatment; support education, training, and work goals; and reduce antisocial behavior.

Brian M. Denietolis, PsyD, is assistant professor of psychiatry at the University of Massachusetts Medical School and a licensed psychologist at the University of Massachusetts Adolescent Continuing Care Unit. His research interests include child maltreatment and interpersonal trauma; evidence-based treatments for trauma and trauma-related disorders; and the intersection between attachment theory and emotion regulation.

Wendy den Dunnen is a PhD candidate in clinical psychology at the University of Ottawa. She received her master's degree in counseling psychology at Western University in 2011 and has been involved in research on residential programs since 2010. She currently works under the supervision of Dr. John S. Lyons.

Richard Dougherty, PhD, CEO of DMA Health Strategies has more than 30 years of consulting experience in improving quality and managing change for public health and human services. He is the lead on several major projects working on SAMHSA's Assessing the Evidence Base series in psychiatric services.

Marc Fagan, PsyD, is the associate director for youth services at Thresholds in Chicago. Dr. Fagan oversees comprehensive programs for young adults with serious mental health conditions (SMHC) and participates in numerous policy groups improving the lives of vulnerable youth. As a National Network on Youth Transition for Behavioral Health (NNYT) Consultant, he trains audiences nationally regarding best practices for young adults.

Sylvia Fisher, PhD, is the director of the Office of Research and Evaluation, Office of Planning, Analysis and Evaluation, in the U.S. Health Resources and Services Administration. Areas of professional expertise include evaluation, survey design, LGBT youth, and children's mental health. She co-edited *Improving Emotional and Behavioral Outcomes for LGBT Youth: A Guide for Professionals.*

Deborah Green, MSW, program administrator, DFPS Child Protective Services, has more than 30 years' experience in child welfare. She has held multiple leadership positions and was Texas's first disproportionality division administrator. Ms. Green is published in journals, articles and co-edited *Challenging Racial Disproportionality in Child Welfare: Research, Policy, and Practice.*

Kaitlyn Harrington, MPA, MA, is a public health advisor at the Substance Abuse and Mental Health Services Administration (SAMHSA) in the Center for Mental Health Services, Child, Adolescent and Family Branch. She serves as a government project officer on the Children's Mental Health Initiative System of Care grants. Previously, Ms. Harrington provided direct service to youth and young adults involved with the child welfare and juvenile justice systems. She holds a master's degree in public administration from American University and a master's degree in clinical psychology from Fairleigh Dickinson University.

Kevin Ann Huckshorn, PhD, RN, MSN, CADC, is the Delaware director of the Division of Substance Abuse and Mental Health. Ms. Huckshorn is a licensed and certified mental health nurse and substance abuse clinician with 30 years of experience, working in a variety of public and private behavioral health organizations. She has published on topics including violence, treatment adherence, trauma-informed care, and workforce development and co-authored a book with William Anthony, PhD, titled *Principled Leadership in Mental Health Systems and Programs,* in 2008. She led the development of the evidence-based best practice titled *The Six Core Strategies* in 2012.

Jonathan Huefner, PhD, is a research scientist in the Boys Town National Research Institute for Child and Family Studies. His recent research has focused on psychotropic medication use in residential-care youth, the impact of family-involvement on youth outcomes, and examining negative peer contagion in residential care.

Joe Anne Hust first entered the world of children's mental health as an advocate for her own child. She managed a peer-to-peer support division for a large mental health agency. Ms. Hust is a national trainer and manager for the Institute for Innovation and Implementation at the University of Maryland School of Social Work and is a co-chair of the National Building Bridges Initiative's Family Advisory Network.

Vivian H. Jackson, PhD, is faculty for the National Center for Cultural Competence and the National Technical Assistance Center for Children's Mental Health, Georgetown University Center for Child and Human Development, where she provides technical assistance and consultation related to cultural and linguistic competence for the Substance Abuse and Mental Health Services Administration's Children's Mental Health Initiative.

Karen A. Johnson is the single parent of a special needs adult son. Karen was orphaned at birth and raised in out-of-home settings. Her life path is an example of grace, perseverance and receiving support from friends, family, and colleagues. Karen has worked for three years as a residential peer advocate for SCO Family of Service in New York City.

Neil Kelly is affiliated with Keene State College in New Hampshire, where he is studying education and science. He has significant experience working with children and youth with an array of needs and has a focal interest in social justice. Mr. Kelly has received numerous awards for leadership and academic excellence.

Lacy Kendrick Burk is the founder and CEO of Youth Engagement Solutions, in Hattiesburg, Mississippi, and current executive director of Youth MOVE National, Inc. Ms. Kendrick Burk obtained her bachelor of arts degree in psychology at Missouri State University and her master's degree in counseling psychology at William Carey University.

Jeremy C. Kohomban, PhD, is the president and CEO of the Children's Village and the president of Harlem Dowling. He has been honored by CWLA for exemplary innovative service resulting in positive and successful outcomes for children and by the Alliance for Children and Families with the Samuel Gerson Nordlinger Leadership Award.

Anne Kuppinger is a national consultant and the director of training and credentialing for Families Together, in New York State. She collaborates on a number of initiatives with IDEAS Center at the New York University Child Study Center and is a member of several workgroups of the Building Bridges Initiative.

Janice LeBel is a licensed, board-certified psychologist with 30 years' experience in public mental health, overseeing a statewide system of care for children and adolescents. She has led several system transformation efforts and has researched, published, and presented nationally and internationally on restraint/seclusion economics and prevention, trauma-informed care, and related topics.

Jody Levison-Johnson is a deputy assistant secretary at the Louisiana Office of Behavioral Health, where she is responsible for leadership and oversight of all publicly funded behavioral health services. Previously, Jody was the vice president of management organization in New York, where she provided consulting on system of care and special initiatives across the country.

Eric Lulow is a public health advisor with the Substance Abuse and Mental Health Services Administration, and an alumnus of the foster care and mental health systems. Eric obtained his bachelor's degree in social work from Middle Tennessee State University and works to promote the voice of young adults.

Thahn Ly is a psychology student at the University of Ottawa.

John S. Lyons, PhD, is a professor and endowed chair of child and youth mental health research at the University of Ottawa and the Children's Hospital of Eastern Ontario. He is the editor of *Residential Treatment for Children and Youth.*

William Mclaughlin is an independent consultant, assisting human services organizations to assess and modify practices to improve outcomes for families, children, and youth. Bill draws from his prior experience with New York State's Child Welfare/Juvenile Justice Agency in senior level positions, where he focused on transforming systems through effective collaboration.

Raquel Montes, the lead youth advocate at Casa Pacifica Centers for Children and Families, has been recognized nationally as a youth advocacy leader. She serves as the co-chair of the Building Bridges Initiative's Family/Youth Partnerships Workgroup and chair of its youth advisory group. Raquel earned her bachelor of arts degree in psychology in 2011.

Jim Nyreen, a graduate of the Columbia University School of Social Work, is the assistant executive director of St. Charles-Ottilie (SCO) Family of Services, in New York, overseeing residential, in-home, young adult, crisis respite, and in-home services. Jim serves on the board of the New York State (NYS) Coalition for Children's Mental Health Services.

Sherry Peters, MSW, ACSW, is the director of the Psychiatric Residential Treatment Facility (PRTF) Waiver Initiative at Georgetown University's National Technical Assistance Center for Children's Mental Health. Previously, Sherry worked in Pennsylvania on statewide children's mental health policy and program development and as a therapist in residential and community settings.

Brenda R. Plante is a parent consultant and has helped build the Parent Partner Program with the New Hampshire Division of Children, Youth and Families. After a successful reunification with her daughter, Ms. Plante has focused her efforts on how to successfully engage and provide support to parents during family team meetings, and making sure the parent voice is heard. Most recently, she was hired by Child and Family Services of New Hampshire as the FAIR (Family Assessment and Inclusive Reunification) Permanency Facilitator. In this role, Ms. Plante facilitates meetings that are designed to ensure the safety and well-being of children by bringing together family support professionals, juvenile protection and probation officers, and child protection staff to work in partnership with the family.

Michael Rauso, PsyD, MFT, is the division chief for the Los Angeles County Department of Children and Family Services, Service Bureau 1—Metro North and West L.A. As part of his responsibilities he oversees the county's residentially based services demonstration project, called Open Doors, and the Wraparound program.

G. Olivia Ríos is a doctoral student in counseling psychology at Indiana University. Her research and clinical interests include sexual health within relationships and the use of language in therapy with bilingual clients. She is a provider of mental health services in Spanish and an advocate for monolingual Spanish speakers.

Thomas L. Sexton is a professor in the Department of Counseling Psychology and the Center for Evaluation and Education Policy (CEEP) at Indiana University. He is author of *Functional Family Therapy in Clinical Practice* (2010) and the *Handbook of Family Therapy* (2003, 2014), a licensed psychologist, a Fellow of the APA, and a board-certified family psychologist and editor for *Couple and Family Psychology: Research and Practice*.

Diane L. Sondheimer is deputy chief for the Child, Adolescent and Family Branch, Federal Center for Mental Health Services, SAMHSA. She is a nationally recognized leader with more than two decades of experience in developing, implementing, administering, and evaluating local, state, and national health and mental health programming to improve the quality of life for children, adolescents, young adults, and their families.

Deborah Strod, MSW, has been an associate at DMA Health Strategies since 2006. She supports the firm's youth residential outcomes work. Previously, Ms. Strod spent 10 years in technology transfer at Partners Health Care System. She received an MSW from Boston University in 1989, and an A.B. from Harvard College in 1986.

Kristin Williams-Washington, PsyD, earned her master's and doctorate degrees in clinical psychology from the American School of Professional Psychology at Argosy University, in Washington, DC. Her areas of interest include underserved populations, cultural disparities, and military and veteran issues. She is currently a public health advisor at the Substance Abuse and Mental Health Services Administration in Rockville, Maryland.

Acknowledgments

Making this book happen was truly a labor of love and could not have occurred without the passion and commitment of so many people along the way. First, we would like to thank and acknowledge the work and dedication of our authors. They had to endure a rigorous editorial process, and it is their collective experience and expertise that makes this volume meaningful. We also want to acknowledge the assistance of our consulting editor, Kaitlyn Harrington. Kaitlyn helped organize the details of the project and kept us on track along the way. We deeply appreciate her efforts.

We want to particularly thank and acknowledge the youth and family members, who, based on their lived experience, provided their expertise, ideas and feedback—some by serving as lead or co-authors, some by reviewing draft materials, and some by helping shape the values and principles that comprise this book. In the creation of this volume, we tried to model partnership and collaboration, and we hope we were successful.

This book would also not have happened were it not for the knowledge, skill, passion and hard work of the national Building Bridges Initiative (BBI) Steering Committee, the members of the many BBI workgroups, the dedicated persons and organizations who have endorsed the BBI Joint Resolution, and the countless hard-working staff who every day operationalize BBI principles. The commitment of the professionals, advocates, families, and youth involved in BBI has contributed in so many ways to make this book a reality.

We also want to say thank you to our families. Gary wants to specifically acknowledge his amazing wife of more than 30 years, Gwenn, and their fabulous children, Jennifer and her husband, Riley, and Andrew and his partner, Kristina. And, by the time this book is printed, Jennifer and Riley will have welcomed a baby boy into this world (Gary and Gwenn's first grandchild). For him, the amount of affection and pride he has for his family is endless. They are a constant source of inspiration and support, and he loves them so very much. Gary also wants to acknowledge his parents, Burt and Louise Blau, and his mother-in-law, Elaine Brittner. During the preparation of this book, Gary experienced the profound and unexpected loss of his mother, and her humor, kindness and compassion serves as a reminder for how the unconditional love of caring parents is the foundation for success. He has been blessed with such love from birth and through marriage.

Beth would like to first thank all of the youth and families she has served over the years, both those who were able to benefit from her supports and those for whom what was offered fell short. If she had had the knowledge in this book—when she was serving Joey, she may have found him a family; she may have truly listened to George's mother; she may have viewed Vinnie's behaviors through a "trauma lens" and not a "behavioral lens."

In addition, Beth would like to thank her amazing parents, Bob and Rose Lepping; they have served as loving role models throughout her life. Her appreciation for her husband (Bob), four children (Carey, Oliver, Maggie and Lia), her son-in-law and daughter-in-law (Chris and Katrina), and her three grandchildren (Sophia, Amara, and Aidan) has no bounds. She is so lucky to have and is so proud of this group of caring, good and healthy family members.

Bob would like to thank his wife Kerrie for her enduring patience with his many professional commitments and long hours, and for her support and perspective on tough issues related to the agency and to the local, state, and national systems. His children, Maggie and Aaron, are an inspiration to him, solid human beings, following their passions, responsible, and compassionate. He would like to especially posthumously acknowledge his parents, Reuben and Sara, who raised his brothers and him to believe that it is their place to stand up with compassion and sensitivity in support of those who are downtrodden in any way, and to advocate and work for social justice and peace in the world.

Bob would also like to recognize the young people and families who have taught him so much over the years, and thank them for their courage and resilience. Finally, influenced by a quote from Albert Einstein that was on his father's wall throughout his career, Bob believes that "man is here for the sake of other men," and that his outer and inner life and work is built upon the labors of countless others, living and dead, to whom he stands in deep gratitude.

We can think of no greater calling than a career dedicated to improving the lives of children, adolescents, and families. If this is your calling, this book is dedicated to your ongoing efforts.

Gary M. Blau, Beth Caldwell, and
Robert E. Lieberman

1 Improving Outcomes in Residential

Kaitlyn Harrington, Kristin Williams-Washington, Beth Caldwell, Robert E. Lieberman, and Gary M. Blau

Introduction

Now more than ever there is a need to ensure that best practices are being used in residential programs. As the focus on costs and outcomes increases, residential programs must demonstrate that the interventions provided are efficient and effective. The good news is that we now know more than ever before about the core components of successful residential interventions and what works. There is research, practice-based evidence, and compelling testimony from children, adolescents and families about what works. For example, we have learned how to:

- create strength-based, empowering, and healing environments;
- better engage and partner with children and adolescents (hereafter referred to as "youth") and families in a meaningful way;
- support those who have experienced trauma and/or loss, and prevent and strive to eliminate restraint, seclusion, and all coercive interventions;
- respect and include cultural indices in practices;
- train, mentor, supervise, support, and empower staff to deliver promising, best practice and evidence-informed, and evidence-based interventions; and
- track long-term outcomes and utilize different funding strategies to better support sustained positive outcomes.

Simply put, we know how to improve residential interventions, and this book was developed to push the field towards implementation of the practices that can achieve the best possible outcomes. Moreover, to assist you, the readers, in implementing best practices, this book contains information, tips, and resources to guide you and inform your work.

Purpose

The purpose of this book is to help organizations, communities, and systems improve the services and the integration of care that both families and youth experience as they navigate residential programs from intake to the transition to community programs and supports. Each chapter is intended to provide practical, specific strategies and promising and best practices that can be used to improve services and outcomes for youth who receive residential interventions due to emotional, behavioral, and/or other life challenges, and their families. The aim is for the readers to gain how-to ideas that will enable them to make a difference in the services and supports provided for youth and families receiving residential interventions. Specifically, the goals of this book are to:

- articulate the values necessary to successfully incorporate residential interventions in the array of services for youth and families;
- identify and describe effective, promising, best and evidence-informed and evidence-based practices that residential leaders can use in partnership with community providers, advocates, families and youth, and funders to improve services and long-term outcomes;
- provide references, resources, and documents that create a blueprint for residential providers to improve practice and long-term outcomes (this how-to approach will include techniques for self-assessment and planning, culture change strategies, benchmark and outcomes management, strategies to incorporate youth and families in services and organizational decision-making, and a framework for policy, financing, and system development); and
- identify the steps and content needed to create action plans to develop and implement principles and practices that will lead to sustained, positive outcomes for youth and families who are touched by residential interventions and systems.

Audience

Generally, this handbook should prove useful to individuals with the desire to learn the fundamental principles of best and evolving residential practices and apply them to their existing knowledge of services and supports in residential settings. The audience for this handbook includes:

- residential and community staff across all disciplines and all levels;
- medical and clinical staff at all levels of an organization;
- residential and community provider executive leadership, including members of boards of directors;
- policy makers at the city, county, state, and federal levels, and within tribes and territories;
- advocates;
- individual families and youth; and
- anyone who is interested in improving residential service delivery and outcomes at the federal, state, local, and provider levels.

The truth is, from our perspective, this book can be used by a whole host of people who are interested in improving residential services. The key is whether and how you, the reader, will use the information to effect real change.

Are Residential Services Even Necessary?

Our belief is that *residential* is an important component of a comprehensive system of care. Thus, the simple answer is yes, although not in the way residential services have historically been delivered. The first chapter of this book delves into the history of residential programs in order to better understand what has worked and what has not. It is important to focus on what does not work to develop alternatives that do and that become best practices. There is also a need to understand the tension and friction that has existed between residential providers and community-based providers. This tension arose due to philosophical differences in approaches, roles, and responsibilities. For example, community-based providers have often believed that residential interventions lack a solid evidence base to validate their effectiveness, and that they keep youth too long. On the other hand, residential providers have believed they are often unsupported by their community-based colleagues, particularly when they are needed to assist with appropriate discharge planning. To address these tensions, and to support the need to include both community and residential programs as part of the service array, the Building Bridges Initiative (BBI) was developed.

Building Bridges Initiative

The Building Bridges Initiative has been a key driver in the development, implementation, and measurement of the practices and strategies contained in this volume. BBI is a national effort to promote a dialogue and provide a framework to address the identified issues through advancing consistent principles and coordinated practices across the full array of residential and community-based services (see www.buildingbridges4youth.org). The initiative emphasizes closely coordinated partnerships and collaborations between residential and community-based service providers, families, youth, advocates, and policy makers to successfully introduce and implement change in both policies and practices in communities across the nation. This framework has resonated throughout the field as states, counties, national associations, residential and community program practitioners, families, and youth have formally or informally used BBI products and principles to improve practices.

The BBI core principles were developed after a summit meeting that occurred in June 2006. As a result of this meeting, which was attended by residential and community leaders, government officials and policy makers, advocates, and families and youth, a joint resolution (JR) was created, reflecting consensus about service delivery values and principles (see www.buildingbridges4youth.org/products/joint-resolution). The JR includes a list of specific values and principles that, if shared and implemented, would result in positive improvements for agencies, communities, and systems, and improved long-term positive outcomes for youth and families served. These core values and principles are shown in Table 1.1. The BBI framework is designed to implement these

Table 1.1 Building Bridge Initiative Joint Resolution Principles

• Youth Guided	• Individualized and Strength-Based
• Family Driven	• Collaborative and Coordinated
• Culturally and Linguistically Competent	• Research-Based
	• Evidence- and Practice-Informed
• Comprehensive, Integrated, and Flexible	• Sustained Positive Outcomes

principles and to strengthen partnerships between community based and residentially based treatment and service providers, policy makers, advocates, families, and youth and to generate an effective approach for all service providers. It has been used as a platform for practice innovation that has led to transformation of residential services in locations across the country and that has galvanized significant work towards long-term positive outcomes.

Terminology

It is important to understand some of the terminology that will be presented in this book. The term *youth* essentially means children and/or adolescents. Furthermore, when the context indicates only *children* or *adolescents* or *young adults*, these terms will be used. Sometimes, for example, in order to mix it up, someone might use *young people* or may want to specify a particular age group. In addition, this book will primarily use the term *residential intervention*, as this book will be applicable to many different types of residential programs (e.g., residential treatment programs, group homes, residential centers). We believe that *intervention* is a term that more accurately reflects the current research regarding residential best practices and moves the use of *residential* away from being a placement, or a place to live. The focus is not primarily about what happens inside a residential program but rather on using the residential resource as a short-term intervention to identify a range of practices that can occur in the homes of families and in their communities.

Chapter Organization and Topics

The following topics will be covered in subsequent chapters within this book. Each section will provide information, guidance, tips, and other resources useful to those providing, funding, licensing, advocating for, or receiving residential interventions:

- *Family-Driven Care—Family driven* means families have a primary decision-making role in the care of their own children as well as the policies and procedures governing care for all youth in their community. Chapter 3 will explore, through tangible and practical examples, the importance and benefits of incorporating family-driven care as well as some of the challenges providers can face and how to overcome them.

- *Clinical Strategies for Engaging Families*—The goal of Chapter 4 is to describe, define, and identify evidence-informed and evidence-based clinical strategies that can be used successfully to engage and motivate youth and families in the entire treatment and support process.
- *Youth-Guided Care*—*Youth guided* means that youth are engaged as equal partners in creating systems change in policies and procedures at the individual, program, and community levels. Chapter 5 will help readers understand the principles, strategies, and challenges in developing and maintaining a youth-guided program.
- *Cultural and Linguistic Competence*—*Cultural competence* is the integration and transformation of knowledge, behaviors, attitudes, and policies that enable policy makers, professionals, caregivers, communities, youth, and families to work effectively in cross-cultural situations. Chapter 6 provides a framework for residential programs to address cultural diversity through the effective infusion of cultural and linguistic competence in all program interactions and engagements.
- *Trauma-Informed Care*—*Trauma-informed care* (TIC) is an evolving organizational approach to recognizing and responding to the impact of trauma. Chapter 7 reviews definitional challenges related to TIC; examines the facets of creating interpersonal and physical environments, services, and supports that are sensitive to the issue of trauma; and provides pragmatic recommendations to successfully implement TIC.
- *Linking Residential With Community*—Residential and community services have historically operated as discrete and separate entities. This separation creates unnecessary fragmentation in treatment, family participation, discharge, and continuity of care. Chapter 8 will discuss the benefits of linking residential and community efforts and provides examples and strategies for doing so in a productive, meaningful, and effective way.
- *Preventing Restraint and Seclusion*—Chapter 9 offers historical and current perspectives on seclusion and restraint (S/R) with children and adolescents, discusses the dangers associated with these interventions, and reviews a strategic framework to prevent their use. In addition, key youth and family roles in innovative S/R reduction approaches and effective pragmatic resources to facilitate practice change are provided.
- *Working With Youth in Transition*—The transition to adulthood is a continuous process of rapid psychosocial change that starts accelerating at age 16 and only begins to slow considerably in the late 20s. Chapter 10 describes the unique needs of youth in transition as well as innovative approaches to supporting the transition to adulthood for youth who have serious mental health conditions and are receiving residential interventions.
- *Promising and Best Practices in Medication*—Chapter 11 will summarize the research and concerns regarding the use of psychotropic medication

for children and adolescents, address research and issues specific to residential programs, discuss youth and family involvement in decisions about the use of medications, and identify best practices in the use of psychotropic medication during residential interventions for youth.

• *Initial Steps in the Culture Change Process*—Chapter 12 adds to the available knowledge base by highlighting examples of how individual programs that have a strong commitment to transformation have initiated the cultural change process that is necessary for achieving long-term positive outcomes for youth and families that are touched by a residential intervention.

• *Transformation Towards Long-Term Outcomes*—Chapter 13 delves further into the transformational change process, discussing the importance of addressing change and transformation at all levels of the organization. It identifies common barriers to change and provides a real-world example of one agency's transformation towards documented long-term positive outcomes.

• *Tracking Long-Term Positive Outcomes*—Chapter 14 discusses the needs for and uses of outcomes information, the selection of appropriate measures, and the use of a practice-based research approach to implement outcomes tracking.

• *Policy and Monitoring: Federal and State Examples of Transformation*— With the growing interest by states, counties, and local providers to operationalize best practices overall, and specifically the BBI principles and best practices in residential transformation efforts, there has been a corresponding interest for information about funding options to facilitate this development. Chapter 15 provides information about different federal, state, county, and local funding options that are currently used or could possibly be used in transforming residential interventions. A range of fiscal and policy best practices are discussed.

• *Successful International Approaches to Residential Services*—Chapter 16 will highlight various residential interventions around the world and identify themes that may impact successful outcomes.

How to Use This Book

This book creates an opportunity for residential providers and their funders to have, in one volume, a host of practices and strategies that have emerged over the past several years, stimulated most especially by the national Building Bridges Initiative, which will improve the outcomes they are able to achieve in partnership with the youth and families they serve. We hope the book stimulates more thought, innovation, and examples about how this work is being extended by:

• forging relationships across all vested parties (families, youth, community, residential providers, policy makers, and advocates);

• creating promising practices and protocols to facilitate positive long-term outcomes;

- supporting and advocating for families and youth while they are receiving residential interventions; and
- endorsing, implementing, and then sustaining adherence to the BBI joint resolution principles.

As you read this book, we encourage you to think strategically about how to implement the core values discussed in it. How can your agency create and implement plans that lead to positive change? How can your agency or community address sustained postresidential outcomes? How can your service system cooperate more effectively and work more collaboratively to improve the lives of children and adolescents who have experienced behavioral, emotional, and/ or other life challenges, and their families? These are the critical questions that we hope this book will help you address in the pages to come. Happy reading!

2 Residential Interventions

A Historical Perspective

Robert E. Lieberman and Wendy den Dunnen

Residential treatment came into existence roughly 70 years ago and has since grown and changed extensively (Abramovitz & Bloom, 2003). These changes, and the proliferation of approaches and vast differences between residential programs, have confounded efforts to define residential treatment (Maluccio & Marlow, 1972). For the purposes of this chapter, the more inclusive terms *residential programs* or *residential interventions* will be used. This chapter will briefly capture the history of what have been considered best practices in residential programs and also identify areas and research that have been missed.

Original Context

Orphanages and reformatories, which came into existence in the 1830s, were the predecessors to residential programs. Their purpose was to find a home for disenfranchised or troubled youth or to protect youth from inept parenting. These programs were designed to provide employment, education, and rehabilitation. Obedience was seen as essential to a functional society, and reformatories were especially well known for coercive approaches, such as isolation and severe corporal punishment. By the early 20th century, it was believed that troubled youth had not yet learned to cope with difficult life situations and authority, and thus these youth could be "cured" through treatment. Problems were then diagnosed as character disorders, such as psychopathic or sociopathic personality disorders, and were viewed as treatable. This perspective on youth problems set the stage for the emergence of residential programs in the United States in the 1940s and 1950s (Abramovitz & Bloom, 2003; Fees, 1998). With the perceived need for psychological treatment, facilities for dependent youth, those with special needs, and juvenile delinquents were converted into residential programs (Leichtman, 2006). As part of this approach, it was also believed that youth problems were a result of unfit parenting, and parents were kept at a distance and not included in treatment (Small, 2003).

Early and Emerging Approaches

Early emerging residential programs/approaches fell into three practice focal points: individual, skills-based, and group/milieu treatment.

Individual

Initially, psychoanalytic individual therapy was the treatment of choice. Programs essentially took long-term psychoanalysis done in individual, outpatient settings and applied it to residential settings. The goal was to provide youth with an emotionally corrective experience through a positive relationship with a mental health professional. The purpose of the institution was to prevent youth from deteriorating between therapy sessions. However, it was quickly identified that this approach neglected daily routines and the impact of the group on youth functioning (Abramovitz & Bloom, 2003). The effectiveness of psychoanalytic/psychodynamic therapy was also not clearly demonstrated with youth in residential programs (Foltz, 2004).

Behaviorism offered another individual approach to treatment, premised on the supposition that youth are motivated to change in response to established rewards and consequences for their actions. There is minimal and only dated support for behavioral approaches to residential interventions, and studies that examine behavioral approaches in isolation and the long-term effects of behavioral approaches are not common in the residential literature (Garret, 1985; Hair, 2005). In addition, more recent literature argues that point and level systems can actually be detrimental to youth because of their punitive nature, negative focus, absence of individualization, and lack of generalization into the home (Mohr, Martin, Olson, Pumariega, & Branca, 2009).

Skills Based

There has been research support for teaching skills actively within residential programs and not focusing solely on individual therapy sessions (e.g., Anglin, 2004). A specific skills-based model, the teaching family model (TFM), developed in 1967, provides residential care in a family-like setting, with behavioral interventions focused on decreasing symptomatic behavior and generalizing positive skills to the home. Studies on TFM have shown improvements in academic and behavior problems and parent–child relationships (James, 2011). However, some studies have highlighted that improvements were not maintained over time, with the suggestion that, in order to maintain gains, aftercare services are needed (Oswalt, 1991, as cited in Frensch & Cameron, 2002).

Another early skills-based milieu model that is still being used in some residential programs is Re-Education of Children with Emotional Disturbance (Re-Ed). Employing a psychoeducational, social learning, ecological approach to change, the model focuses on individual strengths to teach youth more adaptive ways of functioning. Studies of Re-Ed have demonstrated effectiveness up to 2 years postdischarge but were not conducted with control groups (Hooper, Murphy, Devaney, & Hultman, 2000).

Group/Milieu

In early residential programs, a significant focus was on the milieu—the treatment environment—as a key intervention. The belief was that putting individuals in a group and using life experiences and group dynamics in the moment would foster adaptive life skills (Leichtman, 2006). In this approach, still broadly used, intervention is viewed as being more effective at the time problems occur rather than retrospectively in individual therapy. Therefore, direct care workers are essential therapeutic agents (Maier, 2012; Zimmerman & Cohler, 1998), working during the "other 23 hours" (Trieschman, Whittaker, & Brendtro, 1969).

Models of group/milieu treatment that emerged include positive peer culture, which uses the peer group as the main agent of change, and Circles of Courage, a framework that promotes resiliency through instilling values of belonging, mastery, independence, and generosity. Studies of these and other milieu treatment approaches have identified treatment gains while youth are in the residential setting, but with consistent findings that gains are not sustained posttreatment (e.g., Frensch & Cameron, 2002; Lee & Perales, 2005). Rather, posttreatment adaptation has shown to be strongly correlated with the posttreatment environment (Bates, English, & Kouidou-Giles, 1997). Overall, despite some qualified but hopeful results demonstrated from these early approaches and models, a review of residential programs found that the various individual, skills-focused, and milieu/group approaches did not have effect sizes exceeding .30; there has been no real research support for long lengths of stay or separations from family (Hair, 2005).

Growth of Residential Programs Despite Concerns

Despite criticism of the limited evidence of long-term change; the lack of consistently utilized, evidence-supported models; the separation of youth from parents; and the lack of attention to family problems, community adaptation, or aftercare planning, there was still a proliferation of residential programs (Leichtman, 2006; Maluccio & Marlow, 1972). This likely occurred because there was some success of these early approaches/models for youth while they were in the residential setting, and because places to live were needed for youth who were demonstrating increasing problems. However, additional concerns arose, which focused on the violation of youth's civil rights that occurred in institutional settings as well as the longer-term institutional mentality fostered by residential placement. Policy makers codified these concerns with initiatives mandating placement in the least restrictive environment possible and that youth not be removed from the home unless they were at risk of imminent danger. Residential care, while still used, became identified as the "treatment of last resort" (Lieberman, 2004).

With the absence of compelling evidence in the face of these demands, the emphasis of residential programs began to shift to case management, cost containment, and accountability (Small, 2003). The medical model became a common approach; many programs shifted from a social service to a mental health, diagnostic orientation, in which managed care and psychopharmacology were key features. Differing shorter term models came into use as medication made it possible to manage behavioral/emotional problems in outpatient/community settings (Leichtman, 2006).

Another significant criticism of residential programs focused on its use of seclusion and restraint (S/R). In the late 1990s, policy makers began to pay more attention to this practice, stimulated in large part by reports of deaths of youth in residential programs. Inquiries found that the use of S/R often did not meet the standard criteria of danger to self or others. State and federal mandates required reduction in S/R use. Many in the field responded with defensiveness, but, as effective alternatives were identified, S/R began to be used less and is no longer considered a helpful practice in residential programs (Miller, Hunt, & Georges, 2006; Nunno, Holden, & Tollar, 2006).

The absence of clearly identified best practice residential models in the face of the challenges occurred within a context in which residential programs might be described as undesirable but indispensable. The increasing number of youth in the child welfare system and insufficient community-based alternatives to support and treat these individuals led to frequent, nondiscriminating use of residential interventions as the sole alternative, despite the increasing prevalence of concerns regarding its effectiveness and practices.

Recent Best Practice Directions

Family therapy was introduced to residential programs in the 1970s. Research found that family-centered approaches that had begun to emerge were showing effect sizes of .81 (Garret, 1985), the postinstitutional environment was essential to a youth's functioning, and services provided to youth and family following residential care were more related to eventual outcome than to youth symptoms at admission or discharge. Nonetheless, many programs did not implement family/community engagement recommendations until more than a decade later (Leichtman, 2006). Later research further identified that work with the family was crucial in all phases of treatment, and that coordination among agencies administering aftercare to youth and family improved success (Hair, 2005).

While individual agencies sought to apply the implications of this evidence, the field as a whole did not. Families found themselves blamed, and providers struggled to know how to incorporate families in response to what appeared to be "poor parenting" or abuse. However, the evolution of the field was influenced by the emerging family voice, which compellingly insisted that providers regard families as equal partners, and understand that even when families make mistakes with their children, they still love them and want to promote healing.

The field also began to shift as service providers became more community integrated through the provision of linked residential-community services. Of further influence has been the emergence of a robust body of neurobiological science that has demonstrated the impact of adverse experiences on youth throughout the life span and the importance of creating environments that are trauma informed, that foster dialogue with youth and families, and that promote partnerships that will support youth and their families while helping them develop the self-regulatory, relational, and cognitive skills to be successful in the community (e.g., Hair, 2005; Perry, 2002).

The Building Bridges Initiative (BBI), organized initially by the Substance Abuse Mental Health Services Administration, is a significant national effort to identify and promote the compilation of best practices that have been identified for residential programs within the context of a comprehensive community system of care. BBI has done much to reduce the long-standing polarization between residential programs and community proponents, identifying practices based on evidence. This represents the first comprehensive effort to identify a research-supported role of residential interventions in community systems and to provide best practice resources to families, youth, advocates, residential providers, and community partners that will help youth grow and thrive (Blau et al., 2010).

Summary

Although greater numbers of youth and families are served in community settings, residential interventions continue to be widely needed and utilized despite questions about their definition, cost, effectiveness, and linkages to other key services (James, 2011). The challenge for the field is to utilize and implement what is known about best practices, historically and currently:

- Relationships and continuity of relationships are the key to promoting positive experiences.
- Engagement of family and support in the community are critical mediators in producing long-term positive outcomes.
- Being trauma informed and empowering family and youth voice in non-coercive environments supports the development of important long-term skills.
- Outcome monitoring and accountability are essential.

The rest of this book will address the best practices in these many dimensions that will help this important service build on its strengths to make important and enduring differences in the lives of youth and families.

References

Abramovitz, R., & Bloom, S. L. (2003). Creating sanctuary in residential treatment for youth: From the "well-ordered asylum" to a "living-learning environment." *Psychiatric Quarterly, 74*(2), 119–135.

Anglin, J. P. (2004, June). Creating "well-functioning" residential care and defining its place in a system of care. *Child and Youth Care Forum, 33*(3), 175–192. Kluwer Academic-Plenum.

Bates, B. C., English, D. J., & Kouidou-Giles, S. (1997). Residential treatment and its alternatives: A review of the literature. *Child & Youth Care Forum, 26*(1), 7–51.

Blau, G. M., Caldwell, B., Fisher, S., Kuppinger, A., Levison-Johnson, J., & Lieberman, R. (2010). The Building Bridges Initiative: Residential and community-based providers, families, and youth coming together to improve outcomes. *Child Welfare, 89*(2), 21–38.

Fees, C. (1998). No foundation all the way down the line: History, memory and "milieu therapy" from the view of a specialist archive in Britain. *Therapeutic Communities 19,* 167–178.

Foltz, R. (2004). The efficacy of residential treatment: An overview of the evidence. *Residential Treatment for Children & Youth, 22*(2), 1–19.

Frensch, K. M., & Cameron, G. (2002, October). Treatment of choice or a last resort? A review of residential mental health placements for children and youth. *Child and Youth Care Forum, 31*(5), 307–339.

Garret, C. J. (1985). Effects of residential treatment on adjudicated delinquents: A meta-analysis. *Journal of Research in Crime and Delinquency, 22*(4), 287–308.

Hair, H. J. (2005). Outcomes for children and adolescents after residential treatment: A review of research from 1993 to 2003. *Journal of Child and Family Studies, 14*(4), 551–575.

Hooper, S. R., Murphy, J., Devaney, A., & Hultman, T. (2000). Ecological outcomes of adolescents in a psychoeducational residential treatment facility. *American Journal of Orthopsychiatry, 70*(4), 491–500.

James, S. (2011). What works in group care? A structured review of treatment models for group homes and residential care. *Children and Youth Services Review, 33*(2), 308–321.

Lee, B., & Perales, K. (2005). Circle of Courage: Reaching youth in residential care. *Residential Treatment for Children & Youth, 22*(4), 1–14.

Leichtman, M. (2006). Residential treatment of children and adolescents: Past, present, and future. *American Journal of Orthopsychiatry, 76*(3), 285–294.

Lieberman, R. E. (2004). Future directions in residential treatment. *Child and Adolescent Psychiatric Clinics of North America, 13*(2), 279–294.

Maier, H. W. (2012). What's old is new: Fritz Redl's teaching reaches into the present. In W. C. Morse (Ed.), *Crisis intervention in residential treatment: The clinical innovations of Fritz Redl* (pp. 15–27). New York, NY: Taylor & Francis.

Maluccio, A. N., & Marlow, W. D. (1972). Residential treatment of emotionally disturbed children: A review of the literature. *The Social Service Review, 46*(2), 230–250.

Miller, J. A., Hunt, D. P., & Georges, M. A. (2006). Reduction of physical restraints in residential treatment facilities. *Journal of Disability Policy Studies, 16*(4), 202–208.

Mohr, W. K., Martin, A., Olson, J. N., Pumariega, A. J., & Branca, N. (2009). Beyond point and level systems: Moving toward child-centered programming. *American Journal of Orthopsychiatry, 79*(1), 8–18.

Nunno, M. A., Holden, M. J., & Tollar, A. (2006). Learning from tragedy: A survey of child and adolescent restraint fatalities. *Child Abuse & Neglect, 30*(12), 1333–1342.

Perry, B. D. (2002). Childhood experience and the expression of genetic potential: What childhood neglect tells us about nature and nurture. *Brain and Mind, 3*(1), 79–100.

Small, R. (2003). Charting a new course. In *Contribution to residential treatment* (pp. 72–76), compiled from the 2003 annual conference. Washington, DC: American Association of Children's Residential Centers.

Trieschman, A. E., Whittaker, J. K., & Brendtro, L. K. (1969). *The other 23 hours: Child-care work with emotionally disturbed children in a therapeutic milieu.* New York, NY: Aldine de Gruyte.

Zimmerman, D. P., & Cohler, B. J. (1998). From disciplinary control to benign milieu in children's residential treatment. *International Journal of Therapeutic Communities, 34,* 123–146.

3 Moving Toward Family-Driven Care in Residential

Joe Anne Hust and Anne Kuppinger

Overview

Definition and Principles

Family-driven care sees every child as a part of a family, and every family as a valued partner. As fundamental as this seems, practice does not always reflect this vision. Becoming family driven requires that all facets of providers' work with families honor the life each child leads as a part of a family and community.

Each family will approach the process of becoming stronger differently—based on its unique dreams, preferences, challenges, and resources—and that requires that each plan of care and collaboration be individualized and flexible. In many instances, a commitment to family-driven care means taking steps to help the youth and his or her family reconnect. It may mean working to engage, without judgment, families who have lost hope. Sometimes, a commitment to family-driven practice means reaching out to extended family, friends, and community members to support the creation of a new family for a child.

There is a shift in family-driven care to seeing the child in the context of family rather than in the context of treatment. A commitment to family-driven practice requires that the program welcome family members with open arms and make them part of the team. Even if the family is not able to participate fully, staff members "meet them where they are" with every expectation that they can be empowered to play a more active role.[1] Organizations that value family-driven care actively critique common beliefs, biases, and practice habits that stand in the way of developing respectful partnerships with families. Agency leaders consistently communicate that family-driven principles will guide every policy and every interaction with families. They support this philosophy through training, supervision, and quality-improvement strategies that review every aspect of the program to determine if it supports family engagement, invests in family strengthening, empowers families to make informed choices and decisions, and supports the creation of a plan of care that responds to the family's vision for change.

DEFINITION OF FAMILY-DRIVEN CARE

Families have a primary decision-making role in the care of their own children as well as the policies and procedures governing care for all children in their community, state, tribe, territory, and nation. This includes

- choosing culturally and linguistically competent supports, services, and providers;
- setting goals;
- designing, implementing, and evaluating programs;
- monitoring outcomes; and
- partnering in funding decisions.

Guiding Principles of Family-Driven Care

1   Families and youth, providers and administrators embrace the concept of sharing decision making and responsibility for outcomes.
2   Families and youth are given accurate, understandable, and complete information that is necessary to set goals and to make informed decisions and choices about the right services and supports for individual children and their families.
3   All children, youth, and families have a biological, adoptive, foster, or surrogate family voice advocating on their behalf and may appoint them as substitute decision makers at any time.
4   Families and family-run organizations engage in peer-support activities to reduce isolation, gather and disseminate accurate information, and strengthen the family voice.
5   Families and family-run organizations provide direction for decisions that impact funding for services, treatments, and supports, and advocate for families and youth to have choices.
6   Providers take the initiative to change policy and practice from provider driven to family driven.
7   Administrators allocate staff, training, support, and resources to make family-driven practice work at the point where services and supports are delivered to children, youth, and families and where family- and youth-run organizations are funded and sustained.
8   Community attitude change efforts focus on removing barriers and discrimination created by stigma.
9   Communities and private agencies embrace, value, and celebrate the diverse cultures of their children, youth, and families, and work to eliminate mental health disparities.
10 Everyone who connects with children, youth, and families continually advances their own cultural and linguistic responsiveness as the population served changes, so that the needs of the diverse populations are appropriately addressed. (National Federation of Families for Children's Mental Health, 2008)

Research and Impact

Several studies support practices that are consistent with family-driven care in residential. They report improved outcomes when there is increased family involvement, shorter lengths of stay, and stability and support in the postresidential environment (Walters & Petr, 2008). The national Building Bridges Initiative (2007) found that the strongest predictor of posttransition success from residential treatment, after education, is support from the family. Residential leaders who focus on sustained success in the community postdischarge (versus the more limited objective of youth making improvements between admission and discharge) have found that it is imperative that they work with families in their homes and communities to achieve positive long-term outcomes (Dalton, 2011; Hust, 2010; Kohomban, 2011; Leichtman, Leichtman, Barber, & Neese, 2001; Martone, 2010).

Organizations are at different places in their journeys to become more family driven. In some programs, staff members still believe that their job is to "fix" the youth and protect the child from his or her family as they hold tight to the idea that "staff know best." Other programs are moving towards family-driven care, but family-driven practice is not implemented throughout all of the organization's functions. Some programs have spent years developing their family-driven care approaches and continue to learn and transform. This chapter summarizes some key issues for consideration, provides examples of family-driven practice, and explains the critical role that family partners play in engaging families and promoting change.

Every Child Has a Family

In many instances, the child's parent(s) are involved, and they will be the primary partners with the residential program (perhaps with the assistance of other relatives and friends chosen by the family). The expectation is that their child will return to their home or that they will be actively involved as their child transitions to living on his or her own in the community. Sometimes, a relative is actually parenting the child, either through an informal arrangement or as the result of a kinship placement. In these situations, it is important to involve both the child's parent(s) and the individual providing day-to-day care. [2]

For many children, however, the first step will be to find someone who is able to be a permanent family resource. Programs that commit themselves to achieving this goal have developed effective techniques; they are guided by the conviction that this is their responsibility, that it is integral to fulfilling their mission, and that it is possible. They reject the assumption that some children will not have permanent families.

The Family Preservation Team of Catholic Community Services of Western Washington State developed Family Search and Engagement (FSE), a set of practices designed to locate, engage, connect, and support family resources for youth. The underlying goal of this program is to

> move youth from a place where they don't hear "I love you" to a place where they can hear it and feel it every day. This comes from family, relatives, and others who love them. Frequently these youth are involved in the child welfare system, have experienced multiple placements with non-relatives and have lost contact with their extended family members. (Catholic Community Services of Western Washington, 2013)
>
> EMQ Families First, a multiservice agency serving youth and families in over 30 counties in California, describes a process they call Family Finding, which is a program that: helps reconnect children with safe, healthy families and speed their recovery from emotional trauma. Using internet search technology, [they] are able to find biological family members for children in the system. Once [they] have identified family members, [they] work to reestablish relationships and explore ways to find a permanent family placement for the child. (EMQ FamiliesFirst, 2012)

Joining With Families

Empathy is important in this work of becoming family driven. Change comes when providers stand in the shoes of a mother about to leave her child with virtual strangers, a grandmother being asked to come to meetings when she is exhausted, a parent who feels the pull of siblings who need attention, or a father being left to carry out a plan that others wrote that does not seem like it will work for his family. Imagine that this is your family and your child. What would need to change so that you felt safe, trusted, listened to, believed, empowered, and supported? The following are a few examples of strategies that programs are using to change the family experience in positive ways.

A Compassionate Admissions Process

The first contact with families should be welcoming, respectful, culturally and linguistically competent, and sensitive to the issues and challenges the family is facing. This is the foundation for building strong relationships. The following are a few examples of how residential programs are improving the way they interact with families during this very difficult process:

- Family partners conduct a "walk through" and provide feedback to program leadership on the placement and intake procedures from a family perspective.
- Families are offered preplacement visits to determine if the program meets their needs. Youth can stop by in the evening or have an overnight if desired. (Every family receives a follow-up phone call to answer any questions.)

- Staff members review the Building Bridges Initiative's Youth and Family Tip Sheets to help the family ask questions (National Building Bridges Initiative Family Advisory Group, 2010; National Building Bridges Initiative Youth Advisory Group, 2010).
- The date and time of the admission is planned so the youth does not miss a special activity and for the convenience of the family.
- Peer youth advocates and family partners are present. Families are given contact information of a parent who has received services and who has offered to provide information and a family partner (if possible) for ongoing support.

> The first night I left my child at the residential program I received a phone call from the program's family partner. She asked if I had any questions about what would happen next, and explained that she had been in my shoes several years before with her own child. She answered all of my questions and offered to be available to answer any future questions. I felt relieved to know that I was not alone. (Parent)

Partner With Families

The primary responsibility of every staff member is to partner with families, not just to do things for families. This partnership begins as families are encouraged to take a leading role in the development of their family's individualized treatment and care plan. Below are some practices in use by programs to support full family involvement in this process:

- Family members are included in all discussions and decisions about their child.
- All evaluations, assessments, treatment, and service plans include a strong focus on the strengths, talents, skills, and unique family culture as expressed by the youth and family.
- The needs defined in the service plans are based on what the youth and family have identified.
- Child and family team, wraparound, or family team conferencing replaces traditional treatment team meetings.
- Meetings are held only if the youth and family are present.
- Meetings are held at a time and in a location that is acceptable to the family.
- Family members have sufficient time, preparation, information, and support to have a meaningful role in decision making.
- Youth and family are able to invite whomever they want to attend the meetings (e.g., youth's coach, big brother, cousin, mother's sister, father's mother).

- With permission of the family, staff members spend time in the family's home to better understand the culture of the family and community, as well as their needs and strengths.
- Programs acknowledge the impact that placement has on siblings and make sibling support and involvement a priority.

> North Carolina implemented a policy that meetings and discussions about the child do not occur unless the child and family are present. The state facilities also provide transportation for families and have broadened visitation rules to allow families unlimited access, 7 days a week. (Osher & Huff, 2006, p. 14)

Keep the Family in the Parenting Role

There are many opportunities for programs to implement practices that strengthen family relationships when a child is placed outside of the home (National Building Bridges Initiative Family Advisory Group, 2012). This includes maintaining the parent (or other person taking care of the child) in the parenting role even while their child is in placement. This requires frequent communication with the family. For example:

- Families are actively involved in the day-to-day care of their child. As often as possible, families help youth in their own homes with everyday normal family tasks, like helping with homework, reading a book, or playing a game; families are also welcome to come to the residential program to engage in these same tasks. Staff seek out family input about how to handle situations.
- Families schedule and accompany their child to medical appointments. When necessary, staff members provide transportation or other types of assistance.
- Families are full partners in all discussions and decision making related to prescribing and to adjusting medications.
- Schools are notified that the family is the first contact. School meetings are arranged at the family's convenience. Report cards and school documents have the family member's signature.
- If needed, the family is provided with a clothing allowance and asked to shop with their child. Older youth shop for themselves with approval by their family.
- Families take their child for haircuts and styling. If this is not possible, their permission is obtained prior to their children receiving a haircut.

At the Jewish Board of Family and Children's Services' Ittleson Community Residence, families are encouraged to join their child for dinner at the residence, to help with homework, to tuck the child in each night, or to call and read a bedtime story or to just say good night, keeping some of the same routines they had prior to placement. Program staff members call families daily to share something positive that the youth has done or just to inquire about how the family member is doing. (Bette Levy, former NYC Field Coordinator, New York State Office of Mental Health, personal communication, January 23, 2012)

Value and Support Family Time Together

A program's overall strategy should be to minimize the time spent in placement by providing supports in home and in the community, possibly avoiding placement altogether. The role of staff is to enable the child to spend as much time as possible with his or her family and to support positive family experiences, however possible.

- Youth are able to spend time at home during the first week in the program. There are no arbitrary rules about how soon or how often a child can go home.
- Youth never have to earn the right to go home or spend time with their families.
- Youth do not "visit" their homes—they live there and spend time there. If there are safety concerns, alternative plans are made, such as staff going home with the youth so the youth can still spend time with family members.
- There are no visiting hours for families. They can come to the program 24/7. Private space is available for families, including areas for young siblings to play.
- Phones are provided, or youth are allowed to use their cell phones to contact their families and friends as frequently as needed, based on the individual child.
- All celebrations in a youth's life are with their families in their homes and communities.
- The focus shifts from the program organizing fun events for youth to the program facilitating and supporting opportunities for children to have fun with their families.
- If the family lives at a great distance (a practice that should be minimized), budget for travel as well as for staff to transport and support the child while he or she spends time at home. Use Skype or FaceTime to connect with families every day.

At SCO Family of Services, Our Place Community Residence, when staff receives donations or free tickets to attend community events such as Broadway shows and professional sports events, youth are given tickets to invite their siblings, cousins, or friends to go with them. If needed, staff attends to support families. Family outings are planned to amusement parks and movies, and families are encouraged to bring extended family members so the youth does not lose touch with his or her extended family. (Bette Levy, former NYC Field Coordinator, New York State Office of Mental Health, personal communication, January 23, 2012)

Nurture Natural Supports

It is important for all providers to conduct staff training on strategies to support youth and families to build a sustaining network of natural supports. There are many ways to approach this, including the following:

- Encourage thinking beyond the customary formal services to find, involve, and build natural supports (e.g., teacher, coach, friend, neighbor, extended family member) and community resources (e.g., YMCA, women's group, parks and recreation activities, faith-based organizations).
- Engage a large group of extended family and friends to participate in the support plan that increases the likelihood that the youth and family will experience success.
- Connect families with other families in the program and in community-based family support programs close to their homes.
- Connect families to family support groups/family resource centers in their home communities; also, make space available on site for a family resource center, where families can gather and receive support and information.
- Talk with the family and key natural supports about ways in which their culture and beliefs (including their individual family culture) can be a source of support and strength.
- Assist families to identify interests, hobbies, or leisure activities, and connect them to people who can help them get involved in the community. Provide support, as needed, for successful involvement (e.g., mentor to attend with youth; funding to pay registration fee, transportation, and training for program staff).

Improve Cultural and Linguistic Competence

Every family deserves to receive services and supports that take into account their individual cultural, ethnic, and racial backgrounds, as well as their family traditions. The racial disparities in out-of-home placement rates suggest the need to better connect with and serve families of color (National Building

Bridges Initiative Cultural and Linguistic Competence Workgroup, 2011) using a number of strategies, including the following:

- Embrace cultural and linguistic competence, including hiring staff members whose culture represents the diversity of the families served, through which family engagement and collaboration often improves, and complaining about or blaming family members decreases.
- Train program staff to speak with families about their beliefs, values, food, traditions, dress, and grooming so these can be understood and respected.
- Ensure that physical environments reflect the cultural backgrounds of the families served.

Provide Services in the Community While the Family Is Receiving Residential Interventions

The research points to the importance of reversing traditional program practices. Staff should shift their focus so that more work is done with families in their homes and to support youth in clinical and recreational activities with their families and in their communities.

- Provide skills training and support in their homes and communities to help families and youth develop and practice skills in their day-to-day environment.
- Focus on real-world skills that children and families can operationalize after transition back to the community rather than skills that are useful in the milieu but not necessarily applicable in community settings (American Association of Children's Residential Centers [AACRC], 2009).

Focus on Long-Term Success at Home

From the first day, staff, youth, and family members make it a priority to work towards an individualized, well-planned discharge. Examples of practices that support this include the following:

- During the admission process, youth and families decide which services and supports they will need from the residential program and from the community for the youth to return home. Offer as many services as possible in the community and at home.
- At admission, connect the family to peer youth advocates and family partners, both in the program and in the community.
- Utilize a "walk throughout your neighborhood" practice where staff members drive or walk with the youth and family through their community. Everyone shares memories and history to help identify members of a community support team.

- Identify funding to continue to work with the youth and family following discharge.
- Provide seamless family support before, during, and after placement through the coordinated efforts of the residential and community-based family partners.
- Support youth to maintain meaningful connections with their community friends (with permission from the family and courts, if needed).
- Support youth involvement in their neighborhood school while in placement.
- Establish a direct phone line to an identified staff member and family partner for family members to call if they have concerns at any time or do not know how to handle an issue that arises when their child is at home. They should not have to go through telephonic prompts (AACRC, 2009).

Keeping options open for children requires residential programs to invest in *all* families, even highly challenged families, with the hope and expectation that, with the right support, they will be able to care for their children at home. When a parent is not able to provide day-to-day care, every effort should be made (through strategies such as Family Search and Engagement, described earlier) to identify a relative or other individual(s) who can make a lifelong commitment.

At the Institute of Community Living, Linden House Community Residence, to ensure that the transition to home and community is seamless, families are offered a long trial discharge period, where the youth's time at home increases by a day or two each week until they are home 7 days a week. Once the discharge date is scheduled, the youth returns to school in their home-district school while the youth is still a resident at the community residence. The family is able to reconnect the youth in community activities while they still have the support of the community residence staff to guide and assist them with any challenges. This gradual transition takes into account the family dynamics of separation and affords both the youth and the rest of the family time to adjust to having the youth living at home full time. It assists with the youth's reintegration to their home community. (Bette Levy, former NYC Field Coordinator, New York State Office of Mental Health, personal communication, January 23, 2012)

Administrative Practices to Support Family-Driven Care

Becoming family driven involves doing more than just resolving troubling behaviors. It means joining with families and creating complete transparency. Scrutinize every aspect of the organization and move away from practices, policies, and procedures that are not inclusive and respectful of families and youth.

Recognize that this will create major upheaval, and begin to challenge long-held beliefs and values. Will staff members continue to be family driven even when faced with multistressed families, as in the case of parent(s) with mental health challenges or substance abuse issues, or when there has been neglect in the past? The foundation of becoming family driven begins with an unwavering leadership commitment together with strong family and youth voice. Consider the following suggestions to prepare an organization for this change process:

Leadership

- Ensure that the organization's mission and values embrace family-driven care principles and partnership with families.
- Redistribute resources such as personnel, time, space, materials, and money to hire as many diverse family partners as the budget will allow. Ideally, this will include a management-level family partner on the agency's executive team.

Human Resources

- Revise job descriptions to reflect new roles and practice guidelines.
- Hire and promote staff members who demonstrate a family-driven skill set.
- Include family partners in every interview with potential employees.
- Review all agency training curricula and discard training that is disrespectful or blames families. Include family partners on the review team.
- Provide supervision training that includes strategies for promoting family-driven practice, including feedback for supervisors on their personal interaction skills with families.
- Use a variety of methods to obtain feedback from families about their interactions with staff.

Language

- Use language that avoids jargon, judgmental terms, and labels.
- Review the organization's printed materials, Web site, and social media presence to ensure that all language is sensitive to families and promotes family-driven care principles.
- Hire bilingual staff and certified interpreters.

Outcome Data

- Assess adherence to best practices that operationalize family-driven care.
- Look at data elements that are important to families and that signal long-term success, such as:

- long-term recidivism (with recidivism defined as any out-of-home placement that is not part of the long-term support plan);
- number of days each week a youth spends time with the family in their community;
- number of times staff call family members weekly to share strengths and/or positive activities of the youth; and
- number of times youth call family members daily.

Family-driven care principles are guiding the development of a new reper-toire of strategies and supporting a new paradigm for the role of service provid-ers. While there are many strategies suggested in this chapter, there is a simple suggestion that is often overlooked: invite families to share their perspective. Many providers report that the inspiration to think about their relationship with families in a different way came from honest conversations with families about their experience of care.

Hathaway-Sycamores Child and Family Services, a large children's mental health provider in Southern California, has done a noteworthy job of recognizing the work done by parent partners employed by the agency. One example of this is the agency-wide adoption of a data-driven supervision model that was first used in the parent partner program. The supervision model queries the employee, his or her supervisor and families for feedback regarding job skills and the qual-ity of services and supports. Agency leaders, impressed by the data collected in supervision reports and the idea of calling families for feedback, implemented the supervision model for all 650 employees.

Successfully Working With Family Partners

Family partners can transform the way an organization thinks about and works with families that can advance the implementation of family-driven care within the organization. Family partners have different titles. Generally, the first word in their title is *family, parent,* or *peer.* This is paired with *liaison, specialist, advo-cate, partner, support, navigator,* or *coordinator,* terms that also describe some of the activities of the family partner. A family partner draws upon his or her own personal experience to support, guide, and empower other families. Fam-ily partners are also able to provide a consistent family perspective within the organization.

When a hospital, residential, or community program has family partners working as colleagues alongside clinical professionals, it sends a powerful mes-sage that begins to reduce the feelings of stigma and blame that families often feel. Family partners often are able to build trust and engage families more quickly because of their similar experiences. Family partners offer other families hope that they can manage the challenges and attempt to regain a sense of normalcy.

The Unique Role of the Family Partner

Many families discuss the feeling of being brought to their knees by the experience of seeking help for their child while navigating the child-serving system. Many lose confidence in their parenting ability and are afraid to hope that things will ever get better.

> The basic premise of being supported by someone who has lived through a similar experience (and survived) is at the heart of this movement. Parents report over and over again, "I thought I was the only one going through this" and "I could not have done this without the support of my parent partner." (Obrochta et al., 2011, p. 3)

Family partners have the unique ability to engage families and support them with empathy and understanding. It is the peer-to-peer experience that is often so crucial to the healing process for families and at the heart of the family partner's work. Family partners are committed to ensuring families have a voice in their child's care and that they are equipped to navigate the journey ahead.

Patricia Miles (2001) helped a group of California family partners develop an informal code of ethics; this is now incorporated into the national Parent Support Provider Certification (Certification Commission for Family Support, 2013). This provides a good characterization of how family partners seek to interact with families in a manner that is empowering and rooted in a deep belief in the capacity of families:

- We tell our own story when it can help other families.
- We support other families as peers with a common background and history rather than as experts who have all the answers.
- We acknowledge that each family's answers may be different than our own.
- We take responsibility for clarifying our role as family partners and as a parent of a child with special needs.
- We build partnerships with others, including professionals who are involved in the care of our children.
- We commit to honesty with each other and with all involved with the care of a child, and expect the same from others.

- We are committed to a nonjudgmental and respectful attitude in our dealings with and discussions regarding families.
- We are committed to nonadversarial advocacy in our roles within the system.

Family partners can be found in many settings across the country. They often work for family-run organizations, providers, counties, courts, and schools. They may have additional responsibilities and goals defined by the program in which they work (e.g., residential, wraparound, crisis unit, school) or by other agencies involved with the child or family (e.g., child welfare or juvenile justice). While there will be some role differences based on these different contexts, it is very important for the family partner and the organizations for which they work to understand and purposely focus their work on providing family-to-family peer support, educating others on family-driven care, and increasing family involvement within the organization.

> The Parent Advocacy Program in Jefferson County, Kentucky, established in 2004, selects and trains parents, who were previously recipients of child-welfare services to be peer advocates. Advocates and child welfare staff work together to prevent the removal of children from their homes, reunify children with their families, maintain connections between parents and children who are in out-of-home care, and help train workers and foster parents on the needs of birth parents. (Spencer, Blau, & Mallery, 2010, p. 179)

In addition to providing peer-to-peer support, family partners may develop curriculum and provide training for agency staff; participate in program oversight and evaluation; serve on workgroups, committees, and governing bodies; and play many other roles.

> The family partners we hired often interrupt bias toward families in our workgroups and remind us of the family's perspective. One day I realized it was everyone's responsibility to represent the family's perspective. (Agency Program Director)

Organizational Culture and the Successful Integration of Family Partners

It is very important to have a strong, clear leadership vision to support the shift to family-driven practice. Organizations will be much more effective if leaders are fully committed to supporting the level of organizational culture change that is necessary to hire family partners.

While family partners are change agents, they cannot do it alone. Family partners can only thrive in an organization that is engaged in a genuine effort to evaluate its policies and practices to determine if they are consistent with person-centered, strength-based, family-driven care.

Change comes from both the top down and the bottom up and is best accomplished if leaders are dedicated to collaboration and outspoken about their commitment to family-driven care. The leadership team should also make it clear that family partners' perspectives are valued and their input is welcome. Staff should expect family partners to challenge the status quo and to utilize their personal experiences as a tool, and at times disclose information about their own journey.

> When I was first hired as a parent partner, I was expected to instinctively know what to do. Unfortunately, I did what my professional colleagues did: spend more time working with the child than the parent. One day, an experienced parent-partner consultant asked me what I did. When I explained I was spending time with my colleagues helping the child, the consultant said "What's your role?" I answered, "Parent partner." She then asked me, "Who works with the parent?" The light bulb went on. I was hired to support the parent. There were plenty of other workers to help the child, but I was the only one hired to help the parent. It was the clarity I needed to finally begin to do my job. (Anonymous parent partner)

The Benefits of Peer Family Support

Families report that their level of trust and engagement increased and their feeling of stigma decreased through their work with a family partner. Participation and self-efficacy increases as family partners promote family–clinician collaboration and bolster the knowledge and confidence of families. This leads to the development of plans that are more likely to succeed because the family had input, is invested, and has the skills and backup support they indicated they need to carry out the plan.

Family partners can enhance the coordination between placement and treatment settings. They can teach families strategies for how to cope, articulate their needs, connect or reconnect to support networks, and inspire hope. This eventually leads to less reliance on formal services, which is everyone's goal.

A Consistent Approach

Moving an organization toward family-driven care is a transformational process that impacts all aspects of an agency. Leaders who embrace family-driven care are beginning a journey that requires staff to reevaluate long-held beliefs and practices and to embrace shared decision-making. This includes the clinical staff's philosophy and approach to treatment.

Many programs still support practices that are inconsistent with family-driven care. Some examples of these problematic practices include not allowing youth to go home for an arbitrary period of time after admission; making time at home contingent on behavior; using point and level systems; and holding treatment team meetings without families. Fortunately, progressive programs are challenging the assumptions behind these practices and exploring new approaches grounded in mutual respect and partnership.

In the handbook *Collaborating With Families: How to Enhance Engagement, Discover Strengths, and Talk About Problems*, DuBrino and Irsfeld (2010) described their belief in the effectiveness of peer family support:

> In our programs, the single most important advantage we had was the work of parents and caregivers providing parent-to-parent support for those families with which we worked. What 9 years ago was thought of as a "nice little addition" to our programs turned out to be a powerful and key component to our work. Over time, we have come to realize how quickly and efficiently our Family Partners can engage families in our process, thus helping to overcome many of the challenges discussed in this Handbook. In our view, the role of Family Partners represents an enormous advantage in helping to establish effective engagement with families. (p. 49)

The next chapter will explore specific clinical strategies that promote family engagement and family-driven care.

Contact Information:

Creating Positive Cultures of Care
Massachusetts Department of Mental Health
Central Office, Child/Adolescent Division
(617) 626-8090
dmhinfo@dmh.state.ma.us

Darrell Evora, MCP, MBA
President/CEO
EMQ Families First
(408) 379-3790
devora@emqff.org

Joe Anne Hust
Peer Support & System of Care Implementation Manager/National Trainer
The Institute for Innovation and Implementation—University of Maryland, School of Social Work
(443) 610-6853
jhust@ssw.umaryland.edu

Bette Levy, MA, EdM
Former NYS OMH NYC Field Office Staff
(917) 593-9342
betteslevy@aol.com

Jim Nyreen, MSW
Assistant Executive Director/SCO Family of Services
(718) 523-2227
jnyreen@sco.org

Mary Stone Smith, MA, LMHC
Vice-President and Director of Family Preservation
Catholic Community Services of Western Washington
(800) 566-9053
MarySS@ccsww.org

Notes

1 The Massachusetts Department of Mental Health provided permission to the authors to reprint content from two chapters of the manual *Creating Positive Cultures of Care: A Resource Guide* (3rd ed.), Boston, MA: Massachusetts Department of Mental Health (J. LeBel, personal communication, May 3, 2013). The two chapters are "Embracing Family-Driven Care" (Caldwell, Kuppinger, Hust, Lambert, & Levy, 2012a) and "Successfully Working With Family Partners" (Caldwell et al., 2012b).
2 The term *parenting* refers to the day-to-day care, decision making, and support of a child, whether provided by the legal parent, a relative, or other individual who has made a long-term commitment to the child. The recommendations in this book frequently refer to work with "the family" or "family members" instead of "parent," because sometimes the individual who is relating to the residential program is not the parent but a relative or other person who is caring for the child. The intention is for the program to define *family* broadly (and based on the child and family's perception of who that includes), and identify and work in close partnership with the child's parent(s) or other individuals who have made a long-term commitment to parent the child.

References

American Association of Children's Residential Centers. (2009). Redefining residential: Family-driven care in residential treatment—Family members speak. *Residential Treatment for Children and Youth, 26*(4), 252–256.

Caldwell, B., Kuppinger, A., Hust, J., Lambert, L., & Levy, B. (2012a). Embracing family-driven care. In J. LeBel & A. Lim (Eds.), *Creating positive cultures of care: A resource guide* (3rd ed.), Boston, MA: Massachusetts Department of Mental Health.

Caldwell, B., Kuppinger, A., Hust, J., Lambert, L., & Levy, B. (2012b). Successfully working with family partners. In J. LeBel & A. Lim (Eds.), *Creating positive cultures of care: A resource guide* (3rd ed.), Boston, MA: Massachusetts Department of Mental Health.

Catholic Community Services of Western Washington. (2013). *Family search and engagement.* Retrieved October 25, 2013, from www.ccsww.org/site/PageServer? pagename=families_familypreservation_fse

Certification Commission for Family Support. (2013). *Code of ethics.* Retrieved July 13, 2013, from http://certification.ffcmh.org/apply

Dalton, J. (2011, August). *Modernizing residential treatment: Indiana & Damar Services* [PowerPoint slides]. Presentation at the New Hampshire's Transition to Permanency for Youth Project Kick-Off Event, Concord, NH.

DuBrino, T. M. & Irsfeld, J. A. (2010). *Collaborating with families: How to enhance engagement, discover strengths, and talk about problems.* Worchester: University of Massachusetts Medical School.

EMQ FamiliesFirst. (2012). *Family finding.* Retrieved October 25, 2013, from www.emqff.org/services/family_finding.shtml

Hust, J. (2010, October). *Hathaway-Sycamores residential transformation: A parent's perspective—Changing the metaphor of help* [PowerPoint slides]. Presentation at the Massachusetts Interagency Residential Provider Forum, Marlborough, MA.

Kohomban, J. (2011, May). *The Children's Village: Keeping children safe and families together* [PowerPoint slides]. Presentation at the Massachusetts 11th Annual Provider Forum on Restraint & Seclusion Prevention, Shrewsbury, MA.

Leichtman, M., Leichtman, M. L., Barber, C. C., & Neese, D. T. (2001). Effectiveness of intensive short-term residential treatment with severely disturbed adolescents. *American Journal of Orthopsychiatry, 71*(2), 227–235.

Martone, W. (2010, October). *Hathaway-Sycamores Child and Family Services* [Power Point slides]. Presentation at the Massachusetts Interagency Residential Provider Forum, Marlborough, MA.

Miles, P. (2001). *Individualized and tailored care/wraparound parent partner manual.* Unpublished manuscript.

National Building Bridges Initiative (2007, March). *Innovative practices for transformation.* Unpublished internal workgroup document summarizing comments made by Mark Courtney on a workgroup webinar, p. 26.

National Building Bridges Initiative Cultural and Linguistic Competence Workgroup. (2011). *Cultural and linguistic competence guidelines for residential programs.* Retrieved October 25, 2013 from www.buildingbridges4youth.org/sites/default/files/BBI_CLC_Guidelines_FINAL.pdf

National Building Bridges Initiative Family Advisory Group. (2010). *Tip sheet for families considering a residential program.* Retrieved July 15, 2013, from www.buildingbridges4youth.org/workgroups/youth-family/products-resources

National Building Bridges Initiative Family Advisory Group. (2012). *Engage us! A guide written by families for residential providers.* Retrieved July 15, 2013, from www.buildingbridges4youth.org/workgroups/youth-family/products-resources

National Building Bridges Initiative Youth Advisory Group. (2010). *Your life your future—Inside info on residential programs from youth who have been there.* Retrieved July 15, 2013, from www.buildingbridges4youth.org/workgroups/youth-family/products-resources

National Federation of Families for Children's Mental Health. (2008). *Working definition of family driven care.* Retrieved July 28, 2013, from www.ffcmh.org/sites/default/files/Family%20Driven%20Care%20Definition.pdf

Obrochta, C., Anthony, B., Armstrong, M., Kalil, J., Hust, J., & Kernan, J. (2011). *Issue brief: Family-to-family peer support: Models and evaluation.* Atlanta, GA: ICF Macro, Outcomes Roundtable for Children and Families.

Osher, T. W. & Huff, B. (2006).Working with families in the juvenile justice and corrections systems: A guide for education program leaders, principals, and building administrators. Washington, DC: National Evaluation and Technical Assistance Center for the Education of Children and Youth Who Are Neglected, Delinquent, and At-Risk. Retrieved March 7, 2012, from www.neglected-delinquent.org/nd/docs/Family%20involvement%20Guide_FINAL.pdf

Spencer, S. A., Blau, G. M., & Mallery, C. J. (2010). Family-driven care in America: More than a good idea. *Journal of the Canadian Academy of Child and Adolescent Psychiatry, 19*(3), 176–181.

Walters, U. M., & Petr, C. G. (2008). Family-centered residential treatment: Knowledge, research, and values converge. *Residential Treatment for Children & Youth, 25*(1), 1–16.

4   Clinical Strategies for Engaging Families

Thomas L. Sexton, G. Olivia Ríos,
Karen A. Johnson, and Brenda R. Plante

Residential programs are increasingly finding that successful engagement strategies help increase family involvement and child and adolescent (hereafter referred to as "youth") motivation, thereby reducing the length of stay and time out of and time away from the natural environment of the youth. There is good evidence that shifting the focus to community-based treatment has significant benefits. For example, Barth, Greeson, Green, Hurley, and Sisson (2007) found that youth in intensive, in-home therapy were more likely in the future to live with family, make progress in school, not have trouble with the law, and have better placement permanence than youth in residential treatment. It is also becoming increasingly clear from the literature that the best residential programs partner with families, make sure there is meaningful family involvement during residential intervention, and keep the focus of treatment on natural environments and communities. Residential stays are shorter and outcomes are improved when families are involved (Jivanjee, Friesen, Kruzich, Robinson, & Pullmann, 2002; Leichtman, Leichtman, Barber, & Neese, 2001). Even with those youth who do participate in treatment, we now know that if youth do not find something relevant in the discussions, that is delivered by someone who is creditable and matches to their need, the outcomes of even the best evidence-based treatment programs are poor (Sexton, Datachi-Phillips, Evans, LaFollette, & Wright, 2012).

Much of the current work on engagement has focused on family involvement and having family youth and parent representatives embedded within organizations and treatment decisions. This important work is described by Hust and Kuppinger (2014) and Building Bridges (National Building Bridges Initiative Family Advisory Group, 2012). Yet, when working with youth with behavioral and/or emotional challenges and their families, getting started with the seemingly simple goals of all therapies—families, youth, and clinician creating an alliance, developing shared goals, and understanding and assessing the problem—are more difficult than one might imagine. Lack of successful clinical engagement strategies can result in families not trusting staff, not wanting to work with staff, not continuing with work together, and/or not following through with agreed-upon strategies at home.

Clinical engagement strategies, the focus of this chapter, go beyond the broad principles of engagement of youth and families and venture further into the specific clinical approaches, interventions, and interactions between therapists, youth, and families that are linked to successful engagement and motivation when families and youth agree to participate in therapy. Clinical engagement strategies are purposeful interventions that are embedded into—are an integral part of—or are a "module" added to a treatment program with the primary goals of therapeutically engaging youth and families into treatment. One of the ways in which clinical engagement strategies are different is that they are focused on the way in which the treatment approaches, whether they be specific, evidence-based models or more general approaches, integrate engagement as a central goal in the clinical change process.

There is a category of universal clinical engagement strategies. These strategies are the attitudes and behavior that can be adopted by clinicians to help facilitate families and youth being part of treatment together. Many of these universal strategies can also be used at the organizational and treatment delivery levels of residential programs to further build an engaging environment for youth and families. There is also another category of specific clinical engagement strategies that have come from some of the current evidence-based family treatment models. Because of the extensive research into the mechanisms of these models, we have learned even more specific ways to build engagement within the specific clinical interventions used by the treatment program. One of the ways in which the specific engagement strategies differ is that they expand the concept of engagement to include the development of therapeutic motivation. Viewed this way, clinical engagement strategies also serve to promote treatment motivation while fostering family alliance. In fact, it is becoming clear that therapeutic motivation develops as part of the intervention and can be enhanced by a variety of specific clinical strategies that go beyond the universal strategies (Sexton et al., 2012).

The goal of this chapter is to describe, define, and identify the current clinical strategies that can be used to systematically facilitate youth and family engagement in the treatment process. Our goal is not to promote any one treatment program, but instead to identify the universal and specific ways to clinically engage and motivate youth and families in any treatment program. To do so, we begin by defining the meaning of *clinical engagement* as focusing on what families need—because these needs must be addressed by any engagement skills and strategies—and then identify those core attitudes and clinical behaviors that contribute to engaging youth and families into treatment and building therapeutic motivation. We review universal clinical strategies shared by all successful programs, and the specific engagement methods from two systematic models that have integrated engagement and motivation, as central elements in the treatment process, in 10 common keys to successful clinical engagement of youth and families.

This is a chapter focused on clinical change strategies from the perspective of the clinician. The term *clinician* is used to describe the persons who are working with families—including Family Partners, mental health therapists, and others in the role of implementing the clinical treatment strategies as part of the residential intervention. It is important to note that even with research-based clinical strategies at hand, the most successful clinicians do not see themselves as "having the answers" but instead as collaborators in a complex change process with youth and their families. Yet, at the same time, our role is to have a specific process, or pathway, to help families follow so that they can reach the kinds of changes they seek. That process is a complex one in which therapists focus on the mechanism of change—those ways of talking, ways of working with emotions, and ways of helping solve problems.

We also know from research literature that not all engagement strategies are equally effective in facilitating engagement and, ultimately, successful outcomes. As the range of clinical engagement skills grows, those working with families must have purposefulness to their work. It is the role for clinicians, therapists, and other professionals to bring to the family pathways that have the highest likelihood of success knowing that it takes a collaborative working relationship among all to successfully follow that path. Consequently, any discussion of therapeutic change can sometimes seem "judgmental" or "clinical." Respectful interactions would not objectify the family but rather focus the youth and family about approaches and mechanisms that build on their unique strengths, needs, and interests and are thus likely to result in a higher likelihood of engagement and specific therapeutic motivation. That having been said, it is clear that the success or failure of any specific clinical engagement strategy is based on having a collaborative working alliance in which both the clinician and the youth and family find ways of working together that fit them and help to build an internal sense of an incentive to take part, try new things, and work towards a different future.

What Do Families Need?

Youth and families served by residential interventions bring with them multiple strengths and talents as well as a complex history of struggles, attempts at solutions, and, at times, hopelessness at the system, other family members, and even themselves when they come to treatment. Some families are forced to the therapy by mandates from judges, probation officers, other mental health workers, or child welfare agencies. In these cases, the family often brings with them anger and concern over the referral itself, in addition to all else. If one can look beyond the specific details of the specific problem or the nature of the referral, families enter therapy in a similar way—bringing the powerful emotional experiences that contribute to the referral right into all the interactions they have with one another and the treatment staff. In order to understand what specific clinical activities can be used to be relevant and interesting, and speak to their needs, we have to begin with an understanding of what families need. *Engage Us: A Guide Written by Families for Residential Providers* (National Building Bridges Initiative Family Advisory Group, 2012) provides a valuable perspective on what families need. Family members whose children were or had been in residential wrote the guide, and it chronicles the areas that families feel increase their capacity to engage and partner with staff. It seems clear that they need to be heard, understood, believed, and involved. Consider what families say about efforts at engagement, when treatment providers put them forth.

- "I value treatment givers, program 'people,' and clinicians who warmly welcome me, make eye contact, and try to make me feel comfortable, right from the start. I worked best with therapists who didn't 'talk down to me' or over enunciate words they thought I didn't understand, or worst yet speak, in that 'much louder than they think' tone to explain something, or answer a question. (Especially uncomfortable in group settings)."
- "The two most honest things I'd ever heard a welcoming treatment team member say to me was, 'I'm glad you're here,' and 'Ms. Johnson, it's not your fault your son has experienced many challenges.' Most clinicians don't realize (or maybe they do) that some parents run a constant background monologue of thoughts about themselves being the reason their children are 'bad,' 'don't listen,' or 'can't learn,' or 'are always in trouble.' We parents think of what we did wrong as kids, or what bad habits we might have had, or even if we were right to have the kids in the first place. All kinds of things go through our heads."
- "The whole prospect of accepting therapeutic treatment for your child opens doors you don't want to open, much less face in the light of day. I honestly thought I could solve our family problems and my son's mental health needs on my own. I was strong willed and just wrong. Eventually I was able to get him the right kind of help just in time, actually . . . ."

What emerges from these stories is that families need not only to be heard but also to be helped; they may be looking for a lifeline, to be accepted, acknowledged as having tried, and as motivated to change. While system-level strategies for involving families is critical, these stories also illustrate the need for making engagement a critical part of the clinical process.

Clinical Engagement Strategies

One way to identify and define engagement is by looking at the behaviors of youth and families who are clinically engaged in treatment. These include the following:

- *Family members seem to trust the therapist*—Family members communicate openly and believe that the therapist understands their perspectives and has the ability to help.

- *Interfamily negativity and blame have been reduced*—Negativity usually thwarts therapist efforts to gain family collaboration and achieving treatment goals.
- *Family members have a shared focus on the presenting problems*—General agreement on the presenting problems (i.e., agreement on the tasks and goals) is essential for progress to be made on these problems.
- *High rates of attendance at sessions*—Assuming that sessions are scheduled at convenient times and locations (i.e., their homes) for family members, and barriers to service access are overcome.
- *Emotional involvement in sessions*—Engagement is indicated when family members are lively and energetic during sessions, and actively debating and planning intervention strategies. Although the absence of emotional involvement does not necessarily indicate the absence of engagement (i.e., some families have very low-key styles but are sincerely motivated), the presence of emotional energy generally reflects engagement.
- *Greater motivation in sessions*—Youth and family are motivated to try new behaviors in search of a common positive outcome.

Over the last decade, there has been increased emphasis on understanding specific clinical mechanisms that have been linked to these outcomes. The clinical engagement strategies that have emerged from that research are all interpersonal processes built on attitudes and purposeful behavior in treatment that draw youth and families into working relationships. Successful clinical engagement strategies also set the stage for, and are an integral part of, the change process by using purposeful interpersonal behaviors to promote feelings by youth and their families that they are a resource and partner for change. They evoke feelings for youth and families that they are working with a credible therapist who really helps, who they believe in, and who acknowledges and challenges so that they have a reason to take part in treatment. Research-based clinical engagement strategies fall into two categories: universal principles and specific clinical principles and skills that enhance youth and family engagement.

Universal Principles of Successful Clinical Engagement

Universal engagement strategies are principles that guide the way in which the therapist thinks about youth and families. These principles guide how therapists think about and interact with youth and family members that are common to all successful clinical interventions. These universal skills are used across therapeutic approaches and by specific treatment programs, such as Multisystemic Therapy (Cunningham & Henggeler, 1999), PCIT (Chaffin et al., 2004), Trauma Systems Therapy (Saxe, Ellis, & Kaplow, 2007), and Collaborative Problem Solving (Greene et al., 2004), as the foundation for engagement modules for the treatment program. It is important to note that just because these strategies are universal, it is not intended to imply that they are in any way unimportant. These are the central foundation for successful clinical engagement.

- *Work from respect*—*Respect* is a core attitude that is the basis of any clinical engagement strategy. The dictionary definition is "a feeling of deep admiration for someone or something elicited by his or her abilities, qualities, or achievements." *Respect* is more than being understood. Instead, respect is being able to acknowledge the struggle of the youth and family, and believing that they are functioning as well as possible within the circumstances— that they have the ability and resources to make it through. *Respect* also means that the therapist is willing to provide help that "fits" the youth and family members (rather than the therapist). Being respectful is having the belief that *resistant* and *difficult to treat* youth and families are understandably hurt, hopelessness, discouraged, and feel a lack of empowerment to solve their problems and, that with help that fits them, they have the ability to cope and solve problems. *Respect* means that the therapist goes beyond understanding and empathy to also providing help that is practical and addresses the individual needs of the family and youth.
- *Build balanced alliance with youth and families*—*Alliance* is a common way to think about therapeutically engaging approaches to working with youth and families. *Alliance* reflects the necessary ingredients to those therapeutic interpersonal interactions with therapists and youth and families that promote successful outcomes, typically viewed as encompassing an agreement on the goals and tasks, and an understanding and supportive bond. It means that everyone is important to involve, everyone's position is to be understood, and everyone's needs must be accommodated in a way that is perceived as balanced. Each family member must believe that the therapist is on his or her side and understands his or her point of view as well as the views of others.
- *Focus on the concerns of both the youth and the family*—All effective therapies are based on collaboration with family members in the identification and prioritization of presenting problems. Yet, youth and family members should not be expected to engage with therapeutic efforts that they do not see as priorities. Thus, a consensus on problem and need identification must be reached before treatment continues. The development of a conjoint consensus on the foci of treatment goes a long way in building the therapeutic alliance. When family members are collaborators in shaping and prioritizing goals, engagement and motivation increase.
- *Maintain a strength focus*—Identifying strengths helps one to recognize protective factors (e.g., family resources, social supports) that can lead to the development of better informed interventions and to solutions that have increased ecological validity. Focusing on family strengths does not mean that therapists should not be realistic or pragmatic by accepting

ideas not grounded in reality. Rather, *staying strength focused* means that therapists should realistically appraise family members' ability to use their strengths to accomplish tasks, while simultaneously working to develop additional strengths needed to attain treatment goals. *Staying strength based* means identifying and relying on unique family strengths through-out change-focused discussions as the therapist also looks for what they are doing well.

- *Be empathetic*—The importance of therapist empathy in client engage-ment cuts across clinical intervention models and approaches. Empathy involves seeing the world through the client's eyes, thinking about things as the client thinks about them, feeling things as clients feel them, sharing in the client's experiences. The process of expressing empathy relies on the client's experiencing the counselor as able to see the world as he or she (the client) sees it. Therapist empathy is also a significant predictor of a strong therapeutic alliance.

- *Provide hope*—Hope is the feeling that youth and family members have when, after a discussion with a therapist, it seems to them like things can improve, and that working with this therapist in this setting and in this program is worth the time and might provide a way out of the difficult struggle of the youth and family. *Hope*, as described in this manner, is cen-tral to engagement and motivation. Hope can come when the therapist finds "evidence" of client effort and improvement, and positively reinforces such, regardless of how small. Hope comes from a focus on now, the future, and "working things out" rather than trying to find out "why."

Specific Clinical Engagement Interventions

There are a number of intervention programs that consider engagement and its accompanying clinical process of motivation as core and central elements in treatment. Each of these builds on the universal as a foundation for more spe-cific and detailed clinical interventions, while at the same time putting engage-ment (as a process) at the center of the therapeutic process from beginning to end. Motivational Interviewing (MI; Miller & Rollnick, 2002) and Func-tional Family Therapy (FFT; Alexander et al., 2000; Sexton, 2010) both provide strategies that may be used in a variety of treatment programs to enhance the engagement and therapeutic motivation of youth and families. Unique to both of these approaches is that engagement and motivation are treatment goals that are the responsibility of the therapist to facilitate rather than a characteristic approach where motivation is placed on the family, almost as a prerequisite for families. Both FFT and MI are collaboratively based and alliance focused, while at the same time specific in their guidance to therapists in how to respond to the issues that families discuss. In addition, MI and FFT are evidence-based approaches, suggesting the likelihood that the specific engagement strategies and approach to engagement has demonstrated outcomes (Sexton et al., 2012).

We suggest there are 10 core lessons that can be drawn from these approaches that have an evidence base that can be added to the universal strategies and integrated into residential programs as they move their efforts into community settings.

1   *Make evidence-based engagement and motivation strategies an integral part of treatment*—With the growth of evidence-based treatment techniques and programs, we now know much more about how to make treatments engagement and motivation focused. At a clinical level, engagement and motivation are inexorably tied, and there are specific strategies based on good research that suggests these are the most likely to result in helping families step into treatment in a collaborative way. Before families can benefit from these strategies, organizations need to promote them. The most successful treatment providers are those that have integrated engagement into the very heart of the treatment process.

2   *Examine your core beliefs*—Successful engagement begins with the staff member being able to look beyond the individual to the family system; know there are very different ways of successfully being a family; focus on the fact that it is what the youth are doing now, and who they are, that is the major focus; accept them for who they are . . . not who he or she wants them to be; and look beyond the behavior to the "noble intention" behind the behavior. Doing so creates a solid foundation for clinical engagement strategies to work. Remember, interventionists should treat youth and families as collaborators and partners in successful treatment.

3   *Understand that the problems families face are not about the people but instead are behavior patterns in which they may be "stuck" (i.e., youth and families' "way" of doing things that may not work but that are understandable, given the circumstances)*—Remember that individuals cannot change the cause but can only understand and acknowledge what is important to them while focusing the treatment goals on everyone's part in the solution.

4   *Be family focused and work from alliance*—The current research suggests that the engagement is significantly enhanced when everyone is seen as part of the change process, and that the change process is shared by all. In a strange way, this requires, without blame and negativity, remembering that every member of the family has a "part" (responsibility without blame)—everyone is involved in some way. Each "part" is linked to the challenge that the family currently faces (family focused). To create a family-focused problem definition, each member of the family has to reattribute perceived motives, intentions, and behaviors. Taking that perspective, the therapeutic goal is to help make everyone responsible for the solution by expanding the focus of the problem to require everyone's participation and change for it to be successful. This is accomplished by responding to youth and families and refocusing those responses such that there is a shifting, redefining, and expanding of family members' definitions of the presenting problem, with

the therapist eliciting more constructive attributions of motivation, emotions, and behaviors.

5   *Actively work to reduce blame and negativity*—Blame and negativity between family members (or to the system) is a major barrier in engagement. Negativity is both the emotional expression of and the overall climate within the family. Blame is the attribution of problems to a particular source. There are a number of research studies that suggest that by reducing and reframing blame, the risk level within the family goes down, allowing alliance and more effective problem solving to emerge (Sexton et al., 2012). When negativity and blaming is reduced, more positive interactions among family members foster hope. When there is negativity, families do not feel there is a reason to participate, and it is a barrier to alliance. When there is blame, family members do not feel they are heard and do not take responsibility. Relational reframing is a useful strategy to reduce blame and negativity.

6   *Take a collaborative stance*—Collaboration is a partnership between the therapist and the client where the focus is on mutual understanding rather than "rightness." *Collaboration* means that therapists draw out the individual's own thoughts and ideas rather than tell the individual what to do or why he or she should do it. Therapeutic collaboration occurs when the expertise and the responsibility for change is shared between therapist, youth, and family. While the family is clearly an expert of their lives, values, and norms, the therapist is the expert of the specific change pathways available for families to choose from. As noted earlier, being purposeful and strategic about helping families does not represent a lack of collaboration. The biggest challenge for therapists is to bring therapeutic collaboration, through which they work together with the family to promote evidence-based ways of addressing the issues they face.

7   *Talk to the future and be change focused*—It is no surprise that both parents and youth want to know "why are we in this mess" or "who and what caused this." Treatments that engage and motivate youth have a problem focus and future focus to them. That means the discussions are aimed at what to do now rather than why problems happened. Change talk, a central component of MI, is a specific way of systematically building a solution focus to conversation. Change talk involves asking evocative questions, considering the strengths and weakness of changing, identifying the positives and negatives of the newly targeted behavior, looking back to find what was different at a time before the target behavior emerged, looking forward at how things will be if change does not happen, asking about the worst things that might happen if the change is not made and what are the best things that might happen if the change is made.

8   *Using strong emotions*—It is not surprising that one of the major barriers that families face in changing is overcoming the hurt feelings that have accumulated between youth and their families. It is a significant challenge

to let the airing of such emotions happen in a way that provides relief and at the same time pulls everyone involved further into a collaborative part of the treatment. Therapists often miss good opportunities to promote engagement and motivation by trying to control, rather than to redirect, emotional discussion. The research suggests that the most useful change mechanism to use with strong emotions is to change the attributions and therefore the meaning given to the event, emotion, or person. This idea is based on the principle that one of the unique characteristic of humans is to put meaning to events that happened and the emotions that they all experience. In a strange way, those very attributions are a barrier to engagement. It is the attributions of "who did it" and "why" that we all make to give meaning to the struggles we face that may get in the way of successfully working together. Helping families to change the meaning they ascribe to the behaviors of their youth (or parent) is a relationally based way of enhancing family engagement and motivation by changing the cognitive and perceptual basis for negative interaction, painful emotions, and unsuccessful change strategies. Change is most successful when it provides motivating and engaging alternative perspectives for clients that help redefine the meaning they attribute to events, thus reducing the negativity and redirecting the emotionality surrounding the events.

The current evidence suggests that changing meaning is complex and requires much more than "making clients aware" of what they feel and want. Instead, specific clinical strategies, such as relational reframing, have been designed to guide clinicians in talk with families in a way that builds a family focus, reduces negativity and blame, and builds engagement (Sexton, 2010). Reframing begins with the therapist *acknowledging* the speaker's position, statement, emotion, or primary meaning. The therapist next makes a *reattribution statement* that presents an alternative theme targeting the attribution scheme embedded in what the client presents. The reattribution statement may offer an alternative explanation for the "cause" of the problem behavior that takes away blame and at the same time promotes individual responsibility for being part of what occurs that resulted in the struggle, or "stuckness," of the family.

9 *Match to the family*—Engagement looks different for different people, and it is the responsibility of the therapist to match and adjust to the different styles of families. Clinical strategies need to be uniquely tailored to each family and family member and done in ways that demonstrate respect to their family structure, values, spirituality, beliefs, and ethnicity. For example, emotions are not always the modality through which families function. Yet, therapists often want to ask about and explore the feelings that are at the core of the struggles. Unfortunately, for families that operate on a more cognitive level, when this occurs there is a mismatch of pathways that stands in the way of successful engagement and motivation.

10 *Make sure the families have a strong "voice"*—Each of the universal and specific engagement skills is based on families having a voice in treatment. In clinical interventions, having a voice means that therapists specifically target collaborative and therapeutic engagement. With engagement comes the youth and family voice that can help drive treatment and help the therapist, family, and youth accomplish the complex tasks of successful treatment. Family voice can be built into the organizational level of treatment, as participants in treatment interventions, and along the way during treatment.

Summary

There is no question that successful engagement is critical to all programs that work with youth and families. Those engagement strategies that involve and are based on family-driven care appear even more powerful. It is important to remember that engagement is a multilevel systemic process that involves the organization, the treatment, the treatment interventionists, and the families and youth all working to the same end. At each level, there are systematic strategies to further promote engagement. In conjunction with other chapters in this volume (see Chapter 3), this chapter provides both general and specific clinical engagement strategies that can be used as a roadmap to successful family and youth engagement. These clinical strategies stand alongside those used by organizations and systems.

References

Alexander, J. F., Pugh, C., Parsons, B. F., & Sexton, T. (2000). Functional family therapy (Book 3, Vol. 2). In D. S. Elliott (Series ed.), *Blueprints for violence prevention. Institute of Behavioral Science*. Boulder, CO: Regents of the University of Colorado.

Barth, R. P., Greeson, J. K., Green, R. L., Hurley, S., & Sisson, J. (2007). Outcomes for youth receiving intensive in-home therapy or residential care: A comparison using propensity scores. *American Journal of Orthopsychiatry, 77*(4), 497–505.

Chaffin, M., Silovsky, J. F., Funderburk, B., Valle, L. A., Brestan, E. V., Balachova, T., & Bonner, B. L. (2004). Parent-child interaction therapy with physically abusive parents: Efficacy for reducing future abuse reports. *Journal of Consulting and Clinical Psychology, 72*(3), 500.

Cunningham, P. B., & Henggeler, S. W. (1999). Engaging multiproblem families in treatment: Lessons learned throughout the development of multisystemic therapy. *Family Process, 38*(3), 265–281.

Greene, R. W., Ablon, J., Goring, J. C., Raezer-Blakely, L., Markey, J, Monuteaux, M. C., . . . Rabbitt, S. (2004). Effectiveness of collaborative problem solving in affectively dysregulated children with oppositional-defiant disorder: Initial findings. *Journal of Consulting and Clinical Psychology, 72*(6), 1157–1164.

Hust J., & Kuppinger, A. (2014). Family-driven care. In G. Blau, B. Caldwell, & R. Lieberman (Eds.), *Residential interventions for children, adolescents and families: A best practice guide* (pp. 15–33). New York, NY: Routledge.

Jivanjee, P., Friesen, B. J., Kruzich, J. M., Robinson, A., & Pullmann, M. (2002). *Family participation in system of care: Frequently asked questions (and some answers).* Portland, OR: Portland State University, Research and Training Center on Family Support and Children's Mental Health.

Leichtman, M., Leichtman, M. L., Barber, C. C., & Neese, D. T. (2001). Effectiveness of intensive short-term residential treatment with severely disturbed adolescents. *American Journal of Orthopsychiatry, 71*(2), 227–235.

Miller, R., & Rollnick, S. (2002). *Motivational interviewing: Preparing people for change* (2nd ed.). New York, NY: Guilford Press.

National Building Bridges Initiative Family Advisory Group. (2012). *Engage us: A guide written by families for residential providers.* Retrieved November 17, 2013, from www.buildingbridges4youth.org/workgroups/youth-family/products-resources

Saxe, G. N., Ellis, B. H., & Kaplow, J. B. (2007). *Collaborative treatment of traumatized children and teens: The trauma systems therapy approach.* New York: Guilford Press.

Sexton, T. L. (2010). *Functional family therapy in clinical practice: An evidence based treatment model for at risk adolescents.* New York: Routledge.

Sexton, T. L., Datchi, C., Evans, L., LaFollette, J., & Wrigth, L. (2013). The effectiveness of couple and family-based clinical interventions. in M. J. Lambert (Ed.), *Bergin and Garfield's Handbook of psychotherapy and behavior change* (6th ed., pp. 587–639). Hoboken, NJ: Wiley.

5   Becoming a Youth-Guided Residential Organization

Eric Lulow, Kaitlyn Harrington,
Marvin Alexander, and Lacy Kendrick Burk

Youth-guided care, as defined by the Substance Abuse and Mental Health Services Administration (SAMHSA), "means that youth are engaged as equal partners in creating systems change in policies and procedures at the individual, community, State and national levels" (SAMHSA, 2013, para. 5). This concept is important because organizations that develop and implement youth-guided strategies increase buy-in and participation from youth, and generate better outcomes for their futures (American Association of Children's Residential Centers [AACRC], 2010).

Engaging and empowering young people through youth-guided care provides opportunities to increase self-efficacy. Perceived self-efficacy, which has been shown to improve a person's functioning, is defined as a person's belief about his or her capabilities to produce designated levels of performance that exercise influence over events that affect his or her life. Self-efficacy beliefs determine how people feel, think, motivate themselves, and behave (Bandura, 1994). Supporting youth in developing a higher sense of self-efficacy, and helping them to take ownership and responsibility for their actions across multiple life domains, allows them to develop the necessary skill sets to enhance their own well-being and futures.

Although the importance of meaningful inclusion of youth was internationally highlighted 2 decades ago, when the United Nations Children's Rights Alliance (CRA, 1992) made "participation" a fundamental right of all young people, research and consensus about conditions, contexts, and impacts related to youth engagement are still in the early stages. Myths about the readiness of youth and adults to engage with each other and what that engagement looks like have inhibited the growth of youth–adult partnerships. This applies particularly to residential programs in which traditional structures have created inherent power differentials between adults and youth.

This chapter will outline the issues related to the application and implementation of youth-guided principles and practices in residential programs across various service delivery levels, and highlight strategies that a residential program can use to expand and sustain a focus on youth engagement and empowerment.

Challenges and Strategies in Residential Programs

Even under the best of circumstances, there are barriers to embracing and implementing youth-guided practices and cultures in residential programs (Mataresse, Mora, & McGinnis, 2005). Some of the most consistently identified challenges include

- low youth buy-in;
- low staff buy-in;
- negative youth/adult partnership dynamics; and
- limited access to time and resources.

In order to address these challenges effectively, it is important to evaluate where your organization currently is in becoming more youth guided.

Evaluating Organizational Levels of Youth Engagement

Building a system that is youth guided requires self-reflection, leadership, persistence, and effective evaluation. Roger Hart (Fletcher, 2011) developed a model, or guidepost, called Harts Ladder, to help organizations gain a better understanding of where their agency currently stands with respect to youth participation and youth engagement. This model can help an organization determine goals and identify strategies to become more youth guided. The goal is for an organization to climb past those rungs that are considered levels of nonparticipation (these levels include *manipulation*, *decoration*, and *tokenism*), and foster an environment that promotes equality and engages young people in higher levels of participation (these levels include *youth consulted*, *youth/adult equality*, *completely youth driven*, and *youth/adult equity*). This will require commitment from everyone, including the youth and staff (Fletcher, 2011). (More information about Harts Ladder is available at www.freechild. org/ladder.htm)

According to Brown, Allen, Barrett, Ireys, and Blau (2010), organizations that engage and empower youth, those at the top of the ladder, share a number of practices, including

- strength-based individualized treatment planning;
- incorporating family members and "natural helpers";
- preserving family relationships through regular contact between youth and their families;
- collaborating with community-based providers to connect youth with home and community-based services and supports;
- mentoring of youth and peer-to-peer supports; and
- participation of youth in oversight activities, such as agency advisory boards, management, staff training and hiring, and quality assurance reviews.

These practices are included on the self-assessment tool of the Building Bridges Initiative, a useful instrument for gauging where you are with youth-guided care at the practice level, so you can start looking at where you need to go. This tool is immediately applicable to residential interventions and is an important resource for self-assessment. To find this tool and many other useful resources, visit www.buildingbridges4youth.org/products/tools. The following sections will take you on a guided process for what to do at the individual, organizational, and system levels to become more youth guided.

What Can Providers Do to Become More Youth Guided at the Individual Care Level?

It is important for every program to develop protocols and practices that will ensure that entry into residential, time while receiving residential interventions, and the transition back into the community are seamless, supportive, and coordinated. In order to facilitate a youth-guided practice, the youth needs to be an *active participant* throughout the entire process, and clinical approaches and models must be consistent with youth-guided care.

Entry phase—During intake and entry, each youth and family should be involved and have an understanding of the service and support options available to them. Youth should be engaged in a conversation about what they hope to achieve and about the particulars of the program so they are better prepared. Knowing the right questions to ask is often the best step in preparing for entry; for help with this, check out the Youth Tip Sheet that can be found at www.buildingbridges4youth.org/products/tip-sheets. To improve the youth-guided practices of your organization, consider

- hiring youth peer advocates as staff to provide youth voice at all levels of the organization and to support the youth served, using language common to young people that youth understand;
- having youth in your program provide feedback on the intake process and how it could be improved; and
- make sure that all intake materials are reviewed and edited by youth and youth peer advocates to ensure that they are written and presented in youth-friendly and youth-empowering terms.

During residential intervention phase—Traditionally, residential programs have been structured with stages and levels, a sort of one-size-fits-all design. To become more youth guided, programs need to be more individualized, taking into account the unique needs and goals of the youth. In order to take on this approach, AACRC recommends the following:

- Staff responses need to be unique and driven by the youth and the circumstances instead of by a set of organizational rules;

- youth and families need to be engaged in all aspects of the youth's individualized plan, including the decision-making and goal-planning processes;
- all treatment plans should put a strong focus on spending time with family and friends in the community, as well as skill-building activities; and
- all staff are trained to *focus on strengths* and to resolve disagreements so that youth are heard and responded to without dismissing adult concerns.

New York City Administration for Children's Services ensures that the following casework practices and services are available to youth in residential care:

- Identification and involvement of permanency resources
- Individualized assessment and treatment planning
- Skills-building for caregivers
- Frequent visiting
- Child-specific services
- Shortened lengths of stay
- Aftercare
- Residential respite.

Transition phase—In traditional residential programs, discharge is often based on the completion of a step or level in the program, not necessarily on whether the youth and family have the supports and skills they need to live together in the community. While it is often required that discharge planning starts at intake, this does not always occur, and youth are not integrally involved in designing their discharge plan. In a youth-guided residential intervention, staff should

- regularly engage youth in conversation regarding their own discharge plan and in identifying the services that they feel would benefit them;
- provide youth and families with choices to extend or reinitiate services that may have been helpful during the residential intervention phase once they return home; and
- find formal as well as natural supports within the community to link youth up with, prior to discharge.

It is also critical that organizations *create a normative environment* that will facilitate transition for the young people in their care. This includes

- supporting practices that *promote integration into the community* (e.g., making it a policy not to use the removal of prosocial activities as a consequence or punishment);
- creating opportunity for activities with prosocial *peers in the community* (e.g., basketball league, church choir, group guitar lessons);

- offering and/or connecting with community educational services that foster *full development* of young people's abilities;
- encouraging and not limiting the use of phone and social media technologies so that youth can maintain strong connections with immediate and extended family members, as well as friends from the community approved by the youth, family, and licensing agencies (if relevant);
- ensuring that programming inquires about, engages, and honors cultural backgrounds and preferences; and
- allowing young people to fail safely to facilitate learning and growth.

The key to creating such an environment is involving the youth in the conversations regarding mutual expectations in a manner in which both the youth and the adult's concerns are heard, understood, and considered when arriving at mutually acceptable decisions (AACRC, 2010).

Clinical Practices Consistent With Youth-Guided Principles

Key clinical models that are consistent with youth-guided practice and can be implemented throughout the previously mentioned phases include, but are not limited to, Motivational Interviewing, Wellness Recovery Action Plans (WRAPs), the 40 Developmental Assets, and Collaborative Problem Solving.

Motivational Interviewing—Motivational Interviewing (MI) is a collaborative, person-centered approach that encourages motivation for change. MI has been proven effective to engage individuals with co-occurring disorders and developing therapeutic relationships. In order for a therapist to be successful at MI, five strategies to incorporate are

- assessing the person's perception of the problem;
- exploring the person's understanding of his or her condition;
- examining the person's desire for continued treatment;
- ensuring a person's attendance at initial sessions; and
- expanding the person's perceptions for the possibilities of successful change.

As youth in residential programs may be characterized by their ambivalence to change, MI techniques, such as counseling, assessment, multiple sessions, and brief interventions, can be a tool to address this ambivalence in a nonhierarchical, noncoercive manner, increase participation in treatment, and encourage positive outcomes. While MI can be used at any stage during treatment, it has been shown to be particularly effective when incorporated early on in treatment as well as for individuals who are experiencing problems but do not recognize the severity of their condition. It is also helpful to determine the individual's goals and functional level (Substance Abuse and Mental Health Services Administration, 2013).

Wellness recovery action plans—Wellness recovery action plans (WRAPs) are self-designed programs that can be adapted and modified to the individual throughout treatment. The objectives of WRAPs are set in a workshop style that includes presentations, demonstrations, interactive discussions, and other activities around the following topics (Copeland, 2013):

- Hope, personal responsibility, education, self-advocacy, and support;
- accessing good health care and managing medications;
- self-monitoring using WRAP—an individualized system for monitoring and responding to symptoms to achieve the highest possible levels of wellness;
- wellness tools, including finding and keeping a strong support system, peer counseling, focusing, relaxation exercises, diet, light, exercise, sleep, journaling, music;
- dealing with the effects of trauma;
- suicide prevention;
- building self-esteem;
- changing negative thought patterns to positive; and
- building a lifestyle that promotes wellness.

40 Developmental Assets—The 40 Developmental Assets are a research-based set of indicators that are positively correlated with youth becoming successful adults. Its lack of "mental health" terminology makes it a potentially useful tool for youth and providers to have a common language to discuss goals that are important to both youth and adults. The assets center on the following components (Search Institute, 2013):

- **External Assets:**
  - Support
  - Empowerment
  - Boundaries and expectations
  - Constructive use of time

- **Internal Assets**
  - Commitment to learning
  - Positive values
  - Social competencies
  - Positive identity

Collaborative Problem Solving—Collaborative Problem Solving (CPS) is an approach that has a fundamental underlying philosophy of "young people do well if they can," and if they are not doing well, we need to understand why. It involves engaging youth and families in dialogue from which they learn to solve problems they are experiencing. Key to CPS is hearing the youth's concerns first, and working diligently to understand where they are coming from before putting adult concerns on the table. The approach empowers youth in individual and group conversations, looking to forge the partnership from which solutions can emerge. The process helps youth, and the adults, develop a host of enduring skills and can be used in all settings—residential, home, community, and school.

What Can Providers Do to Become More Youth Guided at the Organizational Level?

Over the past decade, providers in residential programs have realized the benefit of positive youth engagement in provision of services to youth. In a study conducted by the National 4-H Council (Zeldin, McDaniel, Topitzes, & Calvert, 2000), researchers found that youth involvement in organizational decisions helps organizations in a variety of ways, including

- bringing clarity to their mission;
- enhancing staff responsiveness to young people served; and
- strengthening staff commitment to the work.

Embracing youth engagement as a principle of service provision and embedding youth involvement practices into organizational processes enhances the commitment and energy of the adults, improves staff-resident collaboration, and assists young people in the development of real-life skills as they transition out of residential programs and back into the community (Zeldin, et al., 2000).

As practices in residential interventions continue to shift away from authoritative models and towards a culture of partnership and collaboration guided by the youth and families served, the need to identify and address related challenges becomes apparent. Though some providers of residential interventions have embraced the concept of youth engagement and have implemented youth-guided practices into service provision, others struggle to identify strategies to overcome their challenges. The purpose of this section is to introduce the reader to strategies to address these challenges at the organizational level, including youth peer support, trauma-informed approaches, positive youth–adult partnerships, youth leadership groups, and peer recreation and networking.

Youth Peer Support

Youth peer support/advocate staff are young people—typically 18 to 30 years old—who have had experience in similar service-delivery systems. A current study from the Pathways Research and Training Center, in Portland, Oregon, found that service providers are increasingly exploring the use of one-on-one peer support as a strategy for engaging emerging adults in treatment and other services, and for helping to ensure that the services that are provided feel helpful and useful to the young person (Pathways RTC, 2013).

Developing youth peer supports within your organization is a great way to generate better buy-in to program activities and will also help improve the self-efficacy of youth who are involved in the program (Bandura, 1994). Youth peer supports should be individuals with lived experience who

- are part of the intake process to explain the ins and outs of the program;
- facilitate conversations between youth and staff;

- prepare youth in the program for important meetings;
- assist in the development and implementation of youth activities and conduct outreach to community partners; and
- remain a support for the youth postdischarge.

Having youth peer support on staff is a great way to gain buy-in from youth, increase their self-efficacy, and become a more youth-guided organization.

A great resource on developing these types of positions is the *Building Bridges Initiative (BBI) Peer Youth Advocates in Residential Programs Handbook* and appendices. These documents were developed by the BBI Youth and Family Partnership Workgroup in collaboration with the BBI Youth Advisory Group. The purpose of the handbook and appendices are to provide a conceptual framework and links to specific tools and technical assistance resources for organizations interested in expanding youth voice and adding Peer Youth Advocate (PYA) positions to their teams. For more information on this resource, visit www.buildingbridges4youth.org/products/tools.

> The New York State Office of Mental Health New York City–based staff developed and implemented a BBI plan to incorporate youth-guided practices into all community residential programs. Youth advocates have been hired; youth have become part of staff hiring and evaluation; youth serve as cotrainers in orientation and staff training; practices stressing youth empowerment and leadership have been developed/implemented (e.g., youth have access to training as peer mentors; meaningful youth councils).

Trauma-Informed Approaches

Another strategy to increase your organization's youth-guided practices is the use of trauma-informed care (see Chapter 7). Active listening and providing a supportive environment helps young people develop relationships centered on trust. Many young people in residential programs have experienced traumatic life circumstances that contribute to strained relationships with adults, particularly in regard to trust. Understanding trauma and how it affects youth in the engagement process can help to overcome these barriers. To obtain more information on how to make your program more trauma informed, visit the National Child Traumatic Stress Network (http://nctsn.org) and refer to Chapter 7 of this book.

Positive Youth–Adult Partnerships

Youth–adult partnerships require structural changes in the way adult organizational leaders conduct business. Accommodations must be made in order for youth to develop competence in performing tasks that are normally reserved for adults. Experienced youth advocates have suggested that such changes in structure will only come about when policy makers work with adult leaders to persuade them of the benefits of a more open and democratic relationship with children and young people (Jennings, Parra-Medina, Messias, & McLoughlin, 2006). Some solutions to address these needed changes in organizational structure would include

- restructuring organizational bylaws to require youth participation on boards and committees;
- providing training for youth to serve in these roles and to staff to appropriately prep and engage youth for these types of meetings;
- holding meetings during times that youth can attend (e.g., after school hours); and
- making sure that youth have the information and resources to attend meetings (e.g., transportation or Internet access for online meetings).

For some organizations, it is believed that young people are unwilling or unable to become involved in their own care, or are too emotionally or behaviorally challenged. However, young people may appear unwilling to be involved simply because they have never been given the chance or invited to the table before. Providing training opportunities for young people (by adults/other youth with experience) to participate on boards and committees, and educating adults about the power and benefits of authentic youth engagement is a strategy for implementation of youth-guided practices in residential programs (Mataresse et al., 2005). Examples of where to find training opportunities include the following:

- Youth MOVE (www.youthmovenational.org/opportunities).
- National Resource Center on Youth Development (www.nrcyd.ou.edu/).

Implementation of youth-guided practices in residential interventions will be a successful venture when young people have support and training opportunities and when organizational leaders demonstrate commitment to youth partnership. This success is indicated in residential programs when an empowered youth voice is systematically interwoven throughout the entire program. This may be evidenced by

- a meaningful resident/youth/student council that is valued for its experience and expertise;
- having youth served as advocates and educators;
- having youth served on organizational boards and committees, who are treated the same as other members (with appropriate developmental support);
- having youth served who are able to go to meetings (transportation and schedule); and
- having a culture of equal partnership and shared respect.

Youth Leadership Groups

Forming a youth group within your organization, such as a youth advisory council, can give youth voice and encourage them to be part of the change towards a more youth-guided program. Giving youth leadership opportunities and allowing them to be a part of the decision-making process is key to a program becoming more youth guided. A youth group can also help to foster an environment of peer support, and encourage youth to work with each other through their recovery process. Youth MOVE Kairos is a great example of a youth group developed within a residential setting. To find out more about this group, visit them online at http://kairosnw.org/home.

To develop an effective youth advisory council within your organization, consider using the "Developing and Sustaining a Youth Advisory Council" tip sheet from the National Building Bridges Initiative. This tip sheet provides excellent strategies and guidelines and can be found at www.buildingbridges4youth.org/workgroups/youth-family/products-resources.

Recreation and Peer Networking

It is important to allow youth opportunities to connect with one another in a positive environment with their peers, not only in the program but more especially in the community. Networking can be structured (such as with team-building exercises) or unstructured (such as a dinner and movie night, inclusive of community peers). When youth have the opportunity to network with other prosocial young people, it can provide them with positive peer role models and help them develop a better sense of self-efficacy. Such opportunities will also help youth to naturally develop peer support relationships. Though each young person's overall experiences are unique, they will often have a strong, supportive connection to other youth with similar experiences. When youth enjoy being a part of a group structure, they will have an increased buy-in to their overall activities. They are also likely to increase their commitment when they see how other youth are benefiting from participation in positive youth development types of activities that are available as part of the organization's approach to services and supports.

What Can Providers Do to Become Youth Guided in Local Systems?

As youth are developing skills and improving their ability to advocate for themselves, it becomes important for them to have opportunities to participate in advocacy efforts outside of their individual services and supports. *Youth guided* means that youth are involved at all levels of decision making, so a good place to start this process is by getting youth involved in natural opportunities in the community, from which they might decide to engage in greater system involvement. The following areas are examples.

Interacting in the Community

Building a sense of community and creating awareness about important community issues is extremely important in the life of a youth. Community creates a sense of belonging, and having an active role in the community can help influence the priorities of decision makers, educate community members about the needs of young people in systems, and help other young people realize that they are not alone. As part of the process, youth can learn social marketing practices that are intended to

- recruit other youth to support and advocacy activities;
- inform community leaders of important issues that affect youth involved in systems;
- encourage community members to support young people by donating their time, treasures, and talents to organizations that support youth and families; and
- recruit mentors, foster parents, advocates, and other volunteers.

There are many negative stereotypes and assumptions about youth and families receiving services. When youth engage in social marketing practices, it can reduce prejudice and discrimination that youth in systems often face.

Personal Development and Leadership Training

Activities and trainings in the community, and those related to systems, promote essential, positive life skills. As youth and young adults see themselves improving their skills and achieving goals, they start gaining confidence in their own abilities and begin to view obstacles as tasks to complete rather than as barriers preventing them from success, with a positive impact on a their experience of self-efficacy.

Opportunities to develop leadership skills are critical. It is important to avoid the "pop up" or token youth at a committee meeting or speaking event. Young adults need to be adequately trained and properly prepared to ensure maximum effectiveness. Leadership development trainings should include

- public speaking,
- strategic sharing,
- trauma-informed method of engagement,
- policy advocacy,
- social marketing,
- leadership,
- community organizing,
- board development,
- fundraising, and
- technical writing.

These skills will help a youth succeed and will help youth participants become successful in other areas of their lives.

In addition, youth need to be given the opportunity to develop and practice these skills in a safe and structured environment. Part of their personal development should be learning how to target specific tasks. For example, youth should learn how to develop and maintain a portfolio of themselves and the work that they have done; when supportive adults assist youth in this capacity, it shows that they have a real interest in their personal growth and development. Youth establishing leadership skills should have a biography, résumé, curriculum vitae, and professional portfolio. Many of the tasks that young leaders participate in and that are reflected in their portfolio will help them with whatever direction they choose to go in their later work life.

Positive Self-Advocacy

Another part of increasing the personal development of youth and young adults in your program is to help them develop positive self-advocacy skills—the first youth-guided step in supporting the development of young people. The origin of self-advocacy stems from the intellectual and developmental disabilities movement, asserting an individual's rights to speak up, to be in control of their own resources and how they are directed, and to make life decisions without undue influence or control by others (West et al., 1999). Van Reusen, Bos, Schumaker, and Deshler (1994) defined *self-advocacy* as "an individual's ability to effectively communicate, convey, negotiate or assert his or her own interests, desires, needs, and rights. It involves making informed decisions and taking responsibility for those decisions" (Van Reusen et al., 1994, para. 2). In an environment where youth voice is encouraged, students develop the self-advocacy skills necessary to effectively participate in community and system conversations.

Engage Youth Groups in Community Forums

Youth groups established in residential interventions should work on developing partnerships with organizations within the community to make sure that their training programs for staff or volunteers include at least a panel of young people who share their experiences on what it is like to receive the types of services they provide. There are many organizations and groups that would benefit from receiving such trainings, such as

- state-level child welfare organizations;
- the state administrative office of the courts;
- court-appointed special advocates—CASA (volunteers, case supervisors);
- the state juvenile justice department (case workers, probation officers);
- mental health providers in the community (therapists, counselors, systems of care);

- schools in the community (guidance counselors, teachers, administrators, student organizations);
- residential staff; and
- other youth in systems.

Additionally, youth working in this area should be trained on policy advocacy, which is often a tricky and difficult area to navigate. When youth and young adults know more about how certain policies impact them, it can help them form ideas on what could be changed for the better. It is often easier to join forces with another group that is more seasoned in this area rather than beginners. However, it is very important that policy makers on local, state, and national levels be informed about how their decisions will impact youth receiving services and supports. Youth who have been or are receiving residential interventions are in a unique position to do so.

Practical Implementation Considerations

Building a youth-guided organization, especially in residential programs, does not happen overnight. Adopting youth-guided practices and principles will be both challenging and rewarding. No matter where an organization is in this process, the goal should be to become more youth guided every day. The following steps will move an organization along this path:

- Develop relationships with the youth in your program and provide them with trainings and resources on how they can use their voice and experiences to be impactful in various ways, including on committees.
- Partner with youth and youth peer advocates to develop a strategic plan to build a more youth-guided process within your organization (doing so will help generate buy-in from youth in your program).
- Train staff on the community resources that are available for the youth they serve. In addition, train staff to promote and encourage involvement from the youth in the decision-making processes.
- Identify and engage with other, more experienced youth advocates that can serve as peer mentors and supports, and help the youth you serve develop the skills necessary to take on these peer-support roles.

As you are developing these youth–adult partnerships, take into account youth-friendly engagement strategies, such as scheduling meetings after school hours, providing transportation, and making sure meals are covered for youth participants.

To make certain that your services are youth guided, avoid a one-size-fits-all approach, make sure that your staff is taking time to learn about the youth and what works for them as individuals. Be certain to include the youth and their identified family in all of the decision-making processes that involve their lives. Provide youth with opportunities to be involved in their communities, and train them to develop their self-advocacy and leadership skills.

It is important to keep in mind that there will be bumps in the road and that this process will not always happen smoothly. Continue working with your staff to engage youth in every aspect of the decision-making process, from intake to discharge, and in setting the policies and procedures that govern how services and supports are provided. Following the steps and suggestions outlined in this chapter will help to ensure that your organization or program is on its way to becoming youth guided.

> By framing goals in ways that are about the young person's future, the work automatically focuses on the positive, something hopeful, which yields more active engagement. Also, this future's focus encourages an emphasis on youth strengths rather than deficits. (Rusty Clark, Director, National Center on Youth Transition)

Resources

There are many tools and frameworks that can be used to promote youth-guided care. The Building Bridges Initiative has many recently developed and helpful tools:

- Peer Youth Advocates in Residential Programs Handbook and appendices.
- Self-Assessment Tool, including the tool for Youth & Families, and the accompanying Instructional Guide.
- Your Life Your Future—Inside Info on the Residential Programs from Youth Who Have Been There—both the brief and expanded versions, as well as the recommendations for use.
- Promoting Youth Engagement in Residential Settings—Suggestions for Youth.
- Promoting Youth Engagement—What Providers Should Know.

Each of these resources are available for download at www.buildingbridges4y outh.org/products/tools.

References

AACRC. (2010). *Redefining residential: Youth guided treatment.* Retrieved June 27, 2013, from www.aacrc-dc.org/sites/default/files/Paper%207%20FINAL.pdf

Bandura, A. (1994). Self-efficacy. In V. S. Ramachaudran (Ed.), *Encyclopedia of human behavior* (Vol. 4, pp. 71–81). New York, NY: Academic Press. (Reprinted in H. Friedman [Ed.], *Encyclopedia of mental health.* San Diego: Academic Press, 1998).

Brown, J. D., Allen, K., Barrett, K., Ireys, H. T., & Blau, G. (2010) Family-driven youth-guided practices in residential treatment: Findings from a National Survey of Residential Treatment Facilities. *Residential Treatment for Children & Youth, 27*(3), 149–159.

Copeland, M. E. (2013). WRAP and recovery books. Retrieved June 27, 2013, from www.mentalhealthrecovery.com/

Fletcher, A. (2011). *Ladder of youth voice.* Retrieved June 27, 2013, from www.freechild.org/ladder.htm

Jennings, L. B., Parra-Medina, D. M, Messias, D. K. Hilfinger, & McLoughlin, K. (2006). *Toward a critical social theory of youth empowerment.* Retrieved July 6, 2013, from www.milcahferguson.com/MEF/Home_files/CriticalSocialTheoryYouthEmpowerment.pdf

Mataresse, M., Mora, M., & McGinnis, L. (2005). *Youth involvement in systems of care: Guide to empowerment.* Washington, DC: Technical Assistance Partnership, American Institutes for Research.

National Resource Center on Youth Development. (2013). *Youth engagement: Positive youth development.* Retrieved June 30, 2013, from www.nrcyd.ou.edu/youth-engagement/positive-youth-development

Pathways RTC. (2013). FAQ: Defining, supporting, and sustaining the peer support specialist role. Retrieved October 20, 2013, from www.pathwaysrtc.pdx.edu/pdf/proj4-peer-support-FAQ.pdf

SAMHSA. (2013). *System of care core values.* Retrieved June 27, 2013, from www.samhsa.gov/children/core-values.asp

Search Institute. (2013). 40 developmental assets for adolescents. Retrieved July 16, 2013, from www.search-institute.org/content/40-developmental-assets-adolescents-ages-12-18

Substance Abuse and Mental Health Services Administration. (2013). *Motivational interviewing.* Retrieved June 27, 2013, from www.samhsa.gov/co-occurring/topics/training/motivational.aspx

Van Reusen, A. K., Bos, C. S., Schumaker, J. B., & Deshler, D. D. (1994). The self-advocacy strategy for education and transition planning. Lawrence, KS: Edge Enterprises.

West, L. L., Corbey, S., Boyer-Stephens, A., Jones, B., Miller, R. J., & Sarkees-Wircenski, M. (1999). Transition and self-advocacy. *LdOnline.* Retrieved June 30, 2013, from www.ldonline.org/article/7757/

Zeldin, S., McDaniel, A. Kugen, Topitzes, D., & Calvert, M. (2000). *Youth in decision-making: A study on the impacts of youth on adults and organizations.* Madison, WI: Innovation Center/Tides Center, University of Wisconsin Extension.

6 Cultural and Linguistic Competence in Residential Programs

Why, What, and How

Vivian H. Jackson, Sylvia Fisher, and Deborah Green

Introduction

This chapter provides a framework for residential programs to address cultural diversity through the effective infusion of cultural and linguistic competence in all program interactions and engagements. Children and adolescents (hereafter referred to as "youth") and their families who receive residential services reflect a broad range of cultural diversity including race, ethnicity, sexual orientation, gender identities/expressions, faith communities, socioeconomic class, national origin, primary language, and geographic community. These cultural factors influence the youth and families' attitudes and behavior in their day-to-day interactions with residential staff in all delivered services and supports (e.g., investment and approach to education, response to authority, interaction with peers).

In the context of growing cultural diversity of the American population and the existing disproportionality of youth of color in residential programs, it is incumbent upon all residential programs to be proactive in creating, sustaining, and improving services to incorporate the role of culture and language into all aspects of their work. Residential programs reflect society at large, and these cross-cultural dynamics can influence healing and helping experiences for youth and families either positively or negatively. Programs that create an environment that accounts for culture can facilitate engagement and participation in the therapeutic process and contribute to successful clinical and functional outcomes. This chapter provides a range of practices, grounded in cultural and linguistic competence (CLC), to support residential programs in increasing their competence in this area and is informed by the Building Bridges Initiative's *Cultural and Linguistic Competence Guidelines for Residential Programs* (n.d.) and the National Center for Cultural Competence's (NCCC) *Planning for Cultural and Linguistic Competence in Systems of Care* (2004).

Why Cultural and Linguistic Competence?

An important reason for a residential program to address cultural and linguistic competence is to ensure the quality of interactions by establishing authentic, helping relationships with youth and their families that are built on mutual respect and trust. Programs need to (1) respond to the current and changing demographic trends among youth in the United States, territories, and tribal communities; (2) enhance the quality, effectiveness, and success of interventions by ensuring they are executed with particular attention to cultural and linguistic competence; and (3) address organizational self-interests related to compliance with regulatory or accrediting mandates as well as limiting liability.

Demographics—The United States population is becoming increasingly diverse; 47% of youth under the age of 18 are youth of color (U.S. Census Bureau, 2012). Current immigration and birth rates suggest that the growing diversity of this age cohort will continue. Many, but not all, of these youth communicate in English; the number of English language learners in kindergarten through 12th grade is approximately 4.7 million children, representing 10% of the K-12 population (Ramsey & O'Day, 2010). Although there is limited demographic data for residential programs available, about 0.9% of the U.S. 12- to 17-year-old population receives services in residential programs (Substance Abuse and Mental Health Services Administration, Office of Applied Studies, 2008). Moreover, 69% of youth in residential programs come from juvenile justice and child welfare systems, which serve a disproportionate number of children of color (Dale, Baker, Anastasio, & Purcell, 2007). Residential programs also serve cultural groups that may require focused and individualized attention, such as lesbian, gay, bisexual, transgender, and questioning (LGBTQ) youth; and youth who are refugees, deaf or hard of hearing, or observe specific religious practices.

Quality—The incorporation of CLC has the potential to improve engagement—indeed; the CLC of providers has been shown to improve mental health outcomes (Halliday-Boykins, Schoewald, & Letourneau, 2005). Furthermore, understanding cultural context and traditions related to conflict, respect, and other potential triggers can enhance a staff's ability to support youth in their work to achieve self-regulation and to avoid aggression. Accuracy of cross-cultural communication can also reduce the likelihood of treatment errors and adherence problems.

Compliance—Multiple regulatory and accreditation mandates specify legal and licensure requirements around CLC services,[1] and there are multiple reasons beyond legal ones for residential organizations to integrate and embed CLC in services, supports, and practices. Similarly, quality communication facilitates positive relationships and increased satisfaction, which in turn reduces the likelihood of malpractice suits (Office of Minority Health, U.S. Department of Health and Human Services, 2013).

What Does CLC Look Like?

A CLC residential program embodies the definition of cultural competence as described by Cross and colleagues (1989) and adapted by the NCCC (n.d.) through policies, structures, and practices that support the behaviors and attitudes of staff to engage in effective cross-cultural practice. At all organizational levels, including youth and families and the larger community, diversity is valued, and the dynamics of difference that arise as a natural outgrowth of diversity are managed. Furthermore, the program engages in self-assessment to discover its strengths and challenges and adapts policies, procedures, and practices as indicated (NCCC, n.d.). A CLC program assesses how CLC informs (1) service functions, (2) human resource functions, (3) fiscal requirements and allocations, (4) collaboration and community engagement, and (5) contracts (National Center for Cultural Competence, 2004). Each of these elements affects the integration of CLC in residential programs.

Service Functions—What We Do

Perspectives related to culture and language can be incorporated within every aspect of operations and routine functions of a residential program.

Creating a CLC Living Environment—Residential programs create their own cultural identity with norms, traditions, values, and rituals that are unique to the program. Programs can and should offer elements to help youth stay connected to meaningful, positive, and prosocial cultural traditions and practices. Acknowledgment of youth and family cultural identities includes culturally oriented decorations, reading materials, music, social activities, recreational activities, and hair-care and grooming options. Access to reading materials, music, television programs, and movies in preferred languages can address linguistic needs. Programs can be responsive to spirituality and various religious traditions by offering youth opportunities to engage in their religious practices; accommodating religious holidays and relevant dietary requirements; providing appropriate space for prayer or meditation; and supporting engagement in their practices in their home communities. Families are also affected by the design and décor of facilities.

Clinical Services—A cultural lens can be applied to the assessment process, treatment, and discharge planning. For example, the initial assessment would include the role of cultural factors to determine how cultural background and experience has contributed to challenges or served as protective factors for the

---

FACILITIES DÉCOR

EMQ Families First Parent Advisory Board shared that the agency's lobbies were not as family-centered as they wanted. They redesigned the lobby, reflecting the culture of children and their families, as well as using artwork and pictures made by some of the children. This change contributed to families reporting that they were welcomed and that it was a safe place to visit.

For more information, contact EMQ Family First (www.emqff.org).

youth and family. Treatment decisions should include an assessment of whether a particular evidence-based treatment is culturally and linguistically appropriate for the youth and/or family. Comprehensive "family-finding" that expands the youth's viable support network should be a priority; this also ensures that family of origin, family of choice, fictive kin, foster family, and/or others are included in the treatment, support, and discharge planning process, as appropriate. Discharge planning would contain preparations for the cultural context of the next stage of the youth and family's experiences including preparation to address bias and discrimination youth and families may encounter in school, employment, and community services and supports.

Educational services—Assessment tools and processes for academic placement should be culturally informed and conducted in the primary language of the youth. Curricula should reference the history, challenges, victories, contributions, and perspectives of the youth and family's cultural group(s). Advocacy and intervention should be implemented if youth experience bias, discrimination, bullying, or other negative behavior from peers or personnel related to their cultural identity. Ideally, youth and families should be connected to an educational environment in the community or in the residential program that reflects a respect for cultural and linguistic diversity.

Language access—A crosscutting objective for residential programs is to ensure appropriate language access for youth and their families by identifying (1) persons who need assistance, (2) how language needs will be provided, and (3) needed procedures, policies, and processes to ensure access to services that meet the linguistic needs of youth and families. Multiple strategies, such as the availability of bilingual/bicultural or multilingual/multicultural staff and interpreters (including American Sign Language [ASL]) and the production and/or translation of relevant materials into languages of service populations can be instituted. Interpretation and translation services should be deemed qualified to accurately relay the content, emotion, and degree of emphasis for all parties in the communication process. Residential programs may also experience high demand for non-English language access services within their service communities. The DePelchin Center embarked upon a focused staffing strategy to accommodate these language needs.

CREATING A DIVERSE WORKFORCE AND ADDRESSING LINGUISTIC COMPETENCE

DePelchin Children's Center recruits staff from diverse communities by advertising in community newspapers and magazines, and targeting publications in diverse communities. The agency also provides a scholarship grant with the University of Houston to support master's-level social worker training of Spanish-speaking students. The agency gives a $1,000 bonus to any staff who are fluent in Spanish.

For more information, go to www.depelchin.org.

Quality indicators and CQI process—A crosscutting process enables the program to discern strengths and challenges in services to specific populations. Data are collected by cultural group (e.g., race, ethnicity, tribal/clan affiliation, language, sexual orientation, gender identities/expression, geographic locale, faith community, immigration/refugee status) and knowledge is gained through the disaggregation and analysis of the data for those groups. Data analysis by cultural/linguistic group for items, such as clinical and functional indicators, placement decisions, levels of restrictiveness, permanency decisions, length of stay, clinical interventions, medications prescribed, disciplinary actions, and discharge plans will help programs assess overall progress as well as how each of these groups is faring on each of these dimensions.

The program needs to understand the needs, preferences, strengths, and challenges of youth and families based on their cultural contexts. Tools such as a *Community Resource Assessment* (Deeds et al., 2008) can be used to gain knowledge of available beneficial services and supports within the youth and family's community environment. This accumulated data can be used to inform program goals and objectives, guide program improvements, and align resources to support those improvements. Youth and family members, advocates, community representatives, and relevant staff should collaborate to interpret findings and develop recommendations for any needed corrective action.

Regular collection, analysis, and reporting of performance indicator data is necessary to enhance organizational-level monitoring and decision making around improving cultural and linguistic competence throughout the organization. Performance measurement, along with thoughtful, committed, and effective performance management will result in continuous improvement of organizational cultural and linguistic competence, an approach identified by the Building Bridges Initiative (BBI).

THE BUILDING BRIDGES INITIATIVE EMPHASIS ON CLC

The BBI has identified crosscutting performance guidelines and indicators that encompass the entire spectrum of experience for youth and their families involved with residential care, including the referral/entry stage, during/within residential placement, and postresidential placement (Building Bridges Initiative Performance Guidelines and Indicators Matrix). The BBI specifies that communities embrace, value, and celebrate the diverse cultures of their children, youth, and families and work to eliminate mental health disparities. Further, CLC and diversity are infused as preeminent values throughout the continuum of care for youth who participate in residential care. Accordingly, CLC will be demonstrated throughout all aspects of service planning and delivery, including assessment process and tools, Child and Family Team (CFT) process, staff diversity, training, provider choice, use of evidence-based practices (EBP) demonstrated to be effective with specific populations and/or modified based on practice-based evidence, respect for culturally-based healing practices, and so forth.

An integral activity to be conducted upon program entry is the completion of a cultural inventory (e.g., cultural/ethnic identity, language, values, spiritual life, family traditions, gender and sexual identity issues, other relevant preferences) used to develop the treatment and support plan for the youth and family. A Community Resource Assessment (CRA) and a strength-based assessment should also be completed to develop and customize services and supports to address the unique CLC needs of individual youth and their families.

For more information, go to www.buildingbridges4youth.org.

Human Resource Functions—Who We Are

The goal of a diverse workforce should be included in the organizational strategic plan. Human resource functions should advance CLC by addressing recruitment, preparation, and accountability, and the workforce must be prepared to implement CLC services and supports at all levels.

Diversity—Programs are encouraged to develop a workforce at all levels of the organization that reflect the cultural diversity of the youth and families served. Family partners and youth peers reflecting the diversity of the service population can be particularly effective staff members and can function as cultural brokers between other program staff and youth, and their families. Staff diversity contributes to the trust and comfort that youth and family members have in the program. Recruiting materials should emphasize the importance of cultural and linguistic competence as part of hiring criteria, and announcements of available positions should be included in culture specific media and culture specific organizations in relevant languages.

CLC of the workforce—Workforce diversity alone does not mean that the workforce is CLC. All staff, volunteers, board members, and executive leadership need to be offered learning opportunities and receive supervision, mentoring, and/or coaching, as indicated, by internal assessments and other means. CLC content should be included in orientation activities and ongoing professional development activities as stand-alone sessions, and embedded in other training content. Reflective supervision, coaching, and mentoring offer useful approaches to help individuals with the application of knowledge, skills, and attitudes in actual situations.

Training content should include basic overview of CLC policies, processes, and principles; information about culture-specific groups that are reflected in the service population and community at large; and opportunities to increase self-awareness and address issues such as bias, prejudice, discrimination, and privilege. Employees with data collection responsibilities can be trained how to collect race, ethnicity, and language data, and clinicians can be trained about the cultural implications in psychopharmacology and other clinical interventions. Training can be led by training staff, community partners, family partners, youth peers, external trainers, and consultants. Including the experience of staff, volunteers, youth, and family members, as members of the teaching team, is

---

CULTURE-SPECIFIC STAFF TRAINING FOR LGBTQ YOUTH

Hathaway-Sycamores Children and Family Services participates in RISE, a pilot program supported by the Permanency Innovations Initiative with a goal of securing permanent homes for LGBTQ children and youth in foster care and their families. RISE has created a specially trained and certified team of clinicians, parent partners, youth specialists, case-managers, and evaluators that employs wraparound, family search and engagement, and Family Acceptance Project (FAP) technologies and materials. The FAP, based on the work of Dr. Caitlin Ryan and her team, is a research-based, culturally grounded approach to help culturally and linguistically diverse families decrease rejection and increase support for their LGBT children. The RISE pilot program offers training to stakeholder staff in the community and residential programs, and includes a coaching component to its operations.

Contact Hathaway-Sycamores at www.hathaway-sycamores.org; see Family Acceptance Project at http://familyproject.sfsu.edu/.

---

also beneficial. Self-directed study can also be an appropriate training option. Hathaway-Sycamores Children and Family Services participates in RISE, which offers a model pilot program that adopts a comprehensive training approach to address the needs of LGBTQ children and youth in foster care and their families.

Workforce accountability—Job descriptions should clearly describe how CLC applies to specific work or volunteer functions. Performance evaluations should reference these functions and prescribe goals for personal development and contribution to the integration of CLC within the program. Staff accomplishments in this effort should be recognized and celebrated.

Fiscal Resources and Allocation—Where Does the Money Go?

Programs need to be purposeful in allocating both financial and staff resources to components that support and promote CLC. Fiscal plans should include provisions for the hiring/availability of personnel required to guide, implement, and monitor the CLC work in the organization. These plans should include funds for trainers, consultants, information technology modifications, interpretation and translation services, and community engagement activities, among other program components and features. Allocation of existing resources and infusion of new funds will support these activities and ensure their sustainability.

Collaboration and Community Engagement—Who Are Our Partners?

Residential programs are challenged to establish knowledge of and meaningful relationships with youth, families, and their home communities, regardless of distance. These efforts include forging strong relationships with culturally and linguistically diverse community-based services and supports available to youth and families, both during the residential intervention and following their discharge into the community. Organizations, family partners, youth peers, and leaders from various cultural communities can assist by identifying resources, offering consultation on program strengths and areas for growth, creating new services, and offering strategies to improve effectiveness. Representatives from these cultural communities on program boards, advisory committees, and so forth, can ensure representation and voice that can help guide programs in identifying resources, supports and services for diverse youth and families. The need for community partnership extends to youth and families from communities that are geographically distant from the residential program. Programs should develop knowledge of resources and potential allies on behalf of youth and families in these communities.

Contracts—Whom Do We Entrust to Deliver Services on Our Behalf?

Residential programs engage institutions and businesses (e.g., school programs, food services, cleaning services, clinical services, language access services) to provide services to the program, youth and families. All services offered in the name of the residential program, including those offered through contracted services, should be held accountable for CLC. Contracts should specify expectations that services would be appropriate for populations being served, by a workforce prepared to serve those populations, and with sufficient and appropriate infrastructure in place to facilitate ongoing professional growth and development in CLC. In sum, residential programs can specify what is expected of contractors to ensure that CLC is embedded fully within the fabric of the organization and addresses cultural needs and preferences across a wide spectrum of diversity.

How to Move the CLC Agenda Forward in Programs

Champions who promote and advance CLC within organizations are frequently frustrated with the slow pace of change due partly to normal resistance to change but, more profoundly, because race, ethnicity, religion, difference, privilege, gender, or immigration status are frequently highly emotionally charged topics in the United States (Brantley, Frost, & Razak, 1996). Given the challenges that surround even a conversation about culture, a fully developed strategy needs to be employed to embed CLC in organizations as described in preceding sections.

Organizational Change

The promotion of CLC challenges members of the organization to reconsider past beliefs, engage in different behaviors, and work within different structures.

Organizational change theories, such as Lewin's force field analysis (Lewin, 1951), Kotter's eight stages of change (Kotter, 1996), or Prochaska's transtheoretical model of change (Prochaska, Prochaska, & Levesque, 2001) offer guidance on how to establish a process that will assess organizational readiness for change and provide an approach to (1) motivate and mobilize change while facilitating emotional safety of organizational members, and (2) institutionalize changes (Mayeno, 2007). These models recognize the pivotal role of persons in positions of authority to help ensure that change becomes institutionalized, including board members and executive leadership teams and leaders at all levels.

A critical step in the change process is an assessment of the organization's strengths and areas for growth. A checklist, such as the one in Appendix can be used to (1) identify perceived program strengths and areas for growth, (2) begin conversations about CLC, and (3) discuss ways to elicit the opinions of youth and their families about how their cultural preferences and needs are being addressed. Providing opportunities for staff and partners to internally process and engage in dialogue about these issues are important first steps to achieving meaningful and actionable outcomes.

Leadership

Leaders express the vision for change, are champions for change, use their position and personal influence to encourage change, and engage leadership from different departments and levels, youth, family members, and community representatives to shepherd the necessary changes. Leadership frequently entails ensuring that resources are available to facilitate the acquisition of knowledge and skills required to serve a culturally and linguistically diverse population, instituting necessary policy and procedural changes, and establishing appropriate structures, practices and interventions, which constitute the nuts and bolts of change processes.

Change efforts around CLC require a change in "values, beliefs and habits of behavior," or what Heifetz calls an "adaptive challenge" (Heifetz, 1994, p. 3). Change efforts related to culture and language can surface ongoing issues that have been present, but not openly addressed, such as cross-cultural conflicts, power differentials, and conscious and unconscious biases. Movement on these issues requires attitudinal change or changes in values, beliefs, and habits of behavior. Some organizations have discovered that tackling these underlying challenges directly has resulted in significant change. Several state child-welfare systems have incorporated *undoing racism initiatives* as part of the effort to address disproportionality in their systems. Similarly, residential programs can take similar steps to identify and address racism within their program, an approach undertaken by Children's Village and the Jewish Board of Family and Children's Services.

An intentional, multifaceted approach to organizational change must be employed to create an organizational culture that welcomes the challenge and

---

THE EXERCISE OF LEADERSHIP TO ADDRESS ADAPTIVE CHALLENGES: UNDOING INSTITUTIONAL RACISM

Jewish Board of Family and Children's Services mandated all 80 program directors (PDs) to attend the People's Institute for Survival and Beyond's *Undoing Racism Training*. PDs gained an enhanced understanding of what racism is, where it comes from, how it functions, why it persists, and how it can be changed. After completing the training, PDs reported they were better prepared to address their internal systems and the role that the organization plays in perpetuating racial and ethnic disparities.

For more information, see the Jewish Board of Family and Children's Services at www.jbfcs.org.

After attending a Peoples Institute's *Undoing Racism Training,* the Children's Village developed an institutional racism committee, co-lead by a parent advocate and the chief operating officer. The committee included diverse departments, programs, races, and organizational positions. Committee members shared their stories, developing trust and honest dialogues, met monthly to examine internal policies and procedures, examined direct practice with youth and families, and participated in advocacy within the larger community. A key early stage outcome was revision of hiring policies to better identify potential personnel with appropriate attitudes for the work and to implement new approaches to addressing equity in internal career ladder opportunities.

For more information, see Children's Village at www.childrensvillage.org, and Peoples Institute for Survival and Beyond at www.pisab.org.

---

benefits of serving diverse youth and family members and fully integrating CLC in serving and supporting these youth and families.

Summary

As culture is pervasive and language is key to effective communication, residential programs should emphasize the roles of culture and language in every single service and support they offer for youth and families. Residential programs are uniquely positioned to discern the role of culture in the lives of youth, particularly to give new insights into problem formation and to discover resources for recovery. When CLC is addressed effectively in residential programs, it can be a launch to an empowered life for youth and their families.

Many policies, structures, and practices need to be employed to embed CLC into programs, and these efforts will only bear fruit if the attitudes and actions of all constituencies align with the goal of effective cross-cultural practice. A thoughtful and purposeful change management strategy can be developed, instituted, and fully integrated to create an environment that truly values and respects diversity and the many cultural gifts that youth and their families bring to bear while in care. Program staff, volunteers, and community organizations and individuals affiliated with the program are all enriched by these gifts.

Additional Reading

American Association of Children's Residential Centers, CAFETY, and Youth MOVE. (2010). *Redefining residential: Youth guided treatment.* Retrieved October 3, 2013, from www.cafety.org/resources/804-redefining-residential-youth-guided-treatment

Becker, J., & Kennedy, M. (2003). Tapestry: A wraparound program for families of color facilitated by parent partners. *Focal Point: Research, Policy, and Practice in Children's Mental Health: Quality and Fidelity in Wraparound, 17,* 26–28.

Connor, D. F., Doerfler, L. A., Toscano, P. F., Volungis, A. M., & Steingard, R. J. (2004). Characteristics of children and adolescents admitted to a residential treatment center. *Journal of Child and Family Studies, 13*(4), 497–510.

Goode, T. D., Dunne, M. C., & Bronheim, S. M. (2006). *The evidence base for cultural and linguistic competency in health care.* Retrieved October 3, 2013, from www.commonwealthfund.org/Publications/Fund-Reports/2006/Oct/The-Evidence-Base-for-Cultural-and-Linguistic-Competency-in-Health-Care.aspx

Matarese, M. (2012). Improving outcomes for LGBT youth in out-of-home care settings—Implications and recommendations for systems of care. In S. K. Fisher, J. M. Poirier, & G. M. Blau (Eds.), *Improving emotional and behavioral outcomes for LGBT youth: A guide for professionals* (pp. 173–187). Baltimore, MD: Brookes.

Osher, D., Cartledge, G., Oswald, D., Artiles, A. J., & Coutinho, M. (2004). Issues of cultural and linguistic competency and disproportionate representation. In R. Rutherford, M. Quinn, & S. Mather (Eds.). *Handbook of research in behavioral disorders* (pp. 54–77). New York, NY: Guilford Press.

Smith, B. D., Duffee, D. E., Steinke, C. M., Huang, Y., & Larkin, H. (2008). Outcomes in residential treatment for youth: The role of early engagement. *Children and Youth Services Review, 30,* 1425–1436.

Resources and Web Sites

Achieving Cultural Competence: A Diversity Tool Kit for Residential Care Settings (Ministry of Children and Youth Services; www.children.gov.on.ca/htdocs/English/documents/topics/specialneeds/residential/achieving_cultural_competence.pdf)

Alliance for Racial Equity in Child Welfare, The Center for Study of Social Policy (www.cssp.org/reform/child-welfare/alliance-for-race-equity)

Building Bridges Initiative Guidelines for Cultural and Linguistic Competence in Residential Settings (BBI CLC Workgroup; www.buildingbridges4youth.org/)

Knowing Who You Are: Helping Youth in Care Develop Their Racial and Ethnic Identity (Casey Family Programs; www.casey.org/Resources/Initiatives/KnowingWhoYouAre)

National Center for Cultural Competence (http://nccc.georgetown.edu/)

Race Matters Institute (www.racemattersinstitute.org/)

Appendix A

Cultural and Linguistic Competence Self-Assessment Checklist for Staff of Residential Programs Providing Behavioral Health Services and Supports to Children, Youth, and Their Families

How to use this checklist: This checklist is designed for staff to indicate the extent to which they believe their residential programs demonstrate an environment that values cultural diversity and supports cultural and linguistic competence. Concrete examples of the kinds of values, practices, and resources that foster such an environment are included in checklist items.

This checklist can be completed by program administrators, staff, providers, and other personnel. Respondent feedback can provide information about the extent to which program staff perceive that practices which support cultural diversity and cultural and linguistic competence are incorporated within many daily program operations.

Results can be used (1) to identify perceived program strengths and areas for growth, (2) as a basis to engage program staff in discussion and planning efforts to enhance cultural and linguistic competence, and (3) to discuss ways to elicit the opinions of youth and their families about how their cultural preferences and needs are being addressed. Results can also be used to position the residential program to conduct an organizational self-assessment process that will yield a rich fund of information that can improve service utilization, outcomes, and satisfaction.

It is recommended that program administrators introduce the checklist to staff and clearly delineate the purpose and intended outcomes. Staff should be informed that the checklists will be completed anonymously. Staff should also be guaranteed that the process is safe and that they are encouraged to share their opinions in a candid manner. NOTE: Administering this type of checklist is only an initial step in a comprehensive process to examine cultural diversity and cultural and linguistic competence in residential programs serving children, youth, and their families.

There is no answer key with correct responses. If staff frequently responded "C," however, the residential program may not necessarily demonstrate an environment that values cultural diversity and supports cultural and linguistic competence.

Physical Environment, Materials, & Resources

In my view, our residential program:

1 Displays magazines, brochures, posters and other materials that reflect the different cultures, ethnicities, sexual orientations and gender identities of children, youth, families and the larger community are prominently displayed throughout the program.

2 Uses videos, films, CDs, DVDS and other media resources for behavioral health prevention, treatment, and other interventions that reflect the cultures, ethnic backgrounds, sexual orientations and gender identities of children and youth in care and their families.

3 Ensures books, movies, and other media resources are screened for negative cultural, ethnic, or racial stereotypes before sharing them with children and youth receiving program services.

4 Provides meals to children and youth in care that include foods that are unique to their cultural and ethnic backgrounds.

5 Has arrangements for unisex bathrooms, showers, and sleeping accommodations for youth who self-identify as transgender or are gender-nonconforming.

Communication and Linguistic Competence

In my view, our residential program:

6 Provides professional development and training to staff on the principles and practices of linguistic competence.

7 Has staff that have the capacity to apply principles and practices of linguistic competence to their respective roles and responsibilities.

8 Employs behavioral health providers and specialists who are familiar with and use cultural terms during assessment, treatment, or other interventions to communicate:

a. more effectively with children and youth
b. with children and youth who speak languages other than English.

9 Has staff that are able to identify familial colloquialisms used by children, youth, and families that may impact on assessment, treatment, and/or other interventions.

10 Has staff that know how to use visual aids, gestures, and physical prompts in interactions with children and youth who have limited English proficiency.

11   Ensures that bilingual staff and/or multilingual trained or certified interpreters are available during assessments, treatment sessions, meetings, and for other events for families who require this level of assistance.
12   Ensures all notices and communiqués to parents, families and caregivers are written in their language of origin for those who require this level of support.
13   Supports staff to use alternative formats and varied approaches to communicate and share information with children, youth and/or their family members who experience disability or who are deaf or hard of hearing.

Program Practices to Support Cultural and Linguistic Competence

In my view, our residential program has a process to:

14   Periodically review our mission statement, goals, policies, and procedures to ensure they incorporate principles and practices that promote cultural diversity and cultural and linguistic competence.
15   Seek information on acceptable behaviors, courtesies, customs and expectations unique to children and youth in care (and their families) based on race, culture, ethnicity, language, sexual orientation, and gender identity.
16   Adapt services and supports to respond to the preferences and needs of children and youth in care, and their families based on race, culture, ethnicity, language, sexual orientation, and gender identity.
17   Regularly review current research on disparities in behavioral health and health care related to race, culture, ethnicity, language, sexual orientation, and gender identity.
18   Adapt evidence-based prevention and intervention practices to ensure they are effective with children, youth, and their families from culturally and linguistically diverse groups.
19   Recruit, hire, train, and support a workforce that is diverse and culturally and linguistically competent, including parent and youth partners.
20   Discourage children and youth in group therapy, treatment situations and the therapeutic milieu from using hurtful language and slurs based on race, culture, ethnicity, language, sexual orientation and/or gender identity.
21   Intervene in an appropriate manner when staff and/or families engage in behaviors that show cultural insensitivity, bias, or prejudice.

Program Values and World View

In my view, our residential program respects and supports the following values and world view about family:

22   Family is defined differently by different cultures (e.g., extended family members, fictive kin, godparents, etc.).

23 Children and youth may identify and define their family to include individuals that comprise their "family of choice" in addition to, or instead of, their "family of origin."
24 Male-female roles in families may vary significantly among different cultures (e.g., who makes major decisions for the family, play and social interactions expected of male and female children).
25 Age and life cycle factors must be considered in interactions with children, youth and families (e.g., high value placed on the decisions of elders or the role of the eldest male in families).
26 Religion, spirituality, and other beliefs may influence how families respond to mental or physical illnesses, disease, disability, and death.
27 Families from different cultures will have different expectations of their children for acquiring self-help, social, emotional, cognitive, and communication skills.
28 Individuals from culturally diverse background may desire to acculturate into the dominant or mainstream culture in varying degrees, even within a single family.
29 The ultimate decision makers for services and supports for youth in care are parents, guardians, or other authorized adults in the youth's life.

In my opinion, our residential program respects and supports
the following values and world view about behavioral health
services and supports:

30 The meaning or value of prevention, intervention, and treatment for behavioral health challenges may vary greatly among diverse cultural and ethnic groups.
31 Beliefs and concepts about emotional well-being and mental illness may vary significantly from culture to culture.
32 The impact of stigma associated with behavioral health services may vary within culturally and ethnically diverse communities.

Adapted from *Promoting Cultural Diversity and Cultural Competency: Self-Assessment Checklist for Personnel Providing Behavioral Health Services and Supports to Children, Youth, and Their Families,* 2009, by T. D. Goode. Washington, DC: National Center for Cultural Competence (NCCC), Georgetown University Center for Child and Human Development (GUCCHD). © 2009 NCCC GUCCHD. Modified by Tawara D. Goode, Sylvia K. Fisher, and Wendy Jones with permission from the NCCC © August, 2013.

Note

1 Title VI of the Civil Rights Act, the Americans With Disabilities Act, and the Individuals With Disabilities Education Act all have requirements that address the nature of services for specific populations. Accrediting bodies such as the Commission

on Accreditation of Rehabilitation Facilities (CARF), the Council on Accreditation (COA), and Joint Commission on Accreditation of Healthcare Organizations (JCAHO) include requirements addressing cultural and linguistic competence. Several states and jurisdictions also have requirements related to cultural and linguistic competence for facility licensure, professional licensure, or condition of employment (Quality Interactions, 2013; U.S. Department of Health and Human Services, Office of Minority Health, 2013).

References

Brantley, C., Frost, D., & Razak, B. (1996). Success indicators: Action and reaction in the diversity change process. *The Diversity Factor, 4*(3), 11–19.

Cross, T., Bazron, B. J., Dennis, K., & Isaacs, M. R. (1989). Towards a culturally competent system of care: Vol. I. A monograph on effective services for minority children who are severely emotionally disturbed. Washington, DC: Georgetown University Child Development Center, National Technical Assistance Center for Children's Mental Health.

Dale, N., Baker, A. J., Anastasio, E., & Purcell, J. (2007). Characteristics of children in residential treatment in New York State. *Child Welfare, 86*(1), 5–27.

Deeds, B. G., Peralta, L., Willard, N., Ellen, J., Straub, D. M., Castor, J., & Interventions, A.M.T.N.H. (2008). The role of community resource assessments in the development of 15 adolescent health community-researcher partnerships. *Progress in Community Health Partnerships: Research, Education, and Action 2*(1), 31–39.

Goode, T., & Jones, W. (2009). *Linguistic competence.* Washington, DC: Georgetown University Center on Child and Human Development.

Halliday-Boykins, C. A., Shoewald, S. K., & Letourneau, E. J. (2005). Caregiver-therapist ethnic similarity predicts youth outcomes from an empirically based treatment. *Journal of Consulting and Clinical Psychology, 73*(5), 808–818.

Heifetz, R. (1994). *Leadership without easy answers.* Cambridge, MA: Belknap Press of Harvard University Press.

Kotter, J. (1996). *Leading change.* Cambridge, MA: Harvard Business School Press.

Lewin, K. (1951). *Field theory in social science.* New York, NY: Harper and Row.

Mayeno, L. (2007). States of multicultural organizational change. In L. Mayeno (Ed.), *Multicultural organizational development: A resource for health equity* (pp. 221–230). Los Angeles, CA: California Endowment and CompassPoint.

National Building Bridges Initiative Cultural and Linguistic Competence Workgroup. (n.d.). *Cultural and linguistic competence guidelines for residential programs.* Retrieved August 4, 2013, from www.buildingbridges4youth.org

National Center for Cultural Competence. (n.d.). *Foundations of cultural competence.* Retrieved August 4, 2013, from http://nccc.georgetown.edu/foundations/frameworks.html#ccdefinition

National Center for Cultural Competence. (2004). *Planning for cultural and linguistic competence in systems of care … for children & youth with social-emotional and behavioral disorders and their families.* Washington, DC: Georgetown University Center for Child and Human Development.

Office of Minority Health, U.S. Department of Health and Human Services. (2013). *National standards for culturally and linguistically appropriate services in health and health care: A blueprint for advancing and sustaining CLAS policy and practice.* Rockville, MD: Author.

Prochaska, J. M., Prochaska, J. O., & Levesque, D. A. (2001). A transtheoretical approach to changing organizations. *Administration and Policy in Mental Health and Mental Health Services Research, 28*(4), 247–261.

Quality Interactions. (2013). *State licensing requirements for cultural competency.* Retrieved August 27, 2013, from www.qualityinteractions.org/cultural_competence/cc_statelicreqs.html

Ramsey, A., & O'Day, J. (2010). *Title III policy: State of the states—ESEA evaluation brief: The English Language Acquisition, Language Enhancement, and Academic Achievement Act.* Washington, DC: American Institutes for Research.

Substance Abuse and Mental Health Services Administration, Office of Applied Studies. (2008, September 25). *Mental health service use among youth aged 12 to 17: 2005 and 2006.* Rockville, MD: SAMHSA.

U.S. Census Bureau. (2012). *U.S. Census Bureau projections show a slower growing, older, more diverse nation a half century from now.* Retrieved August 4, 2013, from www.census.gov/newsroom/releases/archives/population/cb12–243.html

U.S. Department of Health and Human Services, Office of Minority Health. (2013). *CLAS legislation map.* Retrieved August 27, 2013, from https://www.thinkculturalhealth.hhs.gov/Content/LegislatingCLAS.asp

7 Trauma-Informed Care

Janice LeBel and Neil Kelly

Trauma-informed care (TIC) is an evolving, organizational approach to recognizing and responding to the impact of trauma on people (National Association of State Mental Health Program Directors [NASMHPD], 2013). TIC is also a complex construct and comprehensive process. When practiced well, it is likened to an art form and the "platinum rule": *Do unto others as they wish to be treated* (LeBel, 2013).

Trauma experts have identified five dimensions of change to achieve a trauma-informed system: (1) administrative commitment, (2) universal trauma screening, (3) staff training and education, (4) staff hiring, and (5) modification of policies and procedures (Harris & Fallot, 2001). In residential program operations, these dimensions extend to areas such as systems integration, physical health, child/youth/family inclusion, gender considerations, organizational health, and the environment. This chapter reviews definitional challenges related to trauma-informed care, examines the facets of service (identified above), and provides pragmatic recommendations to successfully implement TIC.

Trauma: Evolving Terminology and Understanding

Understanding trauma and trauma terminology can be as challenging as implementing TIC. The experience and expression of trauma are not uniform (Huckshorn & LeBel, 2013; NASMHPD, 2013). Trauma is situation and person specific. There are also no standard, nationally recognized or accepted operational definitions of trauma or TIC. Trauma-related language is often used interchangeably (e.g., traumatic stress, trauma aware, trauma informed, trauma sensitive, trauma focused) which can confuse communication and the development and implementation of interventions. In addition, trauma verbiage, like the practice of TIC, is continually changing. In an effort to develop a common understanding of trauma, the Substance Abuse and Mental Health Services Administration (SAMHSA) drafted a working definition, which is posted on the SAMHSA Web site for public comment:

> Individual trauma results from an event, series of events, or set of circumstances that is experienced by an individual as physically and emotionally

harmful or threatening and that has lasting adverse effects on the individual's physical, social, emotional, or spiritual well-being. (SAMHSA, 2012, para. 2)

Trauma-Informed Care and Trauma-Informed Approach

TIC is a well-recognized concept that is often used in designing and describing contemporary residential services. TIC is a strength-based framework that emphasizes creating physical, psychological, and emotional safety for service recipients and staff, and opportunities for those affected by trauma to rebuild a sense of control and empowerment (Hopper, Bassuk, & Olivet, 2010). However, TIC is not trauma treatment (Huckshorn & LeBel, 2013).

Recently, the phrase *trauma-informed care* was revised and replaced with *trauma-informed approach* by SAMHSA (2012). This one-word shift acknowledges that several human-service sectors, such as education and juvenile justice/corrections, have adopted trauma-informed practices in their settings but do not identify as "care-giving" industries. SAMHSA's definition of a trauma-informed approach follows:

> A program, organization, or system that is trauma-informed realizes the widespread impact of trauma and understands potential paths for healing; recognizes the signs and symptoms of trauma in staff, clients, and others involved with the system; and responds by fully integrating knowledge about trauma into policies, procedures, practices, and settings. (2012)

Posttraumatic Stress Disorder

Compounding the semantic challenge is the evolving diagnosis most frequently associated with trauma: posttraumatic stress disorder (PTSD), which is the most severe form of traumatic response. The diagnosis was previously criticized for its nonapplicability to youth and lack of developmental sensitivity (Alisic, Van der Schoot, van Ginkel, & Kleber, 2008) and was recently redefined in the *Diagnostic and Statistical Manual of Mental Disorders, Fifth Edition* (American Psychiatric Association, 2013). The new PTSD criteria articulates functional and duration criteria for children, adolescents, and adults and specifies criteria for children under 6 years of age. Since many youth who are referred for residential intervention have experienced trauma, the first pragmatic TIC implementation strategy for residential programs is to stay current in the language that defines trauma and how it is addressed.

Key Principles

Key principles underlie effective TIC practices for residential programs. The most important principle is recognizing that trauma is not a tangential problem; it is considered the central problem (Hodas, 2006; NASMHPD, 2013) and requires active acknowledgment and incorporation into residential interventions. The second most important principle is to presume that children/youth/families and staff have a history of trauma, even if it is not acknowledged. A *universal precautions* approach is recommended by leading trauma experts and trade organizations (American Association of Children's Residential Centers [AACRC], 2010; NASMHPD, 2013). Related to this principle is conducting a trauma assessment—asking those served about their experience of trauma and responding to the information given. In fact, a sensitive, developmentally appropriate inquiry is necessary, and the information must be incorporated into an individual/family-specific treatment plan. Residential services must meet this rising standard of practice in the industry (AACRC, 2010; Huckshorn & LeBel, 2013). Some residential programs attuned to TIC will prepare for a new admission by asking about a child/youth/family's traumatic experience *before* the child/youth comes into care. In Massachusetts, TIC is a cornerstone of the Department of Mental Health services, and all people receiving care must have a trauma assessment conducted at admission (NASMHPD, 2013).

Another important principle of TIC is recognizing that trauma experience represents a profound loss of personal control. The focus is on learning "what happened" to the child/youth/family (NASMHPD, 2013) and building on strengths, rather than focusing on deficits. Therefore, the goal of TIC is to restore personal power and efficacy by providing choice, skills, and tools, and avoiding/preventing those practices that remove control and can be traumatizing/retraumatizing, such as restraint, seclusion, point/level systems, and idiosyncratic policies and procedures (Huckshorn & LeBel, 2013; NASMHPD, 2013).

Relevance of Trauma-Informed Care to Residential Care

Understanding trauma and implementing TIC with children/youth is particularly relevant to residential programs (Hummer, Dollard, Robst & Armstrong, 2010). Children/youth entering residential programs have higher rates of trauma than those entering foster care or kinship care (Hummer et al., 2010; Tarren-Sweeney, 2008). One study found that 98% of youth in residential programs had histories of trauma (NASMHPD, 2013). Moreover, rates of trauma/PTSD in adults who experienced out-of-home care in childhood are nearly double that of U.S. war veterans, and in a large-scale review of more than 500,000 children placed in out-of-home care, an eightfold higher rate of PTSD was reported compared to the general population (Pecora et al., 2005).

Efficacy of Trauma Treatment

TIC is intended to "support and sustain 'trauma-specific' services as they are introduced" (Hummer et al., 2010, p. 82). But, recent research on trauma-specific treatment raises the question of its effectiveness. A 2013 review of trauma treatment for children found that effective treatment is still in its infancy (Forman-Hoffman et al., 2013). The authors' comprehensive review of 6,647 unduplicated publications concluded the following:

With a single exception, studies comparing interventions with active controls did not show benefit . . . far more research is required to produce definitive guidance on the comparative effectiveness of psychotherapeutic or pharmacological interventions targeting children exposed to trauma. (Forman-Hoffman et al., 2013, pp. 23–24)

Similarly, a recent Cochrane Review examined the outcomes of 14 randomized controlled trial studies of PTSD treatment for children and adolescents and also reported equivocal findings. The authors concluded that

at this stage, there is no clear evidence for the effectiveness of one psychological therapy compared to others. There is also not enough evidence to conclude that children and adolescents with particular types of trauma are more or less likely to respond to psychological therapies than others. (Gillies, Taylor, Gray, O'Brien, & D'Abrew, 2012)

Given this limited efficacy, residential providers should invest in a trauma-informed approach that is sensitive to the impact of stress and trauma and embeds trauma-sensitive best practices in order to achieve positive outcomes.

Trauma-Informed Care Considerations, Challenges, and Solutions

Against the backdrop of shifting trauma language, definitional flux, and questionable treatment efficacy, important issues of care emerge—especially those fundamental issues that transcend the bounds of service population or setting, such as systems integration, physical health, and female gender considerations. In the following sections, experts discuss these and other aspects.

Ensuring Systems Integration—Glenn N. Saxe, MD

Trauma-focused care for children/youth necessitates a focus on their dysregulated emotions and behavior and the role of their social environment (Saxe, Ellis, & Kaplow, 2007). Children/youth living in residential programs reside in a unique social environment, often referred to as the "milieu." It is essential for residential providers to engage the child/youth's family as a critical aspect of their environment, while also focusing on the impact of the milieu. This is important because youth in residential settings have two distinct social environments, and each can influence their functioning for better or worse.

Strategies for creating a trauma-informed milieu include the following:

✓ *Creating a common understanding and language for all staff, children, youth, and families*—Staff and families are often taught that children/youths in distress are demonstrating "bad," "manipulative," or "conduct disordered" behavior when actually the child/youth is in a dysregulated state and is reacting either to reminders of traumatic events or significant environmental stressors. In this context, the child/youth should be viewed as overwhelmed and doing the best he or she can at that moment.

✓ *Identifying elements in the milieu that can signal and lead to distress or threat*—Specifically, two types of potential distress or threat are identified for assessment in the milieu. The clearest example is a violation of boundaries. If a staff member verbally or physically threatens or is physically or sexually abusive to a resident, the milieu environment is clearly threatening. A more subtle yet pervasive form of distress within the milieu is a violation of "team integrity." Because residential staff are, in essence, the child/youth's immediate caregivers, the functioning of the team as a "family system" can have a profound impact on the child/youth's functioning. If a team does not have a good communication system, or if team members do not concur about how to support children/youth or consistently uphold residence expectations (e.g., morning staff allowing a child/youth to have "seconds" at breakfast, but evening staff not allowing seconds for dinner even though the administrative rule is that seconds must be allowed), the milieu environment is distressed. Staff members providing care in residential settings are also at risk for contributing to these types of environmental distress due to the prevalence of trauma histories in people who seek out helping roles in child-serving organizations (Bloom & Farragher, 2011).

✓ *Actively engaging and involving families in treatment*—Family engagement and involvement in treatment is an essential component of assessing and addressing the child/youth's social environment. While assessing the social environment, for example, the team considers whether the youth's caregiver(s) has been able to adequately meet the youth's emotional needs (i.e., preventing the child from becoming dysregulated or helping the child sufficiently if it does, indeed, occur). For many children/youth in residential programs, this question is relevant because the child/youth may have phone contact or visits with the caregiver(s). A caregiver who fails to provide agreed-upon calls or time at home with the family is not meeting the needs of the child/youth, thus the environment is distressed. When a child/youth spends time at home (while still in care) but is exposed to conflict/violence or not provided with adequate food, for example, the home environment may become threatening. That is why it is critical for residential service to extend beyond the residential site, and for interventions to be taught and integrated into the home/community and shared with other involved providers. Extending services beyond the residential setting transfers the knowledge and prepares the youth and families for a productive life that is independent of caring systems.

✓ *Creating a vehicle to integrate care*—Historically, residential treatment has followed a private-practice model, where each clinician provides therapy according to her or his own approach based on her or his own training and experience. Differential training can create treatment splits or exacerbate preexisting splits between the clinical and direct-care staff. Implementing a consistent clinical approach creates an integrated, multidisciplinary team in which each member of the team—including the family—understands the approach, follows the plan, and has a clearly defined and equally important role in implementing the treatment plan and is an essential component to effective trauma-informed practice. This means training all staff and families in the same approach, ensuring that families are taught the same skills as direct care staff, and inviting youth/families to participate in staff training to talk about their residential-care experiences, and what helps and what hurts from their perspective (Bloom & Farragher, 2013).

Attending to the Physical Effects of Trauma on Children and Youth Served in Residential Programs—Shairi Turner, MD, MPH

Children and youth in residential programs have unique health care needs. Many have experienced some form of trauma (Nelson et al., 2011). Often, prior to placement, attention to their physical and mental health-care needs has been inconsistent. Once removed from their homes, medical care can become fragmented, exacerbating even mild preexisting conditions.

All children from birth to age 18 years require basic health care. This includes health/vision screenings, dental care, immunizations, and treatment for acute and chronic conditions. In residential programs, the coordination of these services often becomes a joint responsibility between the child's family and the program's staff. However, consistent with effective continuity of care and family/community engagement, residential programs should make every effort to ensure that child/youth's medical care continues with their community health-care providers.

In order to address new or existing medical issues upon entrance into a residential program, physical health-care services should include a health screening; comprehensive medical, vision, and dental assessments; developmental screening; ongoing primary care; and monitoring of a child's existing health status (Nelson et al., 2011). A thorough physical exam should be performed by a physician, ideally the child/youth's pediatrician, as soon as possible with extreme sensitivity paid to the manner in which genital and anal exams are performed. Gynecological complaints in girls, in particular, require extreme sensitivity. Due to the high incidence of rape and sexual assault in this population, girls must be examined by practitioners who are aware that a gynecological exam itself could be retraumatizing. Necessary laboratory tests should be ordered, including screening for pregnancy, HIV, or STDs as indicated (Nelson et al., 2011). The status of chronic illnesses must be documented, with particular attention paid to medication and treatment needs, noting whether subspecialty care is warranted (American Academy of Pediatrics [AAP], 2002). The AAP *Recommendations for Preventative Pediatric Health Care* can be used as a reference. Information on immunizations should be gathered from all available sources (previous medical records, schools, state databases). When uncertainties exist, children/youth should be immunized according to American Academy of Pediatrics guidelines (AAP, 2002).

Children/youth entering residential programs will likely have diagnoses that include asthma, eczema/dermatitis, migraine headaches, acid reflux, scoliosis, chronic headaches, hearing loss, heart murmurs, seizure disorders, hypothyroidism, anemia 1, and obesity. These conditions are more prevalent in this population than in the general pediatric population for several reasons: (1) children/youth in this population come from homes where access to care is limited, and (2) the trauma and chronic psychological stressors that they have experienced cause physiological changes in the body's immune system, which increase the likelihood for disease (Kendall-Tackett, 2009; Nelson et al., 2011).

In order to properly meet the health-care needs of children/youth in residential programs, equal consideration must be given to their mental health. The Adverse Childhood Experiences study is relevant to children/youth served in residential programs and confirms that those who experienced trauma are at a greater risk for chronic health and mental health conditions as adults (Felitti & Anda, 2010). Conversely, children/youth who experienced trauma may also have physical complaints that are not related to an actual medical condition (Kugler, Bloom, Kaercher, Truax, & Storch, 2012). Somatization is the tendency to report physical distress in the absence of physiological indicators of illness (D'Andrea, Sharma, Zelechoski, & Spinazzola, 2011). Typical somatic symptoms include dizziness, restlessness, nausea, stomachaches, vomiting, shortness of breath, racing heart rates, and feelings of unease (Kugler et al., 2012). These symptoms in traumatized children/youth can be a direct response to anxiety, posttraumatic stress disorder, and depression (Kugler et al., 2012). Sexual abuse, in particular, can influence the degree of somatic complaints more so than other types of abuse or neglect (Kugler et al., 2012). However, since these complaints can be associated with legitimate illnesses, the work-up can be exhaustive, making a diagnosis challenging for the clinician. Full exploration of physical complaints needs to occur in the context of treatment for existing mental health diagnoses and symptoms. By addressing both physical and mental health needs in an integrated manner, residential programs are afforded a unique opportunity to provide comprehensive, holistic, trauma-informed service for the children/youth in their care.

Female Gender Considerations to Trauma-Informed Care in Residential Programs—Paige Baker, MS, & Jacqueline B. Brown, PhD

Creating a gender-responsive, trauma-informed culture in residential programs is essential to providing girls with competent, quality care. *Why girls?* Girls are more vulnerable to cumulative and complex trauma compared to their male peers (Smith, Leve, & Chamberlain, 2006). Girls are more susceptible to interpersonal difficulties than their male peers, and they are more likely than boys to report symptoms of internalizing disorders such as depression and somatization when they have a history of complex trauma (Leadbeater, Kuperminc, Blatt, & Hertzog, 1999). The risks for a girl to develop these symptoms increase when she experiences greater interpersonal difficulties, more triggers, and poorer relationships with her family (Leadbeater et al., 1999).

Many aspects of residential programming, such as a loss of privacy, restraint and seclusion (R/S), and staff insensitivity can exacerbate feelings of not being safe as well as symbolize a loss of control among traumatized girls and lead to revictimization and retraumatization in care settings (National Child Traumatic Stress Network [NCTSN], 2004). Unfortunately, the needs and behavior of traumatized girls can be ignored or misinterpreted by staff and result in suicide attempts, self-mutilation, lashing out, and seemingly "irrational" responses (NCTSN, 2004).

The following are some practical suggestions for working with girls in a residential program from a TIC perspective. Many of these suggestions are simple. Other suggestions are more complex and are mentioned as starting points for further exploration:

✓ Groups should be facilitated by trained, competent staff and designed to address topics related to victimization, exploitation, identity, trust, safety, body image, self-care, affect regulation, peer group selection and engagement, and sexuality (Hennessey, Ford, Mahoney, Ko, & Siegfried, 2004).

✓ Pregnant girls should have access to parental education (e.g., education on prenatal care, addressing self-defeating behaviors that can expose her and/ or her child to danger, postpartum depression, family conflict or conflict with the father of the child, visitation issues, legal support, child support, parenting skills, coping strategies).

✓ Minority girls are overrepresented in the juvenile justice and caring systems. As such, TIC requires cultural competency and culturally appropriate services to meet the needs of minority girls (Hennessey et al., 2004).

✓ When working with LGTBQ girls, be affirmative and comfortable discussing heterosexist attitudes, examining internalized homophobia, and acknowledging the different cultural experiences of homosexual youth as compared to their heterosexual peers (Safren, Hollander, Hard, & Heimberg, 2001).

✓ Do not just focus on challenges (Hodas, 2006). Challenges are obvious. Everyone has focused on these. Be different. Focus on her dreams and aspirations.

✓ Use strength-based assumptions. Do not assume the girl is acting out of malice. Many of the skills she learned in order to survive in her home, neighborhood, or school may cause her problems in a different environment. The girl will need to be taught appropriate behavior. She will need practice, reminders, and positive reinforcement.

✓ Develop individualized comfort/safety plans with girls upon entering the program. Make this a collaborative process, and allow girls to set goals and help measure their own successes. Girls more than boys rely on social and parental support to increase coping skills, so be sure to involve peers/ friends/family as much as possible (Leadbeater et al., 1999).

These strategies are responsive to the specific vulnerabilities and needs experienced by traumatized girls. Addressing previous histories of trauma and abuse is essential. In addition, communication, relationships, and internalizing symptoms must be a focus of treatment and TIC at the core of every interaction every staff person has with every girl, from intake to transition.

The Youth Perspective: What Residential Programs Do That Helps or Hurts Recovery From Trauma—Neil Kelly

Youth voice, choice, and perspective are essential components of youth-guided, family-driven care that must be respected and incorporated when designing, delivering, or evaluating trauma-informed residential interventions (Transformation Center [TC], 2010). By listening to what youth have to say about their experience in residential programs, one can assess the effectiveness and impact of these services through the magnified lens of those directly served.

Recently, graduates of residential services were hired by the TC, a peer support/advocacy agency in Massachusetts, to survey nearly 100 youth, ranging in age from 12 to 23 years, who reside in residential programs throughout the state as part of the mental health and child welfare agencies joint effort to redesign residential services for children/youth. The majority of surveyors and youth interviewed had histories of trauma. The youth in care represented various cultural backgrounds, resided in different programs, and were interviewed individually and collectively with fellow program residents and without staff present. They offered honest, articulate opinions based upon their personal experience in residential programs (TC, 2010).

The youth reported a variety of positive outcomes of residential service that they felt would benefit them for the future, which included learning how to handle feelings and emotions and learning new skills, like applying for a job, self-advocacy, and good self-care. The youth also identified specific interventions that were effective and helped them feel better, including (1) being able to regularly communicate and spend time with family, friends, and peers in the community and program; (2) having free time outdoors and being able to be physically active every day; and (3) having genuine staff support when they needed someone to talk to or felt unhappy or fearful, such as witnessing someone being physically restrained or secluded. Others indicated that when they formed positive relationships with staff, their residential experience was more meaningful and helpful in the long run. Some youth indicated that what they learned in the program helped them feel prepared to return home, reenter their previous school, and resume their life in the community (TC, 2010).

However, many youth commented on aspects of programming that they considered harmful, that triggered negative memories, and were retraumatizing, such as harsh or indifferent staff behavior, point and level systems and different expectations of youth in the program (unfairness/inconsistency), and the appropriateness (or lack thereof) of rules and procedures. The youth also reported that peer-to-peer support was often discouraged, time out of the program was extremely restricted or limited, rarely were they able to see family or friends from home or have the ability to go home, and those who were aware of their human rights oftentimes felt that their rights were infringed upon.

The survey also elicited specific recommendations from youth for residential providers, including the following:

- replacing level and point systems with effective alternatives that promote safety and individual growth;
- giving incentives to staff to organize program activities that replace rigid and ineffective rules with trauma-informed practices that are consistent with the needs of community life;
- giving youth and staff the opportunity to debrief program violence/R/S;
- hiring people based on their life experience and skills that are relevant to building relationships with youth rather than prioritizing educational credentials;
- interviewing youth and families 30 to 90 days after leaving a program to incorporate their perspective into current program operations;
- establishing youth-led monitoring of program cleanliness and care for the physical space;
- hiring young adult peer mentors/specialists;
- providing staff guidance and support for regularly scheduled youth-led meetings and activities;
- going beyond the regular school curriculum and class schedule to teach basic reading and writing;
- teaching life skills and recovery skills, including how to advocate, combat negative self-talk, face one's fears, and solve problems; and
- providing resources for recreation, peer support, and recovery, including information about addiction, self-inflicted violence, and trauma (TC, 2010).

The professional and family perspective of residential intervention is important, but youth's direct experiences are often overlooked. The important work for residential program staff is to support, teach, and ensure that the youth's and family's perspective is the treatment/service compass. Ultimately, healing happens in positive relationships (TC, 2010).

Organizational Considerations—Brian Farragher, LMSW, MBA

Trauma is not an uncommon experience in the lives of children/adolescents and families receiving residential services, or the staff who serve them. The collective impact of trauma also affects organizations. Therefore, it is no surprise that providing TIC in organizations that are already challenged by the demands of service provision is even more difficult when the collective impact of stress on staff and the organization is not recognized and responded to. Leaders must build in protections to ensure staff and the organization are not overwhelmed by the impact of cumulative trauma and repetitive stress (Bloom & Farragher, 2013).

One strategy to mitigate the impact of stress and trauma is to change the staff hiring process. Rather than delegate hiring to frontline managers, youth, families and leadership should be involved at the beginning of the process and conduct group interviews with prospective candidates before they are referred to the frontline hiring manager. This approach is more interactive and provides important information about how candidates get along with others—how they respond to stress and whether or not they are playful, engaged, and creative. Involving youth and families with senior leadership at the initial stage also communicates the strong value of inclusion and youth-guided, family-driven practice. By focusing essential staff qualities earlier in the process, there is greater likelihood of a better staff selection (Jenks & Zevnik, 1989).

Another strategy to consider when implementing TIC is creating comprehensive trauma training for direct-care staff. Teaching staff about trauma theory, the impact of trauma and toxic stress on the developing brain, and the impact of toxic stress on functioning is essential. Equally important is educating staff about recognizing stress in themselves and identifying tools they can use to help regulate themselves, such as safety planning, self-care, supervision, and so forth. Also, helping staff understand that changing the fundamental question from "what is wrong with you?" to "what has happened to you?" helps them shift their focus from working on child/youth "problems" to working on skills to mitigate the effect of trauma.

Because direct care staff are often exposed to difficult circumstances and challenging behavior, leaders should also consider limiting the level of exposure staff experience each day. While protocols for processing when staff have been injured or when they can tap in/tap out of stressful situations are typically in place, having a method to recognize the impact of stress and ensuring that adequate restorative breaks occur each day is not the norm, but should be.

Youth and families who have experienced trauma often feel helpless and believe their future will be the same as their past. Helping professionals, including direct-care staff, must provide youth and families with hope to be able to live through their challenges so they can move on to a better life. The capacity and skill of instilling hope is best achieved when staff feel supported, cared for, and prepared to bring that optimistic spirit to those they serve.

Environmental Considerations—Elizabeth Perreault and Jessica Moore

When looking to improve care and outcomes for children/youth that have experienced trauma, an important factor to consider is the physical environment. Research in the field of evidence-based design (EBD) confirms the positive impact of the physical environment on the service and people receiving care. Until recently, little research was targeted specifically to the physical environment within behavioral health. The section offers pragmatic recommendations for environmental changes that are rooted in EBD principles. These strategies are designed to reduce child/youth stress and anxiety, improve treatment outcomes, and create a positive working environment for staff. The seven strategies outlined below facilitate a youth-guided healing experience, giving opportunities for choice and independence in a safe manageable way. In doing so, these strategies will help organizations provide an optimal trauma-informed environment of care. The summary chart in Table 7.1 outlines modifications to the physical environment related to each strategy below.

Strategy 1—Create an Interior Environment That Fosters Healing

Simple and fairly inexpensive ways to improve the healing qualities of the interior design are to introduce pastoral artwork (Nanda, Eisen, Zadeh, & Owen, 2011); provide flexible/customizable furniture that allows for patient choice (Crowner, Douyon, Convit, & Volavka, 1991); create a calming, acoustical environment through the balance of hard, durable, surface and sound absorptive materials; and, finally, simply cleaning and decluttering the unit.

Strategy 2—Minimize On-Unit Disruption

On-unit disruptions, such as human traffic, unnecessary building maintenance, and overhead paging can increase noise, create visual distractions, and even pose safety risks. Minimizing traffic through the creation of a service zone that provides off-unit circulation routes, off-unit system rooms (such as electrical rooms and data rooms) to eliminate maintenance staff coming on to the unit, and locating plumbing chases with access panels off the bedroom corridor can reduce traffic and unit disruption. Many programs are eliminating overhead paging and switching to phone systems that are not as disruptive and institutional.

Strategy 3—Provide Spaces to Encourage Emotional Self-Management

A variety of spaces should be provided to allow children/youth to get away from the group to emotionally self-soothe, for self-reflection, and for other quiet activities. Spaces such as quiet rooms and comfort rooms provide an opportunity to practice self-calming skills and prevent behavioral escalation. For some, *Snoezelen* rooms can be provided for sensory stimulation therapy as well.

Strategy 4—Create Opportunities for Passive Supervision

An environment free from hiding alcoves and blind spots allows for passive supervision without the use of secondary devices, such as cameras and mirrors, which can be very institutional in appearance, intrusive, and frightening for

Table 7.1 Strategies to Create a Trauma-Informed Environment of Care

STRATEGY #	SUGGESTED MODIFICATION	INITIAL INVESTMENT	NOTES
1	Add pastoral artwork and/or display client art	$	Ensure that installation is done in a safe way with tamper-resistant devices. Consider donations and/or client art work
1	Declutter the unit	$	
1	"Spring Clean"	$	If possible, include patients in minor renovation projects, such painting or furniture reorganization
1	Update furniture to be flexible and adaptable	$$	Choose flexible, moveable furniture so patients have a choice; in higher risk zones, choose furniture that is light enough to not damage anything if thrown and chairs with sled bases for safety
2	Limit or reduce overhead paging	$$	
2	Locate electrical/data closets "off" unit or in staff-only areas of the unit	$$$	
3	Create a quiet/comfort room	$$	
3	Create multi-sensory room	$$	
4	Create an open care station	$$	
4	Install interior glazing into activity spaces from the corridor	$$	Provide-temper laminated glazing
5	Provide private patient rooms and toilet/showers	$$$	Usually this is part of a major renovation or new construction project.
5	Redefine admissions area — consider the experience of being admitted	$	Choose a space for admissions/interview with natural light and calming interiors.
5	Provide a patient medication distribution alcove for teaching and patient privacy	$	Allow for patient privacy/dignity: provide space for teaching and discharge planning.
6	Provide smaller on unit spaces for activity	$$	Allow spaces to double function (e.g., allow patients to use visitor and interview rooms in the evening for television, games, reading)
6	Provide exercise/workout rooms on the unit	$$$	Allows patients to maintain physical wellness including yoga, meditation, stretching
7	Provide porches on each unit that safely allow patients to remain "on-unit" but be outside	$$$	Usually can only be achieved with new construction
7	Provide a visual connection to the outdoors	$$	Frame the view you have; use interior glazing to bring as much light in to the unit as possible.

Courtesy of CannonDesign

children/youth. Clear lines of sight should be provided throughout the program for both staff supervision and so that children/youth can see their staff and feel an added sense of security and safety. Staff work areas should be strategically placed throughout the program to allow for redundant supervision from staff who may be doing work that is not directly engaged with the children/youth.

Strategy 5—Allow for Privacy and Dignity

Single bedrooms can provide a "home base" for children/youth in residential programs. They also create a quieter environment, lead to improved sleep (Baum & Valins, 1979), and can be a haven where children/youth feel safe. Where single bedrooms are not possible, fewer roommates and careful furniture placement to promote privacy and supervision is key. Larger programs with unit bed wings should divide the units into smaller subclusters that can allow for separation by age, gender, and needs, as required.

Strategy 6—Provide a Variety of On-Unit and Off-Unit Therapy Spaces

Providing a variety of activity and therapy spaces encourages choice and allows for differences in child/youth preference. These spaces should be positioned to allow for passive staff visibility through the use of open staff workstations. Therapy, recreation, and wellness spaces should be provided on and off the residential unit to ensure that all children/youth have access to a variety of therapies and amenities.

Strategy 7—Provide Access to Outdoors

There is a robust body of research regarding the impact of natural daylight and views within the realm of health care. Access to daylight/views lowers stress and anxiety, and reduces average length of stays. Benefits extend to the staff, because the longest term occupants are the caregivers and support staff within the facility (Ulrich, 1991). Natural daylight and views assist in way-finding by providing visual landmarks and create a "grounding effect" for patients and staff through the ability to see what time of day it is and what the weather is like. Where possible, a physical, not just visual, connection to the outdoors is of profound benefit. Children/youth should be able to feel sun, wind, rain, and snow as a basic human right. Outdoor spaces can also become active components of therapy through the provision of planting beds for horticultural therapy, walking paths for ambulation, and labyrinths and outdoor group recreational areas for play and skill building. Outdoor recreation should allow for both passive and active spaces (Marcus & Barnes, 1995; Whitehouse et al., 2001).

Summary

Becoming "trauma informed" is a process, not a task; a journey, not a destination. It is a multifaceted process of change that cannot be delegated down the leadership ladder, nor sustained solely by direct-care staff. It is an organization-wide practice and investment in quality of care for those served and staff. Being trauma informed means that an organization has created the conditions through leadership, education, and transparency to do the right thing, at the right time, for the children, youth, and families receiving services. This is a formidable task that requires administrative support, empowerment of staff, and active engagement and inclusion of the children, youth, and families in care. To help with this journey, useful Internet resources and contact information for the content experts who contributed this chapter are provided.

Contact Information:

Glenn N. Saxe, MD
Chair, Department of Child and Adolescent Psychiatry, and
Director, The Child Study Center at New York University Langone Medical
Center
glenn.saxe@nyumc.org
(646) 754-5050

Brian Farragher, MSW, MBA
Formerly affiliated with ANDRUS
bfarragher242@gmail.com
(914) 217-5932

Shairi R. Turner MD, MPH
Former Chief Medical Director, Florida Department of Juvenile Justice
Shairi@TurnerDavis.com
(617) 905-3746

Paige Baker, MS
Research Assistant
Jacqueline Beine Brown, Ph.D.
Licensed Psychologist
Delores Barr Weaver Policy Center
pbaker@thevoiceforgirls.org
jbrown@thevoiceforgirls.org
(904) 598-0901

Elisabeth Perreault
Vice President
Jessica Moore, Assoc. AIA
Associate Vice-President
CANNONDESIGN
eperreault@cannondesign.com
(716) 774-3362
jmoore@cannondesign.com
(716) 774-3298

Recommended Web Sites and Resources

The Adverse Childhood Events Study; www.acestudy.org
Creating Trauma-Informed Care Environments: Organizational Self-Assessment for Trauma-Informed Care Practices in Youth Residential Settings (Hummer & Dollard, 2010); www.trauma-informed-california.org/wp-content/uploads/2012/0
National Center for Trauma-Informed Care (SAMHSA); www.samhsa.gov/nctic/
National Child Traumatic Stress Network; www.NCTSN.org

Child Trauma Toolkits for Educators & Parents in English & Spanish; www.nctsnet.org/
resources/audiences/school-personnel/trauma

Trauma-Informed Organizational Toolkit: A free organizational assessment tool for
providers to assess their organization's implementation of trauma-informed care
principles and practices; www.familyhomelessness.org/media/90.pdf

Trauma Informed Care Tip Sheets (USDOJ); www.safestartcenter.org/resources/tip-
sheets.php

Reducing Adverse Childhood Experiences: Online overview course from the Washington Family Policy Council; www.fpc.wa.gov/acecourse.html

Creating Cultures of Trauma-Informed Care (CCTIC): A Self-Assessment and Planning
Protocol (Fallot & Harris 2009); www.theannainstitute.org/CCTICSELFASSPP.pdf

References

Alisic, E., Van der Schoot, T. A., van Ginkel, J. R., & Kleber, R. J. (2008). Looking beyond
posttraumatic stress disorder in children: Posttraumatic stress reactions, posttraumatic growth, and quality of life in a general population sample. *Journal of Clinical
Psychiatry, 69*(9), 1455–1461.

American Academy of Pediatrics. (2002). Health care of young children in foster care.
Pediatrics, 109(3), 536–541.

American Association of Children's Residential Centers (AACRC). (2010, December).
Redefining residential: Trauma-informed care in residential treatment. Retrieved on
June 7, 2013, from www.aacrc-dc.org/sites/default/files/Paper8final.pdf

American Psychiatric Association. (2013). *Diagnostic and statistical manual of mental
disorders* (5th ed.). Arlington, VA: Author.

Baum, A., & Valins, S. (1979). Architectural mediation of residential density and control:
Crowding and the regulation of social contact. In L. Berkowitz (Ed.), *Advances in
experimental social psychology* (pp. 131–175). New York, NY: Academic Press.

Bloom, S. L., & Farragher, B. J. (2011). *Destroying sanctuary: The crisis in human service
delivery systems.* New York, NY: Oxford University Press.

Bloom, S. L., & Farragher, B. J. (2013). *Restoring sanctuary: A new operating system for
trauma-informed care.* New York, NY: Oxford University Press.

Crowner, M. L., Douyon, R., Convit, A., & Volavka, J. (1991). Videotape recording of
assaults on a state hospital inpatient ward. *Journal of Neuropsychiatry and Clinical
Neurosciences, 3*(2), 59–64.

D'Andrea, W., Sharma, R., Zelechoski, A. D., & Spinazzola, J. (2011). Physical health
problems after single trauma exposure when stress takes root in the body. *Journal of
the American Psychiatric Nurses Association, 17*(6), 378–392.

Felitti, V. J. & Anda, R. F. (2010). The relationship of adverse childhood experiences to
adult medical disease, psychiatric disorders and sexual behavior: Implications for
healthcare. In R. Lanius & E. Vermetten (Eds.), *The hidden epidemic: The Impact of
early life trauma on health and disease* (pp. 77–87). New York, NY: Cambridge University Press.

Forman-Hoffman, V., Knauer, S., McKeeman, J., Zolotor, A., Blanco, R., Lloyd, S., Tant,
E., et al. (2013, February). *Child and adolescent exposure to trauma: Comparative
effectiveness of interventions addressing trauma other than maltreatment or family violence* (Comparative Effectiveness Review No. 107). Rockville, MD: AHRQ.

Gillies, D., Taylor, F., Gray, C., O'Brien, L., & D'Abrew, N. (2012, December). *Psychological
therapies for the treatment of post-traumatic stress disorder in children and adolescents*

(Cochrane Database Systematic Reviews). Retrieved March 20, 2014, from http://summaries.cochrane.org/CD006726/psychological-therapies-for-the-treatment-of-post-traumatic-stress-disorder-in-children-and-adolescents

Harris, M., & Fallot, R. D. (2001). *Using Trauma Theory to Design Service Systems.* San Francisco: Jossey-Bass.

Hennessey, M., Ford, J. D., Mahoney, K., Ko, S. J., & Siegfried, C. B. (2004). Trauma among girls in the juvenile justice system. Retrieved October 1, 2013, from www.nctsnet.org/

Hodas, G. R. (2006). *Responding to childhood trauma: The promise and practice of trauma informed care.* Retrieved October 1, 2013, from www.nasmhpd.org/docs/publications/docs/2006/

Hopper, E. K., Bassuk, E. L., & Olivet, J. (2010). Shelter from the storm: Trauma-informed care in homelessness services settings. *Open Health Services and Policy Journal, 3,* 80–100.

Huckshorn, K. A., & LeBel, J. (2013). Trauma informed care. In D. Svendsen & K. Yeager (Eds.), *Textbook of modern community mental health work: An interdisciplinary approach* (pp. 62–83). New York, NY: Oxford University Press.

Hummer, V. L., Dollard, N., Robst, J., & Armstrong, M. I. (2010). Innovations in implementation of trauma-informed care practices in youth residential treatment: A curriculum for organizational change. *Child Welfare, 89*(2):79–95.

Jenks, J. M., & Zevnik, B. L. (1989). *ABCs of job interviewing.* Boston, MA: Harvard Business Review.

Kendall-Tackett, K. (2009). Psychological trauma and physical health: A psychoneuroimmunology approach to etiology of negative health effects and possible interventions. *Psychological Trauma: Theory, Research, Practice and Policy, 1*(1), 35–48.

Kugler, B. B., Bloom, M., Kaercher, L. B., Truax, T. V., & Storch, E. A. (2012). Somatic symptoms in traumatized children and adolescents. *Child Psychiatry & Human Development, 43*(5), 661–673.

Leadbeater, B. J., Kuperminc, G. P., Blatt, S. J., & Hertzog, C. (1999). A multivariate model of gender differences in adolescents: Internalizing and externalizing problems. *Developmental Psychology, 35*(5), 1282.

LeBel, J. (2013, June 5). *Advocating for a trauma-informed approach: Making theory a reality.* Presentation at the National Disability Rights Network Conference, San Antonio, TX.

Marcus, C. C., & Barnes, M. (1995). *Gardens in healthcare facilities: Use, therapeutic benefits, and design recommendations.* Martinez, CA: Center for Health Design.

Nanda, U., Eisen, S., Zadeh, R., & Owen, D. (2011). Effect of visual art on patient anxiety and agitation in a mental health facility and implications for the business case. *Journal of Psychiatric and Mental Health Nursing, 18*(5), 386–393.

National Association of State Mental Health Program Directors (NASMHPD). (2013). *National executive training institute curriculum for the creation of violence-free, coercion-free treatment settings and the reduction of seclusion and restraint* (11th ed.). Alexandria, VA: Author.

National Child Traumatic Stress Network. (2004). *Trauma among girls in the juvenile justice system.* Retrieved October 1, 2013, from www.nctsn.org/nctsn_assets/pdfs/edu_materials/trauma_among_girls_in_jjsys.pdf

Nelson, T. D., Smith, T. R., Thompson, R. W., Epstein, M. H., Griffith, A. K., Hurley, K. D., & Tonniges, T. F. (2011). Prevalence of physical health problems among youth entering residential treatment. *Pediatrics, 128*(5), e1226–e1232.

Pecora, P. J., Kessler, R. C., Williams, J., O'Brien, K., Downs, A. C., English, D., & Holmes, K. (2005). *Improving family foster care: Findings of the northwest fostercare alumni study.* Seattle, WA: Casey Family Programs.

Safren, S. A., Hollander, G., Hard, T. A., & Heimberg, R. G. (2001). Cognitive-behavioral therapy with lesbian, gay and bisexual youth. *Cognitive and Behavioral Practice, 8*(3), 215–223.

Saxe, G. N., Ellis, B., & Kaplow, J. B. (2007). *Collaborative treatment of traumatized children and teens: The trauma systems therapy approach.* New York, NY: Guilford Press.

Smith, D. K., Leve, L. D., & Chamberlain, P. (2006). Adolescent girls' offending and health-risking sexual behavior: The predicative role of trauma. *Child Maltreatment, 11*(4), 346–353.

Substance Abuse Mental Health Services Administration. (2012). *What do we mean by a trauma informed approach?* Retrieved April 6, 2013, fromwww.samhsa.gov/traumajustice/traumadefinition/approach.aspx

Tarren-Sweeney, M. (2008). The mental health of children in out-of-home care. *Current Opinion in Psychiatry, 21*(4), 345–349.

Transformation Center. (2010, August). *Youth residential report: Respect for peers and connection are the keys to recovery!* Roxbury, MA: Author.

Ulrich, R. S. (1991). Effects of interior design on wellness: Theory and recent scientific research. *Journal of Health Care Design, 3*(1), 97–109.

Whitehouse, S., Varni, J. W., Seid, M., Cooper-Marcus, C., Ensberg, M. J., Jacobs, J. R., & Mehlenbeck, R. S. (2001). Evaluating a children's hospital garden environment: Utilization and consumer satisfaction. *Journal of Environmental Psychology, 21*(3), 301–314.

8   Linking Residential and Community

Jody Levison-Johnson and Jeremy C. Kohomban

Introduction

Residential and community services have historically operated as discrete and separate units. This separation creates unnecessary fragmentation in treatment, family participation, discharge, and continuity of care. In the past decade, residential and community providers have successfully worked together to bridge this historical separation, reduce treatment fragmentation, and, most importantly, ensure stronger integration of family and community during and after the residential phase. This relatively recent development has given rise to a number of effective residential models that can be replicated with success.

Effective residential interventions place an emphasis on reduced lengths of stay *in* a residential program (Hair, 2005; Walter & Petr, 2008). While at times unfairly misconstrued solely as a cost-savings strategy, reduced lengths of stay are predicated on the simple construct that children and youth need a sense of belonging and community. Unnecessarily long lengths of stay in out-of-home group care can cause institutionalized behavior, including greater risk taking, poor educational achievement, disengagement from positive peer influences, and social isolation (Altshuler & Poertner, 2002).

Effective residential interventions view family (however that is defined) and community as nonnegotiable requirements for long-term success. Therefore, in order to preserve all available family and community connections, young people should be offered a residential program as near to their home as possible. This allows family to be part of the treatment process and, in most situations, allows the youth to develop and maintain a peer group in a community setting, thereby laying the foundation for a community of support postresidential intervention. Furthermore, a near or in community placement option makes discharge and required postdischarge follow-up less cumbersome (Hair, 2005; Landsman, Groza, Tyler, & Malone, 2001). When a close-to-home residential program is not an option, emphasis must be placed on connection to family through the use of technology and frequent in-person meaningful contact. Spending time with family at home and active integration in local community settings can be used to promote the acquisition of skills that will be sustained once at home.

Finally, effective residential interventions are sensitive to the disproportionate removal of children from certain communities over others, and the impact that these actions have on families and communities. "Children of color account for 42% of the U.S. child population yet make up 57% of all children in foster care. This overrepresentation and disparate treatment of children of color in the foster care system is referred to as disproportionality" (Casey Family Programs, 2013, p. 1). Placement seems to plague communities of color and those of lower socioeconomic status (Hines, Lemon, Wyatt, & Merdinger, 2004). When children are removed from these homes and communities, the impact is multifaceted. Separation from community and family is the visible impact, but unseen and often conveniently unacknowledged is the resentment and continued mistrust that is bred between marginalized communities and the systems that serve them (Cook, 1992; Courtney et al., 2007; Courtney, Terao, & Bost, 2004; Dworsky & Courtney, 2000; Pecora et al., 2005; Reilly, 2003). Therefore, effective residential strategies focus on reducing length of stay and involving family at each step of treatment. These providers also invest in community integration and development in the areas where these children are from, which supports safe and successful discharge as well as potentially reducing the disproportionate rates of removal from these communities in the long term.

To successfully integrate residential and community-based programming, we must share a common understanding of both, with clarity on when a residential intervention is appropriate and what the residential intervention can deliver. It is important to note that the ideas presented here represent an evolution of thinking and of the field in general. Social and human services, inclusive of residential and community-based programs, have a long history dating back to the nation's founding. Whether provided by religious or charitable organizations, a mix of both, or as a government safety net, these programs have historically been offered in "the way it was always done." Learning from a few examples of effective residential models, this chapter offers a description of residential interventions that link with families and communities to achieve positive long-term outcomes. Strategies are suggested to achieve this integration, and specific programs are described to allow for additional clarity in understanding both what must be done and how it can be accomplished.

Residential as an Intervention, Not a Destination

Residential interventions can play an important part in the service array used for children, youth, and families. Historically, these services were offered as the last resort and touted as the panacea for all that ailed young people and their families who had failed other, less intensive interventions. The services were discrete and distinct from community-based services. As the knowledge base has grown, the purpose for residential interventions and the circumstances for when they are most successful have shifted.

In a redefined approach, residential is viewed as an intervention for an entire family versus a destination for a young person. Rather than considering the residential program as a destination for long-term treatment and progress, the residential program is now viewed as a targeted high-efficacy (and high cost), emergency intervention that diagnoses, stabilizes, and triages. Like a hospital emergency room, residential is one important component of the long-term treatment and support offered to a family. Children and youth can access residential interventions to help ensure safety for triage and diagnostic purposes and for short-term stabilization. As with any community that feels safer knowing that there is an emergency room in case of a medical emergency, the social- and human-service community feels safer with the availability of residential programs for emergency diagnosis, stabilization, and triage when needed. In this framework, residential programs also function as a safe environment and provide an opportunity for focused analysis of past issues of placement. This allows for a thoughtful review of why prior approaches may not have been successful and helps establish realistic next steps for success in the community. Inherent within this approach to residential programming is that the residential intervention is comprised of several components that truly emphasize and actually ensure the generalizability of skills learned within the residential setting to the community. This mutual strategy between the residential program and the community provider for the transfer of gains is the key to long-term success.

Linking Residential to Community

So how is the linkage between residential and community-based services ensured? Programs across the country have helped to shape and inform a new way of offering services in a residential environment. These successful models share similarities that include

- recognizing and espousing a sincere commitment to the belief that residential care is not a destination where children come to live for extended periods of time;
- proven capacity for rapid stabilization, treatment, analysis, triage, and discharge planning;
- placing substantial emphasis on family engagement and involvement;
- acknowledging, understanding, and acting firmly in those instances when family is unavailable, incapable, or unwilling to provide belonging; and
- paying significant attention to ensuring services and supports that begin in residential continue in community.

Child and Family Teams

As a means to achieve these intents, several residential and community programs have begun to use the Child and Family Team (CFT) approach (also referred to as Family Group or Family Team Conferencing in some child welfare settings) for planning, which ensures family and youth voice and choice drive the resulting plan of care. The CFT can also help to ensure continuity for families with active involvement of the team before, during, and after a residential intervention. The CFT process is a best practice approach, defined as "a group of people–chosen with the family and connected to them through natural, community, and formal support relationships who develop and implement the family's plan, address unmet needs, and work toward the family's vision" (Miles, Bruns, Osher, Walker, & National Wraparound Initiative Advisory Group, 2006, p. 9). The CFT is a clear means to ensure that practice is family driven and youth guided (Bruns, Rast, Peterson, Walker, & Bosworth, 2006; Burns, Hoagwood, & Mrazek, 1999; Carney & Buttell, 2003; Clark, Lee, Prange, & McDonald, 1996; Evans, Armstrong, & Kuppinger, 1996; Evans, Armstrong, Kuppinger, Huz, & McNulty, 1998; VanDenBerg, Bruns, & Burchard, 2003). CFTs that begin in the residential program can continue with the family after the young person returns to the community, providing a critical bridge and link between the interventions within the residential environment and the future in the community.

In Rochester, New York, the Monroe County Building Bridges Program (MCBB) convenes CFTs for youth as they enter a residential program. The CFTs are charged with planning an individualized intervention within the residential program, facilitating a return to community as quickly as possible, and ensuring ongoing individualized services and supports and postresidential placement. Initial evaluation suggests that 85% of youth in MCBB had improved functioning on the Child and Adolescent Functional Assessment Scale (CAFAS), and that length of stay for youth involved in MCBB was 31% shorter than a comparison control group. These young people also showed a lower rate of recidivism back to residential than the control group (L. Oinen, personal communication, July 17, 2013).

Without Family—Failure Is Almost Assured

Many payers of residential programs and the programs themselves have shared that a barrier to successful transition back to the community is the lack of available or identified family resources for youth entering the program. In response, programs have initiated efforts to more deliberately engage families and identify alternative relative resources and engage them during the residential intervention. These programs are determined and untiring in their pursuit of creating family and belonging for children, often using formalized approaches for this outreach and engagement. From the time of admission to the residential program, the role of the family in supporting the interventions is defined. Families are welcomed within all parts of the residential program; their beliefs and needs are identified and serve as the basis for the intervention. Many residential programs have developed specific positions for family and youth advocates. These staff have a primary purpose of ensuring that family members are welcomed, respected, and actively engaged in the activities that occur within the residential program and that family and youth voice drives the decisions made and plans for intervention. At the Children's Village, a Parent Leadership Council comprised of family members of children takes the lead role in welcoming new families, organizing events, advocating on behalf of families in treatment situations, and establishing guidelines for communication between treatment professionals and families (see www.Childrens village.org/parents-page/; www.Childrensvillage.org/about/mission/).

Family Finding (Children's Defense Fund, 2010) and Family Search and Engagement (Boisvert, Brimmer, Campbell, Koenig, Rose, & Stone-Smith, 2001; Catholic Community Services of Western Washington, 2008) are two specific frameworks that have demonstrated success by providing a practical how-to approach to locating potential relative resources and linking young people to these relatives for ongoing connection and support (see www.ccsww.org/site/DocServer/ Family_Search_and_Engagement_Guide_CCS-EMQ.pdf?docID=641). Programs that have made identification of family a core component of their services have been surprised to see the outcomes of diligent and deliberate actions to identify potential long-term sources of support for young people. Repeatedly, youth who "had no one" have become youth who have many.

Creating Permeability Between Residential and Community

Related to the CFT approach to individualize care planning is the practice of ensuring that services offered within a residential environment are carried into the community, and that these services are offered at the appropriate intensity. Permeability between residential and community-based environments is a key component of successful integration. Once an organizational culture that values family and community has been established, programs can consider changes to position titles. By simply changing names, from clinical staff to "reunification specialists" or "family/community liaisons," the orientation for particular roles can be significantly altered and place emphasis on family and community. Locating staff in community-based settings or colocating with other community partners can also serve as an important first step to reorienting staff toward the attainment of reunification and community-based goals. Some residential programs have done this by assigning staff to work with specific families regardless of location or to offer the residential services in a home-like setting.

Damar Services in Indiana has long recognized that consistent treatment relationships across time are important in obtaining and maintaining long-term outcomes for children and families. Child and family teams that include direct-care staff are devoted to a family and remain consistent across all levels of care in the organization—from intensive residential care, to an open campus setting, to group home settings in the community, to home-based supports. Recidivism data tends to support this family-driven variable. The deployment of direct-care staff into the homes and community has necessitated additional and different training for these staff, including maintaining appropriate boundaries when delivering services within the family home; crisis management within community, school, and family home; and communication skills training to enhance their ability to share treatment information with the family, school, and involved clinicians. Staff also receive family-specific training, which includes the family's story, familiarity with community resources that are convenient to the family's home, and cultural awareness that is specific to the family's needs and wants. The use of consistent direct-care staff reduces the opportunity for recidivism and optimizes generalization of treatment and success for young people and their families (J. Dalton & A. Knapp, personal communication, July 18, 2013).

There are many other steps that can be taken to break down the walls that have historically existed between residential and community-based programs. Across the country, training and technical assistance for residential and community-based programs is being offered based on the principles of the national Building Bridges Initiative (see www.buildingbridges4youth.org). These efforts provide the opportunity to introduce important concepts for working together to achieve positive long-term outcomes for young people and their families. This can often be complemented by pairing leadership from residential programs with community programs to develop a more in-depth understanding of the capabilities of each and provide the foundation for establishing new ways of working together. Some areas have begun to develop time-limited workgroups with specific groups of community-based providers (schools, outpatient clinics, etc.) identifying the barriers and challenges that impede their ability to actively collaborate. Once identified, potential solutions are developed and advanced to state and/or community leaders for resolution. Each of these examples represents steps that residential and community-based agencies can take to begin to establish and enhance the linkage to these formerly discrete and siloed settings.

An In-Depth Look: FASST, IRTF, the WAY Home

The Family Advocacy Stabilization and Support Team

Several programs have operationalized the concepts articulated here. The Family Advocacy Stabilization and Support Team (FASST) was originally developed in 1993 by the Guidance Center at Riverside Community Care in Dedham, Massachusetts. FASST is an intensive, home-based treatment program designed to support and stabilize families and reduce the length of stay or the risk of out-of-home placement and psychiatric hospitalization. Program leaders describe the program as "a residential program with no beds" (B. Alvarez de Toledo, personal communication, July 11, 2013).

FASST includes intensive, home-based treatment, care coordination, outreach, and advocacy, 24-hour crisis response, as well as referral and linkage.

Out-of-home placement is considered part of the treatment and a component of the array of community-based alternatives available to those enrolled. It is not seen as a different or distinct level of care. When residential is used, the FASST team, comprised of a master's-level clinician and a bachelor's-level staff person (who, whenever possible, represent the same ethnicity and community of each family served), partners with the residential staff to provide continuity, supports their interventions, and continues to assure engagement by the family. FASST clinicians participate in treatment by offering cotherapy with the residential staff and are partners in care and discharge planning.

A key component of FASST is the flexibility that staff must have in their roles. These staff can be partners, coaches, advocates, tutors, and therapists, depending on the family's needs. The bachelor's-level staff person is often directed towards mentoring activities, working with the young person on skill building. Parent partners are available to provide coaching and support to allow families to learn to advocate for themselves as well as successfully navigate the various systems they may be involved with. Services that are provided are highly individualized and flexible. Staff is available during the week and on weekends as needed. Using concepts of the CFT approach, there is emphasis on developing natural supports and ensuring flexible funding is available to provide for a range of potential needs, including food, recreational activities, and basic needs. Respite services, for parents/caretakers as well as for the young person, are available because FASST recognizes that families which include young people with complex needs will need a break.

FASST has demonstrated positive outcomes. According to the agency's report, 85% of children are discharged home. Fifteen percent of the children living at home at intake require short-term, out of home placement, and 84% of the children that required diagnostic or residential treatment at intake were reunified with their families by the third month of enrollment (Alvarez de Toledo, personal communication, July 11, 2013).

Intensive Residential Treatment Facility

Similar to the efforts under FASST is the Intensive Residential Treatment Facility (IRTF) program, developed by Magellan Health Services and Warwick House in Pennsylvania. This pilot program was implemented in 2009 as an innovative, intensive, family-based residential model. The model integrates effective, empirically supported, and alternative mental health treatment modalities into the traditional operations of a child welfare endorsed residential treatment center. The Warwick House program is designed to promote the use of residential treatment as a specific and specialized transformational intervention. The goal is to shift the perception of all involved from "placement of last resort" to "placement for growth and change." Treatment at the Warwick House, rather than being seen as failure, can be seen as an opportunity for families to restore equilibrium and develop healthier and effective ways to live together successfully.

The program has an enhanced rate that allows for small staff/youth ratios. Protocols that value family involvement, establish or strengthen community connections, and yield appropriate and effective discharge plans with follow-up support have been implemented. Rigorous data collection helps the program stay focused on outcomes and be responsive to any need for a shift in course. A key difference in the model is the incorporation of services and supports delivered at home and in the community rather than being solely facility based. Primary therapists are in the home one to two times each week, as are intensive family case managers. Milieu workers who are direct support staff provide support in the facility as well as in the home on a weekly basis. To support family-member skill development, in addition to staff spending considerable time in family homes, overnight accommodations at the residential program are made available to them so they are able to observe and learn the day-to-day approaches used by the trained staff with their children.

Given the pilot status of this effort, Magellan and Warwick focused heavily on data collection and outcomes. The 2-year findings from their efforts have shown that family-based services continue to be the preferred aftercare plan for children discharged from the IRTF program and that natural supports are essential to successful discharge planning. This supports the criticality of family engagement and involvement during the residential stay as well as the role of CFTs in developing a sustainable team that follows a family over time and across settings. Lengths of stay have been reduced by as much as 60%, with 70 to 80% of children returning to and remaining in a family setting. Youth discharged from the program have also demonstrated improvements in functioning, as measured by the Child and Adolescent Strengths Assessment and Massachusetts Youth Screening Inventory 2, as well as decreased use of inpatient psychiatric hospitalization (J. Friedman, personal communication, July 16, 2013; P. Hunt, personal communication, July 16, 2013).

The WAY Home Program

Children's Village offers the WAY Home Program, which provides at least 1 year of aftercare to all youth leaving the agency's residential school, with the opportunity for older youth who have no family resources to apply for an additional 4 years of support. The program is based on the WAY Scholarship model, which was developed by Children's Village in 1984, and has since been implemented at the Children's Village and in sites throughout the country.

The WAY Home employs paid professional mentors who support the youth primarily with school and work issues. It encompasses what much of the field refers to as "youth development," what school officials call "drop-out prevention," and what the child welfare community refers to as "independent living skills." It is also a long-term "aftercare" program. WAY Home provides a full year of support from a paid professional mentor. These mentors provide concrete assistance to the youth. In the past 7 years, Children's Village has provided 1 year of WAY Home aftercare to 551 youth. Of the youth served, 80% of those eligible to graduate (i.e., still in school) have graduated, and 97% have avoided incarceration. Work numbers are considerably lower because many youth are still in school, and on average only about 25% of the teens are employed at any given time.

In 2008, the Children's Village took another step in refining the model. Based on research and reports of recidivism 1-year postdischarge from residential care, Multisystemic Therapy–Family Integrated Transitions (MST-FIT) was added to the WAY Home model to serve the 15% of youth who had been discharged and were considered the most at risk of recidivism to residential care, jail, or both. For more than 30 years, Multisystemic Therapy (MST) has consistently demonstrated positive outcomes, including a reduction in long-term rearrest rates by a median of 39%, decreased out-of-home placements (incarceration, residential treatment, foster care) by a median of 54%, improved family functioning, decreased substance use among youth, fewer mental health problems for youth, and higher levels of client satisfaction. MST-FIT is an adaptation of MST, specifically designed for aftercare developed by Dr. Eric Trupin at the University of Washington (see http://depts.washington.edu/pbhjp/projects-programs/page/mst-family-integrated-transitions-fit).

The combination of short-term family support through a highly trained MST-FIT therapist and a long-term WAY mentor, who acts as the stable adult in the young person's life, has proven to have positive outcomes for youth and their families. Even with this subset of high-risk discharges, 80% of the youth receiving MST-FIT/WAY Home remained in the home versus 30% of the comparison group, and 76% remained in school versus 43% of the comparison group (measured 1 year postdischarge).

These examples offer illustrations of some specific components of a linked residential and community program. There are many more programs nationwide that have made strides to eradicate the silos that residential programs and community-based programs have historically imposed. Through integration, better alignment with the core foundational concepts of family-driven, youth-guided care, as well as shortened lengths of stay, long term positive outcomes are evident.

Difficult, but Not Impossible

Linking residential and community-based services clearly makes sense, and yet effectively accomplishing this is not easy. Funding silos continue to exist in the social and human services arena. Across the country, federal and state regulation and policy dictate separation of funding by types of interventions. The lack of postresidential care funding creates a revolving door of entry and exits from residential care. There are also few fiscal incentives to encourage residential providers to offer high-intensity stabilization, treatment, and triage that result in reduced lengths of stay in residential care. Providers who have not diversified their service array and rely solely on revenue from residential programming are unlikely to survive in a new environment. In some localities, the desire to simply reduce length of stay as a cost-saving mechanism has led to greater fragmentation of the safety net, and has created skepticism among many. This results in a bifurcated system where residential and community providers are viewed as competitors rather than collaborators.

Despite these challenges, strong examples of residential and community collaborations exist, and these models can be replicated. Currently, the most common approach is one where residential and community services cohabitate within an agency. Residential providers who cannot do this within their organizations can seek to form partnerships with community agencies whose service array and funding streams can complement what occurs in the residential environment. Organizations must also diligently work to diversify their funding streams. The use of grant funding and donor support allows agencies to experiment with the concepts presented here. Tracking successful outcomes from these efforts opens the door to approaching existing funders with compelling rationale to review and revise their existing structures.

With this shift in approach, where community networks have grown stronger and investments in preventive interventions have taken root, residential programs are increasingly expected to work with the "hardest to serve" young people. In many cases, residential providers are unprepared to accept these high-risk, high-need youth and families. In the absence of skill development, this residential capacity limitation places youth and families at risk by increasing the likelihood that dangerous situations will escalate at times, requiring law-enforcement intervention. While law-enforcement responses do not have to be inherently negative, it is the authors' opinion that law enforcement cannot become the default "treatment option" due to a lack of capacity or planning by the private provider community and the public sector. When law enforcement becomes the default treatment option, there is an immediate risk of criminalizing mental health. Law-enforcement responses do not always lead to treatment, and time spent in jail or prison without treatment simply leads to a recurrence of the problem at release. As such, it is incumbent upon all involved in a redefined approach to develop the skills and abilities of staff working in both residential and community environments to ensure the capability and capacity to address youth with complex needs and challenging behaviors. By partnering across agencies and systems, access to education and training is enhanced, and staff abilities are more likely to grow.

Summary

Creating an even stronger, interdependent, and verifiable link between residential and community-based programs is the necessary next step in the evolution. Few argue the notion that children belong in homes and communities whenever possible. The challenge and responsibility falls upon the social and human service community, including providers and funders, to create a system that expects and requires such linkages and collaboration. Every program, whether residential or community based, can and must take responsibility for improving partnerships and linkages and for ensuring their values and services are aligned with best practices. While policy and financing reform will ultimately support the move toward a more unified and sustainable service-delivery system, there are important steps that should and can immediately be taken to improve outcomes for young people and their families.

The programs discussed above begin to demonstrate that even in the current climate, innovative work that results in meaningful long-term outcomes can be achieved. These few examples serve as the foundation for a future that looks and behaves very differently than the historical model that the field has been tied to; a model where funding is discrete, siloed, and is still based on process outcomes rather than quantifiable quality-of-life improvements.

The field also has a vast gap in information that proves what works and what does not. The authors suggest that it is time to apply a "proof of concept" to the issue of linking residential and community—to ensure that innovations in residential and community-based services are validated by data and rational decision making, and not simply by history or anecdote. Emphasis must be placed on the development of peer-reviewed research that looks at the outcomes of residential interventions and helps to establish clear standards on what must be measured, how often, and for how long. The authors believe that this can be done and measurable outcomes should begin to define what works, when and with what type of residential care. This will allow the field to know what works, when, and at what cost.

As the research base evolves, preliminary data tells us that providers that focus on creating and embedding a philosophy that includes community treatment and partnerships, engaging families and youth in new and meaningful ways, changing language and focusing outcomes on time in home and community versus time in the residential environment, ensuring postdischarge services, supports, and follow-up, and rewarding creativity and innovation will yield benefits for the young people and families they serve.

Program Contact Information:

Borja Alvarez de Toledo, MEd
President/CEO
Child and Family Services of New Hampshire
Borjaalvarezdetoledo@gmail.com

Jim Dalton, PsyD, HSPP
President and Chief of Operations Damar Services, Inc.
6067 Decatur Blvd.
Indianapolis, IN 46241

Phone (317) 856-5201
Fax (317) 856-2333
JimD@damar.org
www.damar.org/index.cfm

Jeff Friedman, PhD, LCSW, QCSW
Clinical Director Warwick House
1460 Meetinghouse Rd.
Hartsville, PA 18974
Phone (215) 491-7404 x 20
Fax (215) 491-7405
jfriedman@warwickfamilyservices.com
http://warwickfamilyservices.com

Pat Hunt
Director of Child and Family Resiliency Services Magellan
Public Sector Solutions
P.O. Box 395
Turner, ME 04282
Phone (207) 225-2435
Fax (207) 225-2546
pahunt@magellanhealth.com
www.magellanhealth.com

Angel Knapp Reese, MSW
Director of Community Support Services
Damar Services, Inc.
6067 Decatur Blvd.
Indianapolis, IN 46241
Phone (317) 856-5201
Fax (317) 856-2333
AngelKR@damar.org
www.damar.org/index.cfm

Linda Oinen, MSW
Administrator, Child and Family Services
Monroe County Department of Human Services
111 Westfall Road
Room 528
Rochester, NY 14620
Phone (585) 753-6771
Fax (585) 753-6414
linda.oinen@dfa.state.ny.us

References

Altshuler, S. J., & Poertner, J. (2001). The child health and illness profile—Adolescent edition: Assessing well-being in group homes and institutions. *Child Welfare, 81*(3), 495–513.

Boisvert, B., Brimmer, G., Campbell, K., Koenig, D., & Stone-Smith, M. (2001). Who am I? Why family really matters. *Focal Point, 15*(2), 55–58.

Bruns, E. J., Rast, J., Peterson, C., Walker, J., & Bosworth, J. (2006). Spreadsheets, service providers, and the statehouse: Using data and the wraparound process to reform systems for children and families. *American Journal of Community Psychology, 38*(3/4) 201–212.

Burns, B. J., Hoagwood, K., & Mrazek, P. J. (1999). Effective treatment for mental disorders in children and adolescents. *Clinical Child and Family Psychology Review, 2*(4), 199–254.

Carney, M. M., & Buttell, F. (2003). Reducing juvenile recidivism: Evaluating the wraparound services model. *Research on Social Work Practice, 13*(5), 551–568.

Casey Family Programs. (2013). *Disproportionality: The overrepresentation of children of color in the foster care system.* Retrieved July 21, 2013, from www.casey.org/Resources/Publications/pdf/DisproportionalityPolicyBrief.pdf

Catholic Community Services of Western Washington and EMQ Children & Family Services. (2008). *Family search and engagement: A comprehensive practice guide.* Retrieved July 14, 2013 from www.ccsww.org/site/DocServer/Family_Search_and_Engagement_Guide_CCS-EMQ.pdf?docID = 641

Children's Defense Fund. (2010). Promising approaches in child welfare: Helping connect children and youth in foster care to permanent family and relationships through family finding and engagement. Retrieved July 21, 2013 from www.childrensdefense.org/child-research-data-publications/data/promising-approaches.pdf

Clark, H. B., Lee, B., Prange, M. E., & McDonald, B. A. (1996). Children lost within the foster care system: Can wraparound service strategies improve placement outcomes? *Journal of Child and Family Studies, 5*(1), 39–54.

Cook, R. (1992). *A national evaluation of Title IV-E foster care independent living programs for youth, phase 2, final report.* Rockville, MD: Westat, Inc.

Courtney, M. E., Dworsky, A., Cusick, G. R., Keller, T., Havlicek, J., Perez, A. . . . Bost, N. (2007). Midwest evaluation of adult functioning of former foster youth: Outcomes at age 21. Chicago, IL: University of Chicago, Chapin Hall Center for Children.

Courtney, M. E., Terao, S., & Bost, N. (2004). *Midwest evaluation of the adult functioning of former foster youth: Conditions of youth preparing to leave state care.* Chicago, IL: University of Chicago, Chapin Hall Center for Children.

Dworsky, A., & Courtney, M. E. (2000). Self sufficiency of former foster youth in Wisconsin: *Analysis of unemployment insurance wage data and public assistance data.* Retrieved July 21, 2013, from http://aspe.hhs.gov/hsp/fosteryouthwi00/

Evans, M. E., Armstrong, M. I., & Kuppinger, A. D. (1996). Family-centered intensive case management: A step toward understanding individualized care. *Journal of Child and Family Studies, 5*(1), 55–65.

Evans, M. E., Armstrong, M. I., Kuppinger, A. D., Huz, S., & McNulty, T. L. (1998). Preliminary outcomes of an experimental study comparing treatment foster care and family-centered intensive case management. In M. H. Epstein, K. Kutash, & A. J. Duchnowski (Eds.), *Outcomes for children and youth with emotional and behavioral* disorders and their families: Programs and evaluation best practices (pp. 543–580). Austin, TX: PRO-ED.

Hair, H. J. (2005). Outcomes for children and adolescents after residential treatment: A review of research from 1993 to 2003. *Journal of Child and Family Studies, 14*(4), 551–575.

Hines, A. M., Lemon, K., Wyatt, P., & Merdinger, J. (2004). Factors related to the disproportionate involvement of children of color in the child welfare system: A review and emerging themes. *Children and Youth Services Review, 26*(6), 507–527.

Landsman, M. J., Groza, V., Tyler, M., & Malone, K. (2001). Outcomes of family-centered residential treatment. *Child Welfare Journal, 80,* 351–379.

Miles, P., Bruns, E .J., Osher, T. W., Walker, J. S., & National Wraparound Initiative Advisory Group. (2006). *The wraparound process user's guide: A handbook for families.* Portland, OR: National Wraparound Initiative, Research and Training Center on Family Support and Children's Mental Health, Portland State University.

Pecora, P. J., Kessler, R. C., Williams, J., O'Brien, K., Downs, A. C., English, D., et al. (2005). Improving family foster care: Findings from the Northwest Foster Care Alumni Study. Seattle, WA: Casey Family Programs.

Reilly, T. (2003). Transition from care: Status and outcomes of youth who age out of foster care. *Child Welfare: Journal of Policy, Practice, and Program, 82*(6), 727–746.

VanDenBerg, J., Bruns, E., & Burchard, J. (2003). History of the wraparound process. *Focal point, 17*(2), 4–7.

Walter, U. M., & Petr, C. G. (2008). Family-centered residential treatment: Knowledge, research, and values converge. *Residential Treatment for Children & Youth, 25*(1), 1–16.

9 Preventing Seclusion and Restraint in Residential Programs

Janice LeBel, Kevin Ann Huckshorn, and Beth Caldwell

For as long as residential programs serving children and adolescents have existed in the United States, seclusion and restraint (S/R) has been used in these settings (Bertolino & Thompson, 1999). For almost as long, reformers, advocates, and governments have sought to curb, control, and eliminate these high-risk practices. This chapter offers some historical and current perspectives of S/R with children and youth, discusses the dangers associated with these interventions, and reviews a strategic framework to prevent their use. In addition, the importance of youth/family inclusion and key youth/family roles in S/R efforts, innovative S/R reduction approaches, and effective pragmatic resources to facilitate practice change are provided.

Residential care in the United States reportedly started in 1727, when French nuns from the Sisters of Ursula order arrived in New Orleans and opened a school and orphanage for girls (Folks, 1978). Orphanages were designed for poor, homeless children in need of "rehabilitation," which consisted of religious education, structure, compliance, isolation, and punishment (Bertolino & Thompson, 1999). Because early American practice often followed English common law, children over age 7 who committed crimes or had problematic behavior were subjected to the same treatment as adults, including harsh corporal punishment, such as mutilation, confinement, S/R, banishment, or death. As a result, institutions, such as asylums, almshouses, and workhouses often housed adults and children together (McGowan, 1983).

Today, residential programs do not commingle children with adults, but both populations are subjected to S/R, which some consider to be contemporary forms of corporal punishment (LeBel, Nunno, Mohr, & O'Halloran, 2012). Legal advocates and some national and international legal standards define corporal punishment as "any punishment in which physical force is used and intended to cause some degree of pain or discomfort" (American Civil Liberties/Human Rights Watch [ACLU/HRW], 2009, p. 3). Many people who have experienced S/R concur with this definition (National Association of State Mental Health Program Directors [NASMHPD], 2013). Contemporary residential providers would dispute the intention to inflict pain or discomfort but agree that restraint, as currently practiced, is any manual method or device used to restrict freedom of movement—not including devices used for medical purposes, physical support, or orthopedic control. Seclusion is considered involuntary confinement to a room or area from which a child/adolescent is physically prevented from leaving (LeBel et al., 2012).

Fundamental Seclusion and Restraint Truths

Seclusion and restraint are practiced across all child/adolescent-serving settings. More than a decade ago, S/R use was the subject of highly publicized national criticism when Connecticut's *Hartford Courant* newspaper published a five-part comprehensive investigative report titled "Deadly Restraint" (Weiss, Altimari, Blint, & Megan, 1998). The investigation resulted from two restraint deaths of Connecticut children—one in a residential program, the other in a psychiatric hospital. The *Courant*'s report highlighted the injuries, deleterious effects, and deaths resulting from S/R use across child, youth, and adult settings (Huckshorn & LeBel, 2009).

The *Courant* noted that S/R use and related deaths often occurred for seemingly innocuous reasons (e.g., refusing to let go of a picture, ignoring staff directives to move to another seat, or disputing a missing teddy bear; Weiss et al., 1998). The journalists' findings also revealed the lack of (1) formalized reporting of S/R use; (2) standardized, federal regulations; (3) a national database recording deaths and serious injuries; and (4) accountability for S/R use, injuries, or deaths in health-care provider organizations (Lieberman, Dodd, & DeLauro, 1999). As a result of the *Courant*'s investigation, congressional hearings were held, and the United States General Accounting Office (now called the Government Accountability Office [USGAO]) conducted its own investigation and confirmed the *Courant*'s findings (USGAO, 1999a, 1999b). This led to the Substance Abuse Mental Health Services Administration's (SAMHSA) National Call to Action to Eliminate Seclusion and Restraint Initiative, and with it new funding, new resources, new research, and new methods to reduce and prevent S/R use (Huckshorn & LeBel, 2009; NASMHPD, 2013).

Further study of S/R practice revealed fundamental S/R "practice truths" that have been repeatedly confirmed (NASMHPD, 2013). Some of these truths are particularly germane to child/adolescent residential programs and should be taught to all staff, and minimally include that (1) children are subjected to S/R more often than are adolescents; (2) children and adolescents are subjected to S/R more often than are adults; (3) minority children and adolescents are subjected to S/R more often than are nonminorities; (4) children and adolescents with developmental and intellectual disabilities are subjected to S/R more often than are nondisabled children and adolescents; (5) the majority of children and adolescents served in residential programs have experienced some form of traumatic life experience—most, more than once (S/R are traumatizing/retraumatizing procedures); and (6) the injury and death rate for children/adolescents subjected to S/R is higher than the injury and death rate for adults (NASMHPD, 2013; Weiss et al., 1998).

Additional practice truths were also identified that challenge the premise for S/R use, its "safety" label, and the presumption of efficient crisis management.

Most startling of all, despite centuries of use, S/R has not been subjected to formal study. No formal scientific research, such as random controlled trial methodology, has been conducted to establish a body of evidence to support S/R practice as "therapeutic interventions" (NASMHPD, 2013; Sailas & Fenton, 2012). The evidence that does exist establishes the harmful effects to those involved (NASMHPD, 2013; Sailas & Fenton, 2000). Moreover, the attributions that S/R are "safe procedures" that promote "safety" are false. These emergency containment procedures have higher staff injury rates than high-risk industries (Weiss et al., 1998) and often lead to increased S/R use and greater violence and conflict than they attempt to resolve (LeBel, 2011a).

The risk of harm to children and adolescents subjected to S/R are even greater compared to the risk of harm to adults. Both the *Hartford Courant* (1998) and Nunno, Holden, and Tollar (2006) works cite the greater incidence of death, injuries, and significant medical risks. A large-scale review of one state's S/R data found the incidence of injuries to children/adolescents was significantly higher (23%) than injuries to staff (Garinger, 2009).

There are several mechanisms of injury, death, and physical and psychological trauma to both staff and youth associated with the use of S/R. Most often, deaths from physical restraint result from asphyxia (LeBel et al., 2012; Nunno et al., 2006). This occurs when an airway obstruction is caused by compression to the neck, chest, or abdomen; blockage of the nose and/or mouth; or clogging of the airway by vomitus or excess saliva (LeBel et al., 2012).

Finally, the myth that S/R are efficient crisis-management methods is dispelled when the techniques, their implementation, and the impact on program operations are analyzed. In short, S/R are not efficient techniques. They are labor-intensive practices. A 1-hour episode can claim more than 13 hours of staff time, with the majority of time spent after the event has terminated (LeBel & Goldstein, 2005). Additional research identifies that S/R can claim as much as 23% to 50% of total staff time and a program's operating budget (LeBel, 2011a). When these practice truths are considered together, it is no wonder that SAMHSA declared S/R use "disgraceful . . . and a treatment failure" when the National Initiative was launched (LeBel, 2011b).

Importance of Implementing an Evidence-Based Practice for Reducing S/R

For the last 25 years, the behavioral health field, led by SAMHSA and others, has worked hard to develop and implement best practices based on evidence and founded on research (Institute of Medicine, 2005). The need for this move towards science-based practices and away from intuitional and historical practices has rarely been so significant as when addressing the centuries-old interventions known as S/R (Huckshorn, 2004). As has been clearly explicated in the literature, there never has been any evidence base for the use of these widely used, dangerous, and traumatic interventions (Huckshorn, 2013). As such, the NASMHPD worked with professionals and people with lived experience of mental illness and S/R, also referred to as "persons served," inclusive of families and youth, across the United States, from 2002 through 2009, to develop an evidence-based practice called the "Six Core Strategies to Reduce Coercion, Violence and the Use of Seclusion and Restraint" (Huckshorn, 2004; Huckshorn, 2013; NASMHPD, 2013). The Six Core Strategies (6CS) were approved as an evidence-based practice in 2012 by the National Registry of Effective Programs and Practices (NREPP; http://nrepp.samhsa.gov/ViewIntervention. aspx?id = 278).

On the following pages, find both a summary of each of the 6CS as well as examples of how different residential programs have successfully implemented elements of each of the strategies to prevent/reduce S/R. There are many more practices that can be implemented for each of the 6CS.

The Six Core Strategies

1. *Leadership Towards Organizational Change*—This most important organizational strategy is focused on preventing/reducing the use of S/R by executive leadership, defining and articulating a mission, philosophy of care, guiding values, and assuring for the development of a formal and comprehensive S/R reduction plan and plan implementation. The guidance, direction, participation, and ongoing review by executive leadership must be clearly demonstrated, even mandated, throughout the S/R and restraint reduction project and includes senior leaders participating, in real time, after each S/R event. In SAMHSA's eight-state evaluation over a 3-year period, those programs that realized and sustained significant reductions had committed leaders who fully implemented the 6CS to reduce/prevent S/R (NASMHPD, 2013). These leaders also, more importantly, actively engaged, on a daily basis, in activities to transform their programs from those focused on control and coercion to those operationalizing values consistent with TIC and positive outcomes (e.g., family-driven care, youth-guided care; Walters & Petr, 2008).

> To effectively reduce restraints, we found that leadership must begin with clearly defining the mission, values, and program norms of what is acceptable versus unacceptable. Through collaboration with leadership, honest communication, and a consistent approach, program staff feel a true connection to their work, along with a sense of support that helps to shape and guide their interventions. How we treat one another has a direct correlation to how we treat those we serve, and as a program leader, it is imperative to model this transparency. As we continue to work towards the elimination of restraints, regular staff and community meetings center around defining alternatives to restraints, staff and resident safety planning, consistency in staff supervision, and the ongoing focus of trauma-informed, youth-guided, and family-driven approaches must continue. (Personal communication, Amir Asad Mir, Program Director, Madonna Heights Residential Treatment Facility, SCO Family of Services, NY, 2013)

Residential practice examples from around the country:

Executive leaders:

- Revised the agency mission and values to those based on best practices/ research and sustained positive outcomes.
- Modeled the agency values with all staff, youth, and family members daily.
- Recruited staff representing all disciplines, advocates, youth, and families to be part of an agency-wide S/R prevention/reduction team.
- Ensured the development, implementation, and ongoing review/updates of a strategic/action plan based on the Six Core Strategies.
  - Actively, meaningfully—and not in a tokenistic way—included youth/families and staff as team members in developing and overseeing the comprehensive organizational action plan to change practice and program/agency culture.
  - Broadcast and marketed the plan.
  - Several programs had youth name the initiative.
- Updated all policies, forms, and agency documents to reflect new mission/ values and commitment to eliminate S/R.
- Implemented a "witnessing" protocol, where key leaders were part of a rotation to respond to every S/R event—demonstrating their commitment to prevent S/R and compassion for youth and staff.

2. *Using Data to Inform Practice*—Leadership works to reduce the use of S/R by using data in a performance improvement, empirical, nonpunitive manner. This strategy includes using data to analyze characteristics of an organizations' usage by unit, shift day, and staff member; identifying the organization's baseline use of S/R; and setting improvement goals and comparatively monitoring use over time in all care areas, units, and/or state child and youth care programs.

> We collect and disseminate data regularly among our staff in real time, leading to data-informed clinical interventions and care. From 2005 to 2012, we have eliminated mechanical restraints, decreased physical restraints by 86%, and seclusion by 40%. Our mechanical restraint beds were deconstructed by our staff and youth, and transformed in to a "Healing Bench." (Personal communication, Muhammad Waqar Azeem, MD, DFAACAP, DFAPA, Medical Director & Chief of Psychiatry, Albert J. Solnit Children's Center, CT, 2013)

Residential practice examples from around the country:

- Defined and tracked all coercive events (e.g., S/R; AWOLs; police calls; time outs; medication use) by day, week, month, quarter.
- Analyzed data—including day/shift/individual staff members to understand all trends. Analyzed these findings to find solutions (i.e., when two

specific staff members worked together on a unit, there were never any restraints—so observed and interviewed these staff members and had them meet with other staff teams to replicate their practices).

- Viewed existing S/R standards/policies/regulations as *minimal standards* and set program-specific policy to surpass them as practice improved (i.e., reduced maximum physical restraint from 30 minutes to 5 minutes).
- Posted/shared data w/everyone—simple/readable graphs—against last year, last week, all units.

3. *Workforce Development*—Leadership works to create a program environment where policy, procedures, and practices are grounded in and directed by a thorough understanding of the neurological, biological, psychological, and social effects of trauma and violence on humans, and the prevalence of these experiences in children and adolescents who receive residential interventions. This strategy also acknowledges the traumatic experiences of families and of some staff who work in these programs, and an understanding of the characteristics and principles of trauma-informed care systems. This intervention is designed to create an environment that is less likely to be coercive or conflictual, and is implemented primarily through staff training, education, mentoring, and supervision systems, and other organizational human resource activities, such as staff hiring and evaluation practices, and the inclusion of technical and attitudinal competencies in job descriptions and performance evaluations. Focus on frequent and clear staff communication, and support and empowerment of staff, is also an important piece of workforce development. This core strategy includes "safe as possible" S/R and restraint application training, comprehensively reviewing the choice of vendors to ensure the chosen vendor's training is consistent with the values of the organization.

> We implemented weekly meetings to ensure that our agency mission—which is centered on BBI principles—is driving all efforts and programming at the operational level. These weekly meetings are comprised of residential program supervisors, milieu workers, clinicians, permanency coaches, and upper management; we work collaboratively and problem solve any barriers that may impact our success in making our goals and values a reality. A main goal was to reduce restraints—we reduced by 75% in 2 years; these weekly meetings were critical to getting all staff to join together in this effort. (Personal communication, Susan Beck, Executive Director, Mount Prospect Academy/Becket Family of Services, NH, 2013)

Residential practice examples from around the country:

- Revised staff hiring practices/job descriptions/orientation/ongoing training/supervision/evaluation protocols to be consistent with best practice values. Involved youth and family members in all revisions.

- Developed staff competencies specific to both preventing S/R and using a range of family-driven, youth-guided, and trauma-informed practices.
- Focused on multiple ways to empower, partner with, and celebrate staff; examples included
  - each executive leader "adopted" a "unit" and became active on that "unit" to support staff and ensure practices were understood and implemented;
  - executive leaders would work one "cottage" for 2 to 3 hours so that the entire "cottage" team could attend a training together; and
  - CEO held monthly luncheons and randomly invited 10 to 12 staff each month to listen to their concerns and ideas for improvement— sent out monthly updates to all staff on concerns and ideas identified and his follow-up to these.
- Revised and significantly strengthened staff supervision/coaching/ mentoring.
- Included youth and families in staff supervision activities, specifically soliciting their comments, concerns, and praise for staff. This type of "upward" or "360 review" process is used in business sectors and provides a benchmark of good customer service.
- Included youth and families in staff interviews, tours, and recommendations for hiring.
- Hired likable people. (As referenced in the "Trauma-Informed Care" chapter, youth recommended hiring staff with good relationship skills and not overvaluing previous residential experience.)
- Ensured that youth and families participated in staff orientation and all agency training programs; in orientation they shared both their experience of S/R and residential service.
- Ensured that top leadership (e.g., CEO, COO) attended staff orientation and gave the strong message the organization was moving away from S/R and was committed to best practices principles (i.e., Building Bridges Initiative).
- Even if staff were trained how to use S/R at orientation, they were not allowed to participate in S/R for the first 3 to 6 months on the job. Staff were closely supervised, observed, and studied in their capacity to use their own strength-based communication and problem-solving skills to intervene and quell problems before letting them lay hands on. As one provider stated, "If you do not teach staff well and give them a S/R hammer, everything looks like a nail."
- Breaking up how S/R was taught. Increased the verbal de-escalation skills and taught this separately from the hands-on techniques. Taught the physical skills for restraint with cardiopulmonary resuscitation (CPR) so staff understood this is intended to be a *rare* life-saving procedure of last resort.
- Provided real time on the floor support for staff, such as a "schedule of support," so that direct-care staff knew who was on site and available and

present on the units to help if a problem developed, and had telephonic administrative or clinical backup to provide assistance as well.

- Taught staff, children/youth/families dispute resolution, conflict management, and negotiations skills. As the provider who focused on this remedy stated, "S/R only solves one person's problem—the staff's."
- Taught staff how to be respectful, listen, how to take a reflective pause/breath before reacting, and to avoid the word *no,* which is the precursor to conflict.
- Taught staff about the impact of trauma. Had staff take the Adverse Childhood Experiences Test (www.helloquizzy.com/tests/the-adverse-childhood-experience-test) to appreciate their own trauma history and develop their own individual coping/soothing plans (www.cdc.gov/ace/about.htm).
- Taught staff *not* to put hands on youth unless the request was elicited by the youth (e.g., offering a hug or shoulder rub when distressed).

4. *Use of Seclusion and Restraint Prevention/Reduction Tools*—This strategy is designed to prevent, and thus reduce, the use of S/R through the use of a variety of tools and assessments that are integrated into each individual youth's individual care plan, such as

- assessments for violence and S/R history;
- trauma assessments;
- tools to identify persons with risk factors for death and/or injury;
- use of calming/soothing plans, for most youth, to support early identification of personal triggers and warning signs as well as a variety of strategies to promote self-regulation when youth, family members, and/or staff first recognize early signs of distress, as well as de-escalation preferences if dysregulation does occur;
- environmental changes to ensure physical environments are healing and inviting (these may include comfort and sensory rooms or areas); and
- the use of a range of sensory modulation materials and interventions to use in the residential program, in school, community locations, and at home.

At the Mather St. Children's Community Residence, prevention centered on the idea that every moment counted! How the children were awakened each morning, sent to and received from school, transitioned throughout the evening, and assisted through bedtime were all done with intent of preventing and/or supporting them through emotional distress. Individual Support Plans that clearly listed their preferred interventions, PRNs (pro re nata) of chewing gum and low-calorie flavored drinks, and an approach of kindness and support helped us on our journey towards elimination of physical restraints. (Personal communication, Billy Brill, Program Coordinator, Toomey Residential and Community Services, NY, 2013.)

I remember, as a resident at Chauncy Hall, that the staff would carry around sensory items, and it made me interested in what they were playing with and why. Now, as a peer mentor, I do the same thing and also help our teens figure out their sensory preferences. (Personal communication, Meghan Comeau, Peer Mentor, Chauncy Hall Academy, MA, 2013.)

Residential practice examples from around the country:

- Utilized assessment tools to assess risk for violence and high medical risks for injury and death, as well as comprehensive trauma assessments. The information from the assessments was communicated with youth, families, and staff and transferred in a useful manner to safety/soothing plans.
- Once the individual safety/soothing plan was developed, used it in debriefings (if S/R was used) to learn what did not work and then updated the plan. Made sure the family had the plan for use at home and in the community (e.g., e-mailed; printed on small laminated card). With consent, made sure others involved with the youth/family (e.g., coach, aunt, community mentor) knew the plan, had the plan, and agreed to use it.
- Made environmental improvements, with staff and youth working together to improve the "healing/calming/beauty" qualities of every space in the program—one room at a time, including hallways. Most often, painting is done first. Some have asked local college art students to come in and draw murals with the youth.
- Contracted with an occupational therapist who had expertise in sensory modulation to provide trainings for families, youth, and staff.
- Developed a "resident support team" to teach youth dispute resolution, conflict mediation, and negotiation skills, and gave youth the opportunity to keep small problems small and solve them on their own—with peer support.
- Significantly expanded the exercise/movement/large motor/play activities— got everybody up and moving regularly, and doing things they liked to do.
- Utilized psychiatric service and/or pet therapy dogs every day and evening in the program.
- Found monies for vestibular equipment/activities, such as hammocks, glider rockers, and indoor and outdoor swings.
- Found monies for proprioceptive equipment/activities, such as rock-climbing walls, jungle gyms, and climbing rope swings.

5. *Actively Recruit and Include Youth and Families in all Activities*—This strategy assures the full and formal inclusion of youth and young adult peers and family members, with lived experiences of emotional and/or behavioral challenges in out-of-home settings, in a variety of roles in the organization. These roles can be described as assisting in the prevention and reduction of S/R, the implementation

of trauma-informed care principles, improving emotional safety, providing timely advocacy on behalf of youth and families, and modeling skills in building resiliency through the development of individualized wellness plans and pathways. The use of peers as staff in child/adolescent residential programs lags behind the work being done in the adult system. The adult system has found the addition of peer specialists to be extremely valuable and a real driver of system change when these staff are fully integrated into all aspects of an organization.

> Youth Development Institute reduced restraints by 67% in a year. Once a youth-guided culture is established, staff no longer see themselves as "us" and the youth as "them"; likewise, youth begin to feel that they truly belong, a powerful member of their own treatment team. Seclusion, to isolate and lock a youth away, becomes unthinkable and restraint, to forcibly hold a youth to the floor until he capitulates, seems horribly wrong. (Personal communication, Trish Cocoros, Co-Executive Director, Youth Development Institute, AZ, 2013.)

Residential practice examples from around the country:

- Hired multiple family and youth advocates.
- *Before* the child/youth family was admitted, called them, met them, found out the trauma history, found out the last time S/R was used, and began to develop a soothing plan before they walked through the door. Included extended family in the development and implementation of the plan.
- Developed a youth advisory council with real "power" to make change to the program.
- Developed a family advisory council that reports to the CEO; the council conducts on-site reviews twice annually and provides feedback to the CEO and executive committee on their findings and recommendations.
- Involved other youth/young adult peer mentors as preadmission "ambassadors" to reach out to prospective youth and reassure them that S/R was not something the program wanted to use and inquired what could be done to support them through a difficult time.
- Put a strong focus on person-first language—staff agreed to put a quarter into a jar if they referred to youth by their diagnosis or used pejorative language in talking about families (e.g., dysfunctional, manipulative); monies were saved and used for pizza parties.

6. *Use of Rigorous Debriefing Techniques*—Rigorous debriefing reduces S/R through knowledge gained from a rigorous analysis of S/R and restraint events, and the use of this knowledge to inform policy, procedures, and practices to avoid repeats in the future. A secondary goal of this intervention is to attempt to mitigate to the extent possible the adverse and potentially traumatizing effects of a S/R event for involved staff, youth involved in the event, and all witnesses

to the event. It is imperative that senior clinical/medical staff, including the clinical/medical director, participate in these debriefings and that they occur both immediately post the acute event and more formally the day after or a few days afterwards. The goal of this strategy is to "drill down" on the antecedents to the event and identify where prevention or early intervention approaches could have been implemented, but were missed.

> We learned that looking at the events immediately preceding the event was not enough. Our numbers dropped when we began looking at the restraint in the context of each youth's trauma history and identified how traumatic reenactment contributed to the events leading up to the restraint. Once staff better understood the traumatic reenactment, they began to view the triggers in a different way, search for the unmet need and better recognize missed opportunities. We were able to reduce our restraints by 87% in 2 years, from 329 to 44. (Personal communication, Kathy Perkins, LCSW, RTF Director, The House of the Good Shepherd, NY, 2013.)

Residential practice examples from around the country:

- Ensured after every restraint that all of the youth who witnessed the restraint had an opportunity to share their fears/concerns/frustrations, received necessary emotional support to move on, and were able to share their recommendations for avoiding future restraints similar to the one they observed. We used this information in our formal debriefing.
- Identified at least one practice improvement or program change needed after every restraint—even if it was just more frequent minitrainings on individual youth-soothing preferences.
- Used a trauma lens to review each restraint.
- Had the staff who were closest to the youth involved in the restraint discuss the restraint in an informal manner (i.e., while taking a walk or playing basketball). It was sometimes necessary to have three or four discussions to find out what it was that initially triggered the youth to get upset.
- After every restraint, staff involved in the restraint were asked, individually, how they were "emotionally." They were asked whether they needed some time to "recover." At the end of the shift after a restraint, all staff were reminded to take care of themselves and that the supervisor was available if anybody needed any time to process or just share fears/frustrations.

It must be noted that many youth-serving residential and hospital programs have reduced the use of physical restraints to very few events annually (i.e. < 10) using the 6CS; some have stopped using S/R for several years. It must also be recognized that programs have used a variety of formal practice models (e.g., collaborative problem solving, trauma systems therapy, children and residential experiences, risking connections, sanctuary) to support their efforts to reduce S/R. While programs have realized success with different models, some have used the same models without attaining successful reductions of S/R. The authors of this chapter have found that it is not the specific program model chosen that correlates to reduced S/R; rather, it is that common elements (e.g., leadership, debriefing, rigorous data analysis. ongoing staff training and support, use of a variety of tools, respecting and engaging youth and families) have been in place that support the chosen formal models or informal frameworks in being operationalized to their fullest.

Seclusion and Restraint Use in Schools

Many residential programs also operate schools that use S/R. Other programs send youth to day programs or public schools where S/R is used or could be used. Many schools have successfully reduced the use of S/R, with some eliminating this practice. Ensuring prevention of S/R in all settings that youth receive services is imperative. Background on the use of S/R in schools, as well as national policies and directions, are provided below.

Corporal punishment has been used in the classroom for centuries (Butchart, 1998). One expert identifies it as part of pedagogy's "history of warfare with the child" (Raichle, 1978), used not only to punish but also to underscore the authority of the "schoolmaster." Historically, obedience in school could be derived through physical means (i.e., whispering sticks, yokes, unipods, whips, paddles) and psychological measures (name-calling, dunce cap, and other shaming measures; Raichle, 1978).

In response to increased scrutiny from the advocacy community, the USGAO was asked again to investigate S/R practices, this time in public schools. The investigation found hundreds of cases of alleged abuse and death related to the use of these methods on school children during the past two decades and cited specific examples of death and injury to children (USGAO, 2009). Following the release of the USGAO report, the United States Department of Education (USDOE) in 2009 directed each state to review its current policies and guidelines regarding the use of S/R in schools to ensure every student is safe and protected, and if appropriate, develop or revise its policies and guidelines before the start of the 2009–2010 school year. Later, the Department of Education posted a summary of state laws, regulations, policies and guidelines on their Web site (www.ed.gov/policy/seclusion/seclusion-state-summary.html). The United States Department of Education Secretary, Arne Duncan, indicated that many states and territories have begun to work with their stakeholders to develop or revise current practices (United States Department of Education, 2012).

Federal legislators took more strident action and filed two bipartisan bills (H.R. 4247 and S. 2860). The intent of both bills was to create a national minimum practice standard for reducing and preventing S/R use in schools (LeBel et al., 2012). On May 15, 2012, the Secretary of Education published "Restraint and Seclusion: A Resource Document," which describes 15 principles for school districts, parents, and other child/youth advocates and stakeholders to consider when reviewing school policies on the use of S/R (USDOE, 2012). A summation of the 15 principles follows:

1   Every effort must be made to prevent the need for S/R in school settings;
2   mechanical restraint should be prohibited in schools;
3   S/R should never be used except in the face of imminent danger to self or others;
4   policies restricting the use of S/R should apply to all children, not just those with disabilities;
5   all interventions with children need to be consistent with the right to be treated with dignity and be free from abuse;
6   S/R should never be used as punishment;
7   S/R practices should never restrict breathing;
8   multiple usage of S/R on same child should trigger a thoughtful review and assurance that positive behavioral supports are integrated;
9   strategies used to address the use of S/R must address the underlying causes;
10   teacher and other personnel must be trained regularly on prevention of conflict, violence, and use of S/R;
11   S/R use must be visually monitored for the entire event;
12   parents must be informed on school policies on use of S/R;
13   parents must be notified immediately following a S/R event with their child;
14   S/R policies in educational settings should be reviewed regularly and updated consistently; and
15   all use of S/R must be documented and provide for a system-wide collection of data that would assist teachers, principals, and others to understand the issues and implement the preceding 15 principles.

The education resource document also recognized the work done by SAMHSA and reviews the evidence-based 6CS, described previously.

Sustaining Prevention/Reduction/Elimination Efforts

Where residential, community, and school leaders and staff commit to S/R reduction and prevention, great innovation, inspiration, and reductions have followed. Sadly, success is not always permanent. Many residential, community, and school programs have reduced S/R use, but *sustaining the effort is the key to success and ultimate positive outcomes* (LeBel et al., 2012). It is not unusual to see backsliding, a return to past practice, or a fluctuating use of S/R when there is inconsistent leadership and staffing, or some other operational challenge thwarts focused implementation (NASMHPD, 2013). The most important message for each leader is to tap all disciplines and all levels of staff's inherent leadership and creativity and foster their brilliance. Leadership's consistent attention to ensuring that best practice values (e.g., trauma-informed care, youth-guided care, family-driven care, cultural and linguistic competence) are operationalized provides the foundation for sustaining reduction/prevention successes.

Even after significant reduction and prevention of S/R is achieved, it is strongly recommended that executive leadership ensures that the *6CS continue to be operationalized*, with at least quarterly reviews of how the organization is implementing each strategy. Each core strategy should continue to be used on an ongoing basis. The 6CS are a framework to aid leadership in transforming their service cultures through operationalizing best practice values. Leaders who commit to this framework will realize significantly reduced use of S/R and other coercive interventions and will likely see sustained reductions for as long as the framework is used. The good news is the tools to prevent coercive practices are readily available.

Web Site Resources

American Psychiatric Nurses Association (APNA), www.apna.org/i4a/pages/index.cfm?pageid = 3728

Association of University Disability Centers on Disabilities, www.aucd.org/template/page.cfm?id=748

Bazelon Center for Mental Health Law, www.bazelon.org/Where-We-Stand/Self-Determination/Forced-Treatment/Restraint-and-Seclusion.aspx

Department of Education, www2.ed.gov/policy/seclusion/restraint-and-seclusion-resource-document.html

Department of Education, www.ed.gov/policy/restraintandseclusion

National Association of State Mental Health Program Directors, www.nasmhpd.org/TA/SR_TICpractices.aspx

National Registry of Effective Programs and Practices—6CS,http://nrepp.samhsa.gov/ViewIntervention.aspx?id = 278

Positive Behavioral Interventions and Support, www.pbis.org/seclusion/restraint/default.aspx

Presidents New Freedom Commission on Mental Health,http://govinfo.library.unt.edu/mentalhealthcommission/index.html

SAMHSA Seclusion & Restraint, www.samhsa.gov/matrix2/seclusion_matrix.aspx

TASH (APRAIS), http://tash.org/advocacy-issues/restraint-and-seclusion-aprais/

References

American Civil Liberties Union/Human Rights Watch. (2009). *Impairing education: Corporal punishment of students with disabilities in us public schools.* Retrieved October 11, 2013, from www.hrw.org/en/reports/2009/08/11/impairing-education-0

Bertolino, B., & Thompson, K. (Eds.). (1999). *The residential youth care worker in action: A collaborative, competency-based approach.* New York, NY: Haworth Mental Health Press.

Butchart, R. E. (1998). Historical and political perspectives on classroom management. In R. E. Butchart & B. McEwan (Eds.), *Classroom discipline in American schools: Problems and possibilities for democratic education.* Albany: State University of New York Press.

Folks, H. (1978). *The care of destitute, neglected and delinquent children.* New York, NY: National Association of Social Workers.

Garinger, G. (2009). *Annual report 2008.* Boston, MA: Office of the Child Advocate. Retrieved August 11, 2009, from www.mass.gov/childadvocate/about/annual_report.pdf

Huckshorn, K. A. (2004). Reducing seclusion and restraint use in mental health settings: Core strategies for prevention. *Journal of Psychosocial Nursing and Mental Health Services, 42*(9), 22–33.

Huckshorn, K. A. (2013). *Reducing seclusion and restraint use in mental health settings: A phenomenological study of hospital leader and staff experiences* (Doctoral dissertation). Available from ProQuest Dissertations Publishing. (UMI No. 3553916).

Huckshorn, K. A., & LeBel, J. L. (2009). Improving safety in mental health treatment settings: Preventing conflict, violence and the use of seclusion and restraint. In S. S. Sharfstein, F. B. Dickerson, & J. M. Oldham (Eds.), *Textbook of hospital psychiatry* (pp. 253–265). Washington, DC: American Psychiatric Publishing.

Institute of Medicine. (2005). *Improving the quality of health care for mental and substance-use conditions.* Washington, DC: Institutes of Medicine of the National Academies.

LeBel, J. (2011a). *Promoting alternatives to the use of seclusion and restraint: Issue paper: Making the business case.* Rockville, MD: Center for Mental Health Services, Substance Abuse and Mental Health Services Administration.

LeBel, J. (2011b, May 25). *Optimizing treatment: Developing the talent within.* PowerPoint presentation delivered at New York State Office of Mental Health's Positive Alternatives to Restraint and Seclusion Lessons Learned Conference, Poughkeepsie, New York.

LeBel, J., & Goldstein, R. (2005). The economic cost of using restraint and the value added by restraint reduction or elimination. *Psychiatric Services, 56*(9) 1109–1114.

LeBel, J., Nunno, M., Mohr, W. K., & O'Halloran, R. (2012). Restraint and seclusion use in U.S. school settings: Recommendations from allied treatment disciplines. *American Journal of Orthopsychiatry, 82*(1), 75–86.

Lieberman, J., Dodd, C., & DeLauro, R. (1999, March). *Testimony to the senate committee on finance.* Washington, DC: U.S. Senate Proceedings.

McGowan, B. (1983). Historical evolution of child welfare services: An examination of the sources of current problems and dilemmas. In B. McGowan & W. Meezan (Eds.), *Child welfare* (pp. 45–90). Itasca, IL: F. E. Peacock.

National Association of State Mental Health Program Directors. (1999a). *Position statement on seclusion and restraint.* Alexandria, VA: Author.

National Association of State Mental Health Program Directors. (1999b). *Reducing the use of seclusion and restraint: Findings, strategies, and recommendations.* Alexandria, VA: Author.

National Association of State Mental Health Program Directors. (2001). *Reducing the use of seclusion and restraint: Findings, principles, and recommendations for special needs populations. Part 2.* Alexandria, VA: Author.

National Association of State Mental Health Program Directors. (2013). *National Executive Training Institute (NETI) curriculum for the creation of violence-free, coercion-free treatment settings and the reduction of seclusion and restraint* (11th ed.). Alexandria, VA: Author.

Nunno, M., Holden, M., & Tollar, A. (2006). Learning from tragedy: A survey of child and adolescent restraint fatalities. *Child Abuse & Neglect, 30*(12), 1333–1342.

Raichle, D. R. (1978). School discipline and corporal punishment: An American retrospect. *Interchange, 8*(1), 71–83.

Sailas, E., & Fenton, M. (2000). Seclusion and restraint for people with serious mental illnesses. *Cochrane Database of Systematic Reviews 2.* CD001163.

United States Department of Education. (2012, May). *Restraint and seclusion: Resource document.* Washington, DC: Author.

United States General Accounting Office. (1999a). *Mental health: Extent of risk from improper restraint or seclusion is unknown* (No. GAO/T-HEHS-00–26). Washington, DC: Author.

United States General Accounting Office. (1999b). *Mental health: Improper restraint or seclusion places people at risk* (No. GAO/HEHS-99–176). Washington, DC: Author.

United States Government Accountability Office. (2009). *Seclusion and restraints: Selected cases of death and abuse at public and private schools and treatment centers* (No. GAO-09–719T). Washington, DC: Author.

Walters, U. M., & Petr, C. G. (2008). Family-centered residential treatment: Knowledge, research, and values converge. *Residential Treatment for Children & Youth, 25*(1), 1–16.

Weiss, E. M., Altimari, D., Blint, D. F., & Megan, K. (1998, October). Deadly restraint: A Hartford Courant investigative report. *Hartford Courant.*

10 Innovative Residential Interventions for Young Adults in Transition

Marc Fagan, Maryann Davis, Brian M. Denietolis, and Diane L. Sondheimer

Understanding the Unique Needs of Young Adults

The transition to adulthood is a continuous process of rapid, psychosocial change that starts accelerating at age 16 and slows considerably in the late 20s. During this period, young adults take steps to live more autonomously and to depend less on family support. These steps, which involve completing school and training, building peer and romantic relationships, developing independent living capacities, and launching and sustaining work lives, shape their future adult life.

The transition also includes substantial risks with long-term implications. For example, compared to other age groups, young adults have the highest onset rates of substance abuse and dependence (Delucchi, Matzger, & Weisner, 2008). For young adults with serious mental health conditions (SMHC),[1] the changes during this stage of life are exceedingly more challenging and complex. Young adults are in a critical stage of development, during which they are neither children nor mature adults, and their development, functioning, and service needs are different from those who are older or younger. This chapter describes the unique needs of young adults as well as innovative residential interventions to support the transition to adulthood for young adults with SMHC.

Young Adult Development

Starting in infancy and lasting into adulthood, psychosocial development occurs across five main domains: (1) cognition (thinking); (2) moral reasoning; (3) social cognition; (4) sexual orientation and gender identity; and (5) identity formation (see Table 10.1). Research indicates that maturity in these domains is impacted by peers and relationships, and that this influence diminishes with maturity (Steinberg, 2005). As a group, young people who have developed SMHC during childhood or adolescence are delayed in psychosocial development (Davis & Vander Stoep, 1997), though individual levels of maturity vary considerably. The third column of Table 10.1 describes additional challenges young adults with SMHC may face.

Table 10.1 Stages of psychosocial development in adolescence and young adulthood (Transitions RTC, 2011)

Stage of Development	Highlights	Consequences of developmental delay and potential additional challenges for those with SMHC
Cognitive Development	Increased capacities for • thinking abstractly, • thinking hypothetically (if *x*, then *y*), • having insight or self-awareness, • simultaneous consideration of multiple ideas, • future planning, • calibrating risks and rewards, and regulating undue peer influence on judgment.	• Delays can impede abilities to ◆ develop & execute plans, ◆ weigh pros and cons of actions, ◆ make changes based on self-awareness, and ◆ regulate peer influence on judgment. • Additional challenges; high rates of co-occurring learning disabilities and developmental disorders, which challenge cognitive development & learning.
Social Development	• Friendships become more complex, involving mutuality, intimacy, and loyalty. • Increased perspective taking. • Influence of peer relationships peak, then decline into adulthood. • Social context shifts from lots of daily contact with many classmates to smaller social networks and work social settings.	• Delays can impede abilities to ◆ participate in the increasingly complex peer relationships, ◆ put themselves in others' shoes, ◆ think hypothetically about social actions (i.e., plan and anticipate consequences), and ◆ negotiate the nuances of workplace social rules. • Combination of social immaturity and symptoms can inhibit quality and quantity of relationships across settings (e.g., school, work, family). • Social repercussions can produce emotional pain.
Moral Development	• Increased ownership of own set of rights & wrongs. • More able to understand "mitigating circumstances" of moral rules. • More empathic responses/use of Golden Rule. • Ability to see and act on rationale for sacrifice for the greater good.	• Delays in understanding and acting on the nuances of peers' social rules and society's moral standards may contribute to ◆ compromised success in school or work, ◆ increased criminal behavior, and ◆ reduced quality and quantity of friendships.

(continued)

Table 10.1 Continued

Stage of Development	Highlights	Consequences of developmental delay and potential additional challenges for those with SMHC
Social-Sexual Development	• Provides for new forms of emotional intimacy. • Skills to negotiate sexual relationships typically on par with social development. • Sexual behavior can impact roles in peer groups. • Sexual orientation and gender identity resolves.	• Delays can impede abilities to ◆ have healthy sexual relationships and practice safe sex. • Sexual abuse histories can additionally impede abilities to form healthy sexual relationships. • Individuals who have alternative gender identities or sexual orientation are at greater risk of physical abuse, homelessness, and suicide.

Identity Formation	• Seeking answers to the question, Who am I?
	• Is a prerequisite for feeling unique while feeling connected to others.
	• Produces boundary pushing.
	• Some experimentation needed to try out aspects of identify.
	• Rejection of authority facilitates ownership of identity choices.
		• Delays can contribute to
		  ◆ prolonged experimentation and rejection of authority beyond typical ages,
		  ◆ difficulty making role choices (occupation, friend, spouse),
		  ◆ undue influence of others on self-evaluation (not sufficiently distinct from others).
		• Self-image is often poor.

Typical Family Life-Cycle Stages

Family dynamics also change as youth transition to adulthood. As adolescents increase their levels of independence and move into adult roles, parental roles in decision making and nurturing shifts simultaneously with family structure change (see Table 10.2; Carter & McGoldrick, 2005). These changes may vary depending on family cultural background and other dynamics, such as divorce, economic stress, or family relationships.

Today, families play an increasingly critical role during the transition to adulthood, especially in supporting youths' pursuits of educational or vocational opportunities or providing a safety net when young adults need one (Settersten, Furstenberg, & Rumbaut, 2005). The strongest predictor of post-transition success after education is family involvement, and 50% of youth aging out of the system will live with a family member within a couple of years. Maximizing the family role can be complicated; some families of young adults with SMHC may also face disproportionate challenges, including poverty, addiction, incarceration, and intergenerational mental health challenges (Davis & Vander Stoep,

Table 10.2 Stages of the family life cycle

Stage	Family features	Changes	Challenges for families of children with SMHC

Families with adolescents	Increasing flexibility of family boundaries for child's independence and grandparent's frailties	• Parent/child relationships shift to permit adolescents' dependence to wax and wane
		• Refocus on midlife marital and career issues
		• Shift toward caring for an older generation
			• Stresses of raising a child with a chronic health condition
			• Out-of-home care, which restricts parental roles during the time away and may implicitly communicate parental incompetence
			• Higher family rates of
			  ◆ single-parent household & poverty,
			  ◆ mental health conditions,
			  ◆ substance use, and
			  ◆ incarceration.
			• Challenges can impede successful "launch" during transition years

"Launching" children and moving on	Accepting a multitude of exits from and entries into the family system (i.e., birth of grandchildren, passing of elders)	• Marital system renegotiation as dyad • Children and parents develop adult-to-adult relationships • Inclusion of in-laws and grandchildren • Loss of senior generation	

1997). Also, emotional bonding and problem solving in families of youth with SMHC may be compromised (Prange et al., 1992). Given the importance of families in young adults' lives, residential programs must become experts at strengthening family connections while also supporting the young adult's growing independence and self-determination. This delicate balance is a challenge every family must work towards as their children move towards independence.

Overall, these psychosocial development and family life-cycle changes are important to understand because they help (1) describe why residential interventions for young adults must be tailored to address developmental needs; (2) design developmentally appropriate residential interventions; and (3) differentiate between developmentally "typical" and "atypical" aspects of healthy young-adult development.

Important Milestones

Psychosocial maturity is linked to functional capacities. For example, increased cognitive abilities to suppress impulses to pursue attractive immediate opportunities (e.g., go with friends to a party) in order to pursue a longer term goal (e.g., go to a job that provides income for rent) help youth achieve adulthood milestones. Young adults with SMHC in residential programs experience significant struggles in achieving these milestones. High school graduation and employment rates are lowest for youth in highly restrictive service settings compared to youth in mixed treatment settings or community samples (Davis & Vander Stoep, 1997; Vander Stoep et al., 2000). Also, youth who receive public services (e.g., state mental health/child welfare services) are less likely to be living with family and more likely to have been pregnant and to have a history of justice-system involvement (Vander Stoep et al., 2000). Overall, youth with SMHC struggle not only to achieve young adult milestones but also to avoid outcomes, such as homelessness (Embry, Vander Stoep, Evens, Ryan, & Pollock, 2000) or arrests (Davis et al., 2007) that can derail successful adult trajectories.

Developmentally appropriate, effective, and appealing services are lacking for this population (Davis, Green, & Hoffman, 2009). Few established evidence-based practices (EBPs) exist for young adults. Some EBPs are only for adolescents (under age 18), while others are specific to adults and have not demonstrated efficacy with young adults. Because of the developmental uniqueness of young adults, "adult" EBPs should not be assumed to be effective for young adults. Furthermore, there is no research assessing the availability of EBPs or programs that follow systematically designed practice guidelines for young adults (Clark & Hart, 2009; Wagner & Davis, 2006).

Aging Out of the Child Welfare System

Many adolescents in child welfare systems have SMHC, and 42% of them receive treatment in group or residential settings (McMillen et al., 2004). Without a set of developmentally geared interventions, young adults leaving the child welfare system have struggled. In a large longitudinal study of over 700 young adults exiting child welfare in three states, former foster care youth assessed at ages 23 and 24 had greatly compromised 2-year college completion and highly elevated rates of homelessness compared to peers. Furthermore, those exiting residential or group care, as opposed to foster care, were 60% less likely to be employed (Courtney, Dworsky, Lee, & Raap, 2010). Though the presence of a serious mental health condition was not controlled for in this study, these results underscore the importance of well-designed residential interventions for young adults.

Innovative Practices

Successful residential interventions for young adults with SMHC involve creatively gaining an in-depth understanding of the young person (e.g., their culture and familial background, their interests and goals, and their mental health experiences) and planning rapidly for the transition to higher levels of independence. Imperative to supporting young adults in this transition is the ability of residential programs to provide opportunities for increased decision making and personal agency, while simultaneously enhancing lasting bonds with familial and relational supports. While there are programs across the country doing innovative work with young adults in residential settings, this section highlights two particularly innovative programs for young adults using residential interventions.

The Three Bridges Secure Residential Treatment Facility, in Grants Pass, Oregon, is an intensive, voluntary, 12-bed alternative to long-term state hospitalization for 17- to 24-year-olds with acute mental health needs. Three Bridges creates a noncoercive and person-centered approach, emphasizing self-determination to assist young adults of extremely high acuity in achieving stabilization, learning to manage their illness, and making the transition back to their communities. Three Bridges uses collaborative problem solving (CPS) combined with recovery-oriented practices in its treatment and support model. Families are encouraged to participate as partners in the services and supports, and young adults and families identify cultural and linguistic strengths, needs, and preferences.

The Thresholds Young Adult Program (YAP) is a strength-based residential program in Chicago for 16- to 21-year-olds with SMHC, trauma histories, and long-term service refusal. Thresholds specializes in serving young adults with high needs across the state, providing these intensive services between a main program location and housing in three flats embedded in the Chicago community, thus facilitating integrated, community-based programming. Thresholds utilizes the Transition to Independence Process (TIP) model (Clark & Hart, 2009), which supports self-discovery and empowers young adults to collabroate with key supports in reaching goals across the following transition domains: career development, education, living situation, community-life functioning, and personal effectiveness and well-being. Most of the young adults come from restrictive settings and will soon launch to independence or semi-independence with much less support than that provided within the youth service sector. Thresholds strives to create a balance and continuum of skill building between the child-serving and adult-serving world. Departing from a traditional residential approach, the program focuses on self-determination, self-discovery, and community, instead of level systems, containment, and prerequisites for being in the community.

The following identifies key components of residential interventions for young adults, with examples of strategies and practices from these programs.

Early Engagement

Despite a high prevalence of mental health conditions in young adulthood (Copeland et al., 2013), young adults are the least likely age cohort to utilize mental health services (Wang et al., 2005). For those who have histories of multiple placements and/or trauma, initial engagement in residential interventions can be especially challenging. Consistent with what would be expected of this developmental stage, young adults are typically more interested in accessing the community and socializing amongst their peers than they are in actively engaging in treatment. Yet, there is no other time period more crucial for building the skills necessary for adult functioning.

Effective engagement begins with creating choices and providing young adult–friendly information. For example, residential programs can utilize social media to provide information about programming in nonstigmatizing ways that allow young people to formulate questions for their treatment providers. Another key practice is to use the initial interview as a way for young adults to interview the program and become familiar with their future treatment team. At Three Bridges, young adults are offered a choice during the interview as to whether or not to enter the program, even if under legal guardianship or civilly committed. Asking young adults to identify goals about their future can yield more active engagement and encourage an emphasis on strengths, not deficits.

Young adults say they connect best with adults who are interested in engaging around what the *young adults* are interested in. Casual conversation time can provide critical opportunities to learn about the strengths, interests, and dreams of the young person. Such interactions can provide insight into the critical motivators of the young person while also enhancing the staff–young adult connection.

> The difference was that I had more freedom. I had more freedom at Thresholds than I did at (my past residential program). And another difference

would have to be, like, staff that really believe in me and they're not going to tell you, "Oh you can't do this," or "You can't do that," "You have to do this," like not bossing you around, telling you what you have to do. They actually sit down and talk with you. (Quinta Bicanovsky, young adult from Thresholds)

Self-Discovery and Self-Determination

A recovery orientation focused on self-direction; empowerment; individualized, person-centered planning; and hope (Substance Abuse and Mental Health Services Administration, 2011) is critical. Thresholds adapts the adult mental health concept of recovery to the notion of *discovery* for young adults, implementing the belief that, more than ever before in their development, young adults are able to discover their personal motivators and triggers, how they learn and work best, and how they function within a variety of relationships. This self-discovery often leads to more effective goal planning.

When residential programs provide flexibility for young adults to start with attainable goals that have high intrinsic value to them, the young person is more likely to subsequently engage in goals that may be intrinsically less appealing, such as addressing mental health issues. Thresholds works with individuals to pair treatment-based goals with goals that *appear* less treatment focused, such as obtaining a boyfriend/girlfriend or playing sports. While young adults may value staff guidance, they want their voice heard and appreciate making their own choices regarding their services based on individual strengths, needs, and interests.

Empowering young adults in self-discovery and their own decision making brings with it the potential for age-appropriate risky behavior (e.g., sex, substance use). As young adults age, there are fewer opportunities to protect them from real-world outcomes (e.g., STDs, pregnancy, incarceration). Explicitly empowering them to make decisions, even if they involve risky behavior, creates the opportunity for "safe failure" and the learning that can arise from it. Dialogue about decisions helps create a balance of young-adult self-determination and adult involvement, while facilitating partnerships on behalf of the young adult's goals and dreams.

Furthermore, when young adults have the opportunity to take healthy chances (e.g., starting a job) that lead to natural, positive consequences, they can take ownership of that accomplishment, ultimately increasing self-esteem and self-determination.

Community Living Skills

Young adults with histories in residential programs are accustomed to their goals and activities being largely confined to the residential setting. However, individualized coaching outside of the residence is important in maintaining strong engagement and generating ownership of specific skills. Rather than utilizing groups to teach independent living skills, Thresholds engages young adults individually, or in small interest-matched groups, and utilizes in-vivo teaching, or teaching skills through hands-on experiences, in order to shape their community learning process. Staff support young adults in planning activities to do alone (e.g., doctor's appointment) or with friends and family (e.g., local festival) in the community in order to support future community involvement. Three Bridges facilitates independent pursuits focused on community living and life goals, such as volunteering at the animal shelter and attending church groups.

Education and Career Development

> Just them being there and giving us tips on what to do in interviews as far as dressing professional, tips on how to basically sell ourselves, you know, advertise and put us out there that we'll be good workers. . . . They check up on you making sure you know you're doing your work, participating, that you comprehend everything and are keeping you up to date. It's like having that tool in employment and education, it's like a backbone. (Corey Wallace, young adult from Thresholds)

For young adults with SMHC, vocational exploration through work and educational experiences is developmentally significant and essential for future success. These individuals often have not had the same opportunities as their peers to engage in early vocational experiences (e.g., paper routes, babysitting, part-time fast food worker). Furthermore, in cases where young adults have strong family support, lengthy separations from family may further distance them from models of adult careers. Traditional residential practices, such as job introduction groups, on-site job simulations, prerequisites for community interface, and point and level systems can interfere with the unmatched benefit of the real-world experience of applying, interviewing, and starting and ending jobs in the community.

Thresholds uniquely integrates clinical supports with vocational supports. Its special education high school provides a mix of web-based assessments and curricula, experiential learning activities, and transition-based services staged from a small classroom atmosphere. These educational supports provide the flexibility for young adults to succeed in education while pairing those achievements with transition goals. Three Bridges provides similar on-site instruction, and facilitates young adult enrollment at the community college and in community GED classes.

In conjunction with the Transitions Research and Training Center at the University of Massachusetts, Thresholds adapted the evidence-based Individual Placement and Support (IPS) model of supported employment to include supported education and peer mentorship (Transitions RTC, 2012). Engagement in IPS services and subsequent employment are linked to a number of positive mental health outcomes in adult populations (Bond, Drake, & Becker, 2008). Using a "place and train" philosophy, once young people express a desire to work or go to postsecondary school, they are immediately linked to the vocational team—independent of their present mental health status. The vocational team works closely with the clinical team in order to best support young adults in exploring their career options, facilitating job/education applications, planning for interview/enrollment processes, and in providing tailored, ongoing support during school and/or work.

Peer Mentorship and Support

Using peers who are living in the community to teach and model skills and offer support is a critical practice for empowering young people in residential programs (Rogers et al., 2007). It is not uncommon for young adults with SMHC to struggle with pronounced feelings of hopelessness, loneliness, and despair. Due to their lived experiences, peer mentors offer young adults hope as well as a deeper level of empathy and understanding.

Peer mentors at Thresholds meet individually with young adults in community settings and use their own stories and experiences to engage, role-model, and coach young people with a particular focus on work and school-based endeavors. Three Bridges employs a peer-support specialist who works with the young adults to help them learn self-advocacy and to navigate successfully within community settings.

> I really value my work with the Three Bridges staff, but during time I spent with Nicole (the peer-support specialist) I was able to talk about things I never talk about with staff. It was hugely helpful to me. (HP, this young person is from Three Bridges)

Self-Care and Wellness

It is important for residential programs to facilitate wellness routines that are adaptable to community living and can last into adulthood. Residential interventions work best when they provide young adults an opportunity to develop self-care techniques that individually fit for them. Wellness strategies should be woven throughout the fabric of residential programs, including self-soothing activities, frequent breaks, quiet space, and staff who model mindfulness.

Frustration tolerance and individually tailored coping strategies are only effective when young adults have opportunities to adapt these strategies to community life while receiving ongoing coaching. Wellness is best facilitated during times when young adults are doing well. Staff and peer mentors can support young people in identifying what factors contribute to their wellness, how to recognize signs of deterioration, which strategies work best, and which loved ones can be most supportive during times of need. It is critical to purposely focus on adaptations that can last beyond life in residential programs.

Thresholds utilizes dialectical behavior therapy (DBT) to support increased personal awareness, emotion regulation, and distress tolerance. Three Bridges integrates DBT with collaborative problem solving (CPS) to teach self-management skills while addressing the cognitive skill deficits that have resulted from overwhelming trauma histories. CPS equalizes power differentials between staff and young adults, empowering young adult voice in solving problems and enhancing emotional competency.

Trauma and Transition

> It started like a couple of weeks before they told me I had to move [from residential], I ran away because I was nervous about it. I was like, "Oh if I run away they're not going to send me [away]. . . ." And then there was the phase where I was going to leave in September and I ran away again. . . . Because I was leaving in September and I didn't think, I wasn't ready to have to start all over again. (Quinta Bicanovsky, young adult from Thresholds)

Transitions can be overwhelming for any person, but for those who have experienced early trauma and/or neglect, the transition years can be particularly difficult. The ambivalence generated by the attraction of independence juxtaposed against the loss of stability and structure can result in anxiety and confusion. Although young adults often report that they cannot wait to be "independent," the prospect of taking the next step can be terrifying, as it portends a period of isolation, increased responsibility, and real-life consequences. Some young adults cope with this anxiety with unhealthy attempts to control their environment, through aggression, withdrawal, risky actions that precipitate psychiatric hospitalization, or other dangerous behavior that might look like self-sabotage. These behaviors are normative, especially for youth who have experienced significant trauma, yet can get in the way of even the best-planned transitions from residential programs. In addition, utilizing seemingly benign transition-based language (e.g., "when you're on your own"), can trigger unanticipated feelings of abandonment and anxiety.

Engaging in discussions of the anxieties and concerns directly, and normalizing the process helps young adults gain comfort with what they are experiencing. Furthermore, understanding the potential interfering behavior as a need for support, rather than a barrier to transition, can also go further in helping young adults move forward.

Family Relationships

> Since I've been at Thresholds, they've done so much for me. They've reunited me with my mom and everything like that. They gave me therapy,

so I'm excited about being able to stay in touch with my mom. (Quinta Bicanovsky, young adult from Thresholds)

Increased family involvement and stable and supportive post-residential environments are linked to improved youth clinical outcomes (Walters & Petr, 2008). While some young adults may elect to distance or not involve their family at all in residential interventions, others rely heavily on their family's support. There are several practices residential providers can implement to assist families and young adults in negotiating their evolving familial relationships. These include

- supporting young adults in determining who they consider family, which include former foster family members, mentors, siblings, and friends;
- with young adult concurrence, involving families in planning meetings and family therapy;
- convening multi-family groups, ideally in the community, focused on family support and education regarding young adulthood and mental health;
- offering frequent time with families at home and in the community; and
- seeking opportunities to involve family members in building skills geared toward enhancing and sustaining the family relationships beyond the transition.

Peer and Romantic Relationships

Young adults often identify their emotional turmoil as directly tied to the volatility of their relationships. During the transition to adulthood, the focus tends to switch from family relationships to peer and romantic relationships. Due to long histories of relational trauma experienced by many young adults who need residential programs, it is not surprising that these romantic relationships are ever-changing, with a high vacillation between feelings of love and hate as well as confusion regarding sexual orientation and sexual partners.

It is typical for young adults in residential programs to have romantic relationships with their in-program peers and also to engage more than ever in romantic relationships in the community. Strong residential interventions use these relationships as a launching pad for building relational coping skills and addressing self-esteem rather than establishing barriers to these relationships, which distances young adults from discussing these turbulent topics with the staff whom they often trust most.

Additionally, young adults report that relationships with peers whom they met in residential are important to them. Using social media helps in maintaining these connections. While these relationships may appear tumultuous for young adults during residential, treatment providers must also recognize the potential long-term value of these connections.

Transition From Residential Programs

During the time when their same-aged peers typically assert greater independence from their families of origin, young adults leaving residential programs will often be in the process of reestablishing and renegotiating relationships with their families. Some young adults may return to live in the same home where there are memories of past challenges and struggles and, for some, abuse or neglect. Others may be moving into their own housing. Residential interventions offer the opportunity for the family and the young person to identify how the family can be supportive beyond transition, irrespective of where the young adult will be living.

While there are several options for adult services, none matches the level of multidimensional support (e.g., psychiatric, vocational, transitional) received in the youth and young adult systems of care, making the transition even more difficult. Young adults face limited housing options, the confusing navigation of adult services, service eligibility difficulties, and the demands of adulthood, with less preparation than their peers in the general population. In order to prepare them for these realities, residential interventions should involve, from admission, a focus on building a network of supportive community relationships and early connection to adult services.

With continued stability and goal attainment, young adults at Three Bridges integrate into community-based activities. They work with staff and families to identify and prepare for their next living situation, which can be at home, in supportive housing in their home community, or occasionally in a specialized group home for young adults that is less intensive than the more secure setting they are departing.

Thresholds has a tiered housing program, allowing for transition to supported apartments and transitional living programs in preparation for independent living. A transition coordinator works individually with young adults and their support networks to obtain benefits, coordinate housing, and connect to adult services. Staff assist individuals in eventually launching into their chosen living environment and connecting to adult mental health services, both of which are meant to last beyond their time receiving residential interventions. Services and housing begin while young adults still maintain all the supports of the program and continue until their official discharge date. This allows for strong communication between the teams, as well as a smoother transition.

> All the group homes operate differently. They just helped me feel like I should take responsibility for my actions, you know, get on the ball because I'm becoming an adult. They still got their rules, but they're just not as restrictive, you know? There's a lot of freedom within Thresholds. You know, so there was a lot of free will and opportunities, so . . . understand why you're here, understand what you have to do in order to eventually emancipate, you know, leave in good shape. . . . Understanding the program and how it will work with you to still get to where you want to be, you know, independent. So take advantage of where you're at, you know, and

ask for help, and just don't give up whatever you want to do in life. People are going to help you if you start helping yourself, that's the main thing. (Corey Wallace, young adult from Thresholds)

Addressing Policy for Young Adults

Policy Tenets

Pressing policy issues that are unique to young adults receiving residential interventions are centered around their access to *age-appropriate* services as they "age out" of eligibility for services in the youth sector. Davis and colleagues (2009) developed six connected policy guidelines to support young adults with SMHC transitioning to adulthood:

1   Provide continuity of care from ages 14 or 16 to ages 25 or 30.
2   Provide continuous and coordinated care across the many adult and youth systems that offer relevant services.
3   Provide developmentally appropriate and appealing services.
4   Promote a density of good services from which individualized service and treatment plans can be constructed.
5   Promote appropriate involvement of family.
6   Promote the development of expertise in professionals who work with young adults.

These policy tenets highlight the importance of a full range of services and supports, inclusive of residential interventions, that span the transition period and/or provide for a continuum of opportunities that are not bound by artificial age cutoffs. Residential programs implementing these interventions should have automatic, system-based linkages to community-based services and supports—most importantly, naturally occurring support systems—and firmly established coordination practices that connect the various systemic bureaucracies which can otherwise limit young adults' success in adult life.

Residential programs that closely integrate with family and community supports and services provide a unique opportunity to enhance young adult protective and wellness factors, thereby maximizing the capacity for success through the transition to adulthood and toward becoming "satisfied in life."

Success is when you finally reach your point where you're satisfied in life. You accomplished some goals, whether it's school, graduating from high school or getting your diploma or GED. Being successful is when you're doing things that a person should be doing for themselves. Eating every day. At least twice, three meals a day . . . taking time out to enjoy your life. Taking time out to have activities. Taking time out to do your homework. Taking time out to . . . journal. And make new goals. (Brandon Wilcoxon, young adult from Thresholds)

Note

1   Young adults access services in both child and adult mental health systems, which use different diagnostic terminology. We use the term *serious mental health conditions* (SMHC) to capture either serious emotional challenges or disturbance, or serious mental illness.

References

Bond, G. R., Drake, R. E., & Becker, D. R. (2008). An update on randomized controlled trials of evidence-based supported employment. *Psychiatric Rehabilitation Journal, 31*(4), 280–289.

Carter, E., & McGoldrick, M. (Eds.). (2005). *The expanded family life cycle: Individual, family, and social perspectives.* Boston, MA: Allyn & Bacon.

Clark, H. B., & Hart, K. (2009). Navigating the obstacle course: An evidence-supported community transition system. In H. B. Clark & D. K. Unruh (Eds.), *Transition of youth and young adult with emotional or behavioral difficulties: An evidence-supported handbook* (pp. 47–94). Baltimore, MD: Brookes.

Copeland, W. E., Adair, C. E., Smetanin, P., Stiff, D., Briante, C., Colman, I., . . . Angold, A. (2013). Diagnostic transitions from childhood to adolescence to early adulthood. *Journal of Child Psychology and Psychiatry, 54*(7), 791–799.

Courtney, M. E., Dworsky, A., Lee, J. S., & Raap, M. (2010). *Midwest evaluation of the adult functioning of former foster youth: Outcomes at ages 23 and 24.* Chicago, IL: Chapin Hall at the University of Chicago.

Davis, M., Banks, S., Fisher, W., Gershenson, B., & Grudzinskas, A. (2007). Arrests of adolescent clients of a public mental health system during adolescence and young adulthood. *Psychiatric Services, 58*, 1454–1460.

Davis, M., Green, M., & Hoffman, C. (2009). The service system obstacle course for transition-age youth and young adults. In H. B. Clark & D. Unruh (Eds.), *Transition of youth and young adults with emotional or behavioral difficulties: An evidence-based handbook* (pp. 25–46). Baltimore, MD: Brookes.

Davis, M., & Vander Stoep, M. S. (1997). The transition to adulthood for youth who have serious emotional disturbance: Developmental transition and young adult outcomes. *Journal of Mental Health Administration, 24*(4), 400–426.

Delucchi, K. L., Matzger, H., & Weisner, C. (2008). Alcohol in emerging adulthood: 7-year study of problem and dependent drinkers. *Addictive Behaviors, 33*(1), 134–142.

Embry L. E., Vander Stoep, A., Evens, C., Ryan, K. D., & Pollock, A. (2000). Risk factors for homelessness in adolescents released from psychiatric residential treatment. *Journal of the American Academy of Child and Adolescent Psychiatry, 39*(10), 1293–1299.

McMillen, J. C., Scott, L. D., Zima, B. T., Ollie, M. T., Munson, M. R., & Spitznagel, E. (2004). Use of mental health services among older youths in foster care. *Psychiatric Services, 55*(7), 811–817.

Prange, M. E., Greenbaum, P. E., Silver, S. E., Friedman, R. M., Kutash, K., & Duchnowski, A. J. (1992). Family functioning and psychopathology among adolescents with severe emotional disturbances. *Journal of Abnormal Child Psychology, 20*(1), 83–102.

Rogers, E. S., Teague, G. B., Lichenstein, C., Campbell, J., Lyass, A., Chen, R., & Banks, S. (2007). Effects of participation in consumer operated service programs on both personal and organizationally mediated empowerment: Results of multisite study. *Population, 11*, 12.

Settersten, R. A., Furstenberg, F. F., & Rumbaut, R. G. (2005). *On the frontier of adulthood: Theory, research, and public policy.* Chicago, IL: University of Chicago Press.

Steinberg, L. (2005). Cognitive and affective development in adolescence. *Trends in Cognitive Sciences, 9*(2), 69–74.

Substance Abuse and Mental Health Services Administration. (2011). *SAMHSA announces a working definition of "recovery" from mental disorders and substance use disorders.* Retrieved from www.samhsa.gov/newsroom/advisories/1112223420.aspx

Transitions RTC. (2012). *Supported employed adapted for young adults with peer mentors: A feasibility study* (Brief #4 Research in the Works). Retrieved August 22, 2013, from http://labs.umassmed.edu/transitionsRTC/Resources/publications/brief4.pdf

Vander Stoep, A., Beresford, S.A.A., Weiss, N. S., McKnight, B., Cauce, A. M., & Cohen, P. (2000). Community-based study of the transition to adulthood for adolescents with psychiatric disorder. *American Journal of Epidemiology, 152*(4), 352–362.

Wagner, M., & Davis, M. (2006). How are we preparing students with emotional disturbances for the transition to young adulthood? Findings from the National Longitudinal Transition Study–2. *Journal of Emotional and Behavioral Disorders, 14*(2), 86–98.

Walters, U. M., & Petr, C. G. (2008). Family-centered residential treatment: Knowledge, values and research converge. *Residential Treatment for Children & Youth, 25*(1), 1–16.

Wang, P. S., Lane, M., Olfson, M., Pincus, H A., Wells, K. B., & Kessler, R. C. (2005). Twelve-month use of mental health services in the United States: Results from the National Comorbidity Survey replication. *Archives of General Psychiatry, 62*(6), 629–640.

11 Best Practices in Psychotropic Medication Treatment During Residential Interventions for Youth and Families

Christopher Bellonci and Jonathan Huefner

Introduction

The possibility that psychotropic medications may be overprescribed or inappropriately prescribed for children and adolescents (hereafter referred to as "youth") has become a significant public health concern given the relative lack of information on the safety and efficacy of these medications in youth (Mayes, Bagwell, & Erkulwater, 2008; Zito, Safer, & Craig, 2008). This chapter will briefly summarize the research and concerns regarding the use of psychotropic medications for youth, address research and issues specific to residential programs, discuss youth and family involvement in decisions about the use of medications, and identify best practices in the use of psychotropic medications during residential interventions for youth.

Current Research Context

Psychotropic medication rates for youth with mental and behavioral disorders have greatly increased since the early 1990s (Comer, Olfson, & Mojtabai, 2010; Cooper et al., 2006; Heflinger & Humphreys, 2008; LeFever, Arcona, & Antonuccio, 2003; Najjar et al., 2004). Research has indicated that these increases have occurred across demographic groups, geographic locations (Zito & American Society of Clinical Psychopharmacology, 2007), treatment settings (Zito & Safer, 2005), and psychotropic drug classes (Najjar et al., 2004; Patel et al., 2005).

Despite the belief among some professionals that increased rates of psychotropic medications may indicate better identification of mental health problems in youth and improved access to pharmacological treatment (Vitiello, Heiligenstein, Riddle, Greenhill, & Fegert, 2004; Walkup, 2003), the increased use of the full psychotropic medication armamentarium in the absence of adequate efficacy research in youth populations has raised many questions about the appropriateness of current prescribing practices (Brown, 2005; Dean, McDermott, & Marshall, 2006; Vitiello, 2007). Specifically, concerns have been raised due to differences in youth physiology and pharmacokinetics, an increased risk for adverse health effects, and the potentially disruptive impact of these agents on developing body systems (Correll et al., 2006). Additionally, there remains a gap between research and practice, and evidence for the effectiveness of pediatric pharmacotherapy remains rather limited (Correll, Kratochvil, & March, 2011; Mehler-Wex et al., 2009; Mintz & Flynn, 2012).

The growing trend for youth to be on two or more psychotropic medications far outpaces our capacity to evaluate and assess the efficacy and safety of these medication combinations (Safer, Zito, & dosReis, 2003). Potential problems increase with high rates of polypharmacy (Comer et al., 2010; Vitiello, 2005), where drug interactions pose their own unique additional side effects (Duffy et al., 2005; Woolston, 1999). A review of relevant literature found that between 1996 and 2002, polypharmacy increased 5.1 fold, to 27% for youth on a stimulant (Safer et al., 2003), and an examination of Medicaid claims found a 6.2 fold increase in polypharmacy, to 42% for depressed youth between 1996 and 2005 (McIntyre & Jerrell, 2009). Similarly, for youth prescribed psychotropic medication by an office-based physician, the polypharmacy rate increased from 14% to 20% (1996–2007; Comer et al., 2010), and 50% for youth seeing an office-based psychiatrist (Duffy et al., 2005; Staller, Wade, & Baker, 2005).

On the other hand, several studies have indicated that psychotropic medications have effectively reduced mental health and behavioral symptoms. For example, research on the use of psychostimulants for youth with ADHD has demonstrated their effectiveness in reducing symptoms with moderate to large effects (Schachter, Pham, King, Langford, & Moher, 2001); positive effects also have been found when medications and psychosocial treatments were combined for youth with depression (March, Silva, Vitiello, & TADS Team, 2006; Vitiello et al., 2006); and second-generation antipsychotics have been effective for youth with behavioral disturbances and cognitive delay or autism spectrum disorders (Stigler & McDougle, 2008; Van Bellinghen & De Troch, 2001).

Use of Psychotropic Medications in Residential Programs

Residential treatment settings in the United States serve approximately 200,000 youth annually (Child Welfare League of America, 2009). Youth are placed in residential settings for a variety of reasons. Many have a history of trauma, many have learning and emotional challenges, and for many there are insufficient family supports. They manifest severe, and often chronic, emotional, and behavioral impairments (Pottick, Warner, & Yoder, 2005), and history of multiple treatment failures at less restrictive levels of care (Boyer, Hallion, Hammell, & Button, 2009). Over the past decade, the level of clinical needs of youth in residential treatment has increased significantly (Duppong Hurley et al., 2010). One residential program reported that the most common diagnostic categories for youth at admission were disruptive behavioral (49%) and affective and anxiety disorders (31%), and 92% of youth had psychiatric comorbidity (Connor, Doerfler, Toscano, Volungis, & Steingard, 2004).

This clinical picture is paralleled by the use of psychotropic medication in residential programs. The research has found the following:

- Depending on the clinical acuity of the youth served, 31% to 94% of youth entering residential treatment settings are on psychotropic medication (Griffith et al., 2009; Hussey & Guo, 2005; Ryan, Reid, Gallagher, & Ellis, 2008).
- Up to 55% of those on medication enter care on three or more psychotropic drugs (Griffith et al., 2012).
- More complex presentations, including history of abuse or suicide attempts and multiple diagnoses, are associated with higher medication rates (Dean et al., 2006).
- Psychotropic medication rates typically increase further while youth are in out-of-home treatment settings, even when controlling for the severity of clinical issues (Najjar et al., 2004; Pathak et al., 2004; Warner, Fontanella, & Pottick, 2007; Zakriski, Wheeler, Burda, & Shields, 2005).
- Youth on psychotropic medications have 61% longer lengths of stay compared to youth who were not taking medications (Hussey & Guo, 2005).
- Paradoxically, the high levels of emotional and behavioral impairment that trigger out-of-home placement occur in spite of the high rates of psychotropic medication youth are receiving at the time of admission (Connor & McLaughlin, 2005; Duppong Hurley et al., 2009).

The high rate of medication prescribed for youth entering residential programs may be due to their higher acuity and more complex clinical presentation; it may also be due to inappropriate services and/or insufficient supports for the youth and his or her family in the community and/or even in the residential program. Residential interventions create opportunities for thoughtful medication reassessment for youth who are on much higher levels of medication, in the context of a comprehensive evaluation of services and supports that can also nonpharmacologically address the youth and family's needs and strengths.

Best Practices in the Use of Psychotropic Medications for Youth During a Residential Intervention

There are several best practice strategies that have emerged for the use of psychotropic medications for youth in residential programs. Taken together, these are consonant with practice parameters established by the American Academy of Child and Adolescent Psychiatry (AACAP) in 2009, and are responsive to the emerging understanding of the importance of combining psychotropic and non-psychotropic interventions in treatment.

Conduct initial evaluation of clinical needs and medication status from prior treatment attempts while also engaging the family and youth—Care must be taken in initiating a therapeutic alliance with youth and families beginning a residential intervention. Frequently these youth and families have had many prior attempts at rectifying the clinical issues, resulting in the residential intervention. They are likely to feel frustrated that prior attempts to help their child have failed to prevent the need for the residential intervention. Similarly, many medication trials may have been attempted without treatment success. Families may be wary of making any changes that might further destabilize their child's functioning, and the youth may similarly be distrustful of what the medication will do or what might happen if the medication is discontinued. It is critically important that the residential prescriber approach the treatment of these youth and families with an understanding of the clinical journey that has resulted in their referral to the residential program. This will provide the context and basis for a successful therapeutic alliance between the prescriber, family, and youth during the residential intervention.

Entry into a residential program should be seen as an opportunity for a second opinion regarding the biopsychosocial formulation of what drives the behavior that resulted in the need for the residential intervention. Youth at admission are often already receiving medications and frequently are prescribed multiple medications. The prescriber's role is to ensure that any current medications are warranted based on feedback from the youth and his or her family; past treatment providers and community partners; a comprehensive psychiatric evaluation that includes a review of past medication trials and benefits, and side effects of each medication; past test reports; birth and developmental history; medical history, social history, family history, educational history, history and impact of trauma; and cultural concerns.

Ideally, the residential prescriber communicates with past prescribers in order to understand the rationale for the current medication regimen, ensure the effectiveness of the current regimen, and know the response to prior medication trials so as to avoid repeating an earlier failed trial. In truth, obtaining a full understanding of the medication history can be challenging given the often chaotic nature of the youth's treatment trajectory. Residential prescribers may wish to carefully consider withdrawing psychotropic medications to determine if they are still needed. This approach also allows for reassessment of the diagnosis and provides an opportunity for comprehensive multidisciplinary treatment planning to help the youth develop self-soothing, coping, and management skills.

Coordination with the primary care provider and allied health professionals is another core component of the initial assessment. Some residential programs have on-site pediatric consultation, facilitating real-time coordination of care. In addition to medical consultation and evaluation, some have allied health professionals that can include occupational therapists, physical therapists, speech and language therapists, special educators, psychologists, social workers, and behavioral specialists, depending on the population being served. These additional professional perspectives help to provide a holistic understanding of the youth's strengths and needs that can be lacking in care settings more limited in duration or frequency of contact. Insights from the youth, family, and other multidisciplinary team members can lead to new formulations of the youth's emotional and behavioral needs, and a different treatment focus that can result in identifying and eliminating unnecessary medications and/or adding others that will target specific therapeutic needs.

Symptoms must be understood in the context of the youth's lived experience. Many youth referred for residential interventions have experienced trauma. Trauma in youth can present in myriad clinical presentations that are often misdiagnosed as a psychiatric condition warranting a medication intervention (i.e., bipolar or psychotic disorders). The literature supporting a psychopharmacological approach to the treatment of posttraumatic stress disorder in youth is negligible while there is strong evidence for psychosocial interventions (e.g., TF-CBT; Forman-Hoffman et al., 2013; Gillies, Taylor, Gray, O'Brien, & D'Abrew, 2012).

Develop treatment plan—Using the information and observations collected in the process of the initial psychiatric assessment, the prescriber in a residential program works as part of the multidisciplinary team, most importantly including the youth and parents/guardians, to develop an individualized treatment plan. The team solicits feedback from those who know the youth best (e.g., youth, family members), asking whether the working clinical hypothesis "sounds like your child." This becomes the basis of the biopsychosocial formulation. Together the youth, the family, their advocates, and residential staff write a treatment plan based on the formulation, with clear measures that will be tracked in order to monitor the youth's progress. This includes treatment goals for any and all medications and how response to any medication changes will be measured. Medication decisions must be informed by clinical needs via an evidence-based indication or clinical guidelines for psychotropic use, as well as by response to treatment using objective data collected during the residential intervention. There should be clear communication about how long the medication will take to work, alternatives to the proposed treatment, and the best prediction of what might occur if the proposed treatment was not initiated.

Estimates are that 50% to 75% of pediatric prescribing is "off label" (Roberts, Rodriguez, Murphy, & Crescenzi, 2003). It has been long argued that given the unknowns about pediatric pharmacotherapy, nonpharmacological treatments should be prioritized (Foxx, 1998; McKay, 2007; Rhoades, 1982). Providing effective alternative services and supports to psychotropic medications is an area in which residential programs should excel. Nonpharmacological interventions, especially trauma-informed practices, should always be prioritized before a medication intervention is considered unless the youth's symptoms are so severe that a medication is felt to be indicated along with a range of evidence-based psychosocial interventions for both the family and the youth.

Develop monitoring plan—Best practice calls on residential programs to invest in the ability to measure outcomes, both to inform clinical practice with the youth as well as to guide continuous quality improvement efforts. As illustrated in Figure 11.1, data/feedback from youth, families, and staff can be collected to more clearly determine a cause and effect response to any new medication trial or the discontinuation of a medication. Having sufficient time to monitor the effects of medication changes is another advantage residential interventions have over acute hospital stays or crisis stabilization in monitoring response to clinical and psychotropic interventions. Ideally, no treatment interventions should be utilized that cannot be replicated in the home or community. The goal is not to teach the youth to behave better in a residential program but to be able to generalize gains made during residential interventions to home and community settings.

Discharge planning and coordination with community providers should start at admission and continue throughout the residential intervention. Medication interventions need to consider the capacity of the community provider to manage the medication regimen in an outpatient setting. Frequently, outpatient prescribers are reticent about stopping a medication for fear of causing the youth's symptoms to worsen. Using the residential intervention to reassess each medication the youth is taking (unless there is clear evidence the medication continues to serve a critical therapeutic function) can provide valuable information for the transition and beyond. As discharge approaches, and continuing after discharge, communication between the residential prescriber and

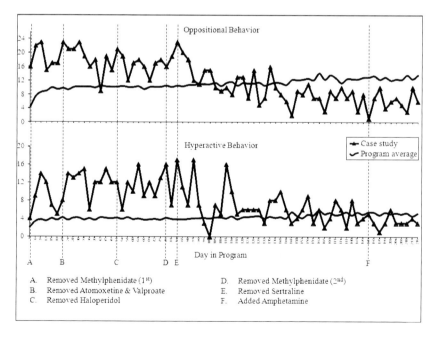

Figure 11.1 Example of daily behavioral data used to monitor the impact of psychotropic medications changes.

community prescriber is critical to ensure the smooth transition of the youth's treatment to the home and community setting.

Communicate/verify with stakeholders—Residential staff and prescribers should be consultants in the care of the youth and family. It is critical that the parents and youth retain the "locus of control" and not be led to believe that the medication will fix everything and/or that they are passive participants in their own or their child's treatment. Youth and family attitudes towards and beliefs about medication should be carefully adhered to and open dialogue should be encouraged. Resulting treatment outcomes can be optimized by thus incorporating youth and family perspectives, including cultural factors influencing beliefs about medication treatment. Therapeutic alliance, patient autonomy, and understanding the meaning of the treatment intervention have positive, powerful, and measurable impacts on the effectiveness of psychotropic medication treatment (Mintz & Flynn, 2012).

Informed consent requires a discussion of what is known and unknown about a medication—for the specific condition for which it is being prescribed and for the specific age group of the youth. The goals of both medication and psychosocial interventions need to be clearly communicated to the youth in a developmentally appropriate way, and their assent should be sought. Similarly, parents and guardians should understand the rationale for the treatment recommendations, both pharmacologic and non-pharmacologic and how a positive response will be measured. Frequent communication about the response to the intervention should occur in order to determine if benefits of the intervention outweigh any side effects that may develop.

Apply sound medication trial practices—Dosage guidelines for many psychotropic medications do not exist for youth. The clinical pearl, "start low and go slow," as regards any new medication trial dosing, is critical when working with youth given the medication unknowns and youth sensitivities to these medications. Using data, as referenced above, to measure and monitor responses to medication and psychosocial interventions can result in rational psychopharmacological trials (including medication tapering, or "washes"). Since objective determination of response to medication and psychosocial interventions can take weeks or even months, it is critical to plan for proper supports and oversight if the youth returns home during the medication trial in order to ensure adequate exposure to the regimen and determination of the intervention's efficacy.

Normal human development is a continual process of youth acquiring new skills, and normative behavior changes over time. Psychopharmacological practice should take this into account and periodically reassess the continuing need for a medication. As the youth develops coping skills to manage what the medication is meant to treat (e.g., anxiety or affect management) the medication may no longer be needed. In fact, psychosocial interventions should specifically promote the acquisition of these skills. The only way to know if a medication continues to be warranted is to stop and assess the response after a period of stable functioning.

Conduct ongoing reassessment—Reassessment of the original formulation developed at admission should occur during every meeting of the multidisciplinary treatment team and include the youth, family, and advocates. This reassessment should be informed by routine clinical data that is being used to measure the youth's ongoing emotional and behavioral progress in relation to the treatment plan goals. This data-driven decision making will allow a medication management process that uses the lowest effective dose of a medication and the fewest number of medications needed to ensure the youth's continued progress.

Two Examples

Two agencies that have implemented these practices provide an example of their impact. Walker and Boys Town have seen a decrease in the use of psychotropic medications from admission to discharge while also seeing a decrease in the need for seclusion and restraint (Bellonci et al., 2013). Specific strategies that have been utilized by both, leading to positive outcomes, follow:

1   Strong medical leadership is empowered to critically assess each psychotropic medication a youth is prescribed at the time of admission and critically assess whether the medication is still indicated.
2   The principle of sufficiency (using just enough medication as clinically indicated) is the foundation for medication management.
3   Prescribers are integrated into the agency and not contracted from another facility, allowing them to truly be a member of the team and earn the trust of the staff, youth, and families in order to be able to make medication reductions.
4   Data are used to guide interventions and refine the work with the youth and family.
5   A comprehensive biopsychosocial formulation is the basis for the treatment plan and informs all clinical work with the youth and family.
6   There is a strong programmatic philosophy of treatment and best practice values (e.g., family-driven; youth-guided; cultural and linguistic competence) that drives the use of evidence-informed best practices that support long-term outcomes for youth and families in their own homes and communities.
7   Multidisciplinary team of professionals formulates the youth's strengths and needs and work collaboratively to support skill development of both the youth and the caretaker.
8   Medication changes are made with feedback from the youth, the family and their advocates, and from the broader treatment team as to the youth's behavioral, emotional, and educational needs, based on ongoing monitoring of the youth's response to treatment (e.g., excessive sedation or other medication side effects, improving/deteriorating behavior, emotional lability).

Conclusion

When the best psychotropic medication practices are in place, residential programs are well positioned to provide thoughtful diagnostic and treatment reassessment (a second-opinion capacity). Done correctly, residential interventions can result in medication consultations (often resulting in lower medication burdens) *and* emotional and behavioral health improvement for youth. Fully integrating prescribers into the clinical and administrative leadership of residential programs leverages their unique skill set and maximizes the possibility for psychotropic medication to play a beneficial role in generating long-term positive outcomes for the youth in care. When the prescriber's only function is to prescribe and they do not have a role in training, clinical care, risk management, and overall administration, programs may see higher rates of medication use—if all you have is a hammer, everything looks like a nail.

References

Bellonci, C., Huefner, J. C., Griffith, A. K., Vogel-Rosen, G., Smith, G. L., & Preston, S. (2013). Concurrent reductions in psychotropic medication, assault, and physical restraint in two residential treatment programs for children. *Child and Youth Services Review, 35*, 1773–1779.

Boyer, S. N., Hallion, L. S., Hammell, C. L., & Button, S. (2009). Trauma as a predictive indicator of clinical outcome in residential treatment. *Residential Treatment for Children & Youth, 26*(2), 92–104.

Brown, R. T. (2005). Recent advances in pharmacotherapies for the externalizing disorders. *School Psychology Quarterly, 20*(2), 118–134.

Child Welfare League of America (2009). *National Data Analysis System: Out of home care* [Data file]. Retrieved May 28, 2013, from http://ndas.cwla.org/data_stats/access/predefined/home.asp

Comer, J. S., Olfson, M., & Mojtabai, R. (2010). National trends in child and adolescent psychotropic polypharmacy in office-based practice, 1996–2007. *Journal of the American Academy of Child & Adolescent Psychiatry, 49*(10), 1001–1010.

Connor, D. F., Doerfler, L. A., Toscano, P. F., Volungis, A. M., & Steingard, R. J. (2004). Characteristics of children and adolescents admitted to a residential treatment center. *Journal of Child and Family Studies, 13*(4), 497–510.

Connor, D. F., & McLaughlin, T. J. (2005). A naturalistic study of medication reduction in a residential treatment setting. *Journal of Child and Adolescent Psychopharmacology, 15*(2), 302–310.

Cooper, W. O., Arbogast, P. G., Ding, H., Hickson, G. B., Fuchs, D. C., & Ray, W. A. (2006). Trends in prescribing of antipsychotic medications for U.S. children. *Ambulatory Pediatrics, 6*(2), 79–83.

Correll, C. U., Kratochvil, C. J., & March, J. S. (2011). Developments in pediatric psychopharmacology: Focus on stimulants, antidepressants, and antipsychotics. *The Journal of Clinical Psychiatry, 72*(5), 654–670.

Correll, C. U., Penzner, J. B., Parikh, U. H., Mughal, T., Javed, T., Carbon, M., & Malhotra, A. K. (2006). Recognizing and monitoring adverse events of second-generation antipsychotics in children and adolescents. *Child and Adolescent Psychiatric Clinics of North America, 15*(1), 177–206.

Dean, A. J., McDermott, B. M., & Marshall, R. T. (2006). Psychotropic medication utilization in a child and adolescent mental health service. *Journal of Child and Adolescent Psychopharmacology*, *16*(3), 273–285.

Duffy, F. F., Narrow, W. E., Rae, D. S., West, J. C., Zarin, D. A., Rubio-Stipec, M., . . . Regier, D. A. (2005). Concomitant pharmacotherapy among youths treated in routine psychiatric practice. *Journal of Child and Adolescent Psychopharmacology*, *15*(1), 12–25.

Duppong Hurley, K., Trout, A., Chmelka, M. B., Burns, B. J., Epstein, M. H., . . . Daly, D. L. (2009). The changing mental health needs of youth admitted to residential group home care: Comparing mental health status at admission in 1995 and 2004. *Journal of Emotional and Behavioral Disorders*, *17*(3), 164–176.

Duppong Hurley, K., Trout, A., Griffith, A., Epstein, M., Thompson, R., Mason, W. A., Huefner, J., Daly, D. (2010). Creating and sustaining effective partnerships to advance research on youth with serious emotional and behavioral disorders. *Journal of Disability Policy Studies*, *21*(3), 141–151.

Forman-Hoffman, V., Knauer, S., McKeeman, J., Zolotor, A., Blanco, R., Lloyd, S., . . . Viswanathan, M. (2013). *Child and adolescent exposure to trauma: Comparative effectiveness of interventions addressing trauma other than maltreatment or family violence* (AHRQ No. 13-EHC054-EF). Rockville, MD: Agency for Healthcare Research and Quality.

Foxx, R. M. (1998). A comprehensive treatment program for inpatient adolescents. *Behavioral Interventions*, *13*(1), 67–77.

Gillies, D., Taylor, F., Gray, C., O'Brien, L., & D'Abrew, N. (2012). Psychological therapies for the treatment of post-traumatic stress disorder in children and adolescents (Review). *Evidence-Based Child Health: A Cochrane Review Journal*, *8*(3), 1004–1116.

Griffith, A. K., Ingram, S. D., Barth, R. P., Trout, A. L., Duppong Hurley, K., Thompson, R. W., & Epstein, M. H. (2009). The family characteristics of youth entering a residential care program. *Residential Treatment for Children & Youth*, *26*(2), 135–150.

Griffith, A. K., Smith, G., Huefner, J. C., Epstein, M. H., Thompson, R. W., Singh, N. N., & Leslie, L. K. (2012). Youth at entry to residential treatment: Understanding psychotropic medication use. *Child and Youth Services Review*, *34*, 2028–2035.

Heflinger, C. A., & Humphreys, K. L. (2008). Identification and treatment of children with oppositional defiant disorder: A case study of one state's public service system. *Psychological Services*, *5*(2), 139–152.

Hussey, D. L., & Guo, S. (2005). Forecasting length of stay in child residential treatment. *Child Psychiatry and Human Development*, *36*(1), 95–111.

LeFever, G. B., Arcona, A. P., & Antonuccio, D. O. (2003). ADHD among American schoolchildren: Evidence of overdiagnosis and overuse of medication. *Scientific Review of Mental Health Practice*, *2*(1), 49–60.

March, J., Silva, S., Vitiello, B., & TADS Team. (2006). The Treatment for Adolescents with Depression Study (TADS): Methods and message at 12 weeks. *Journal of the American Academy of Child & Adolescent Psychiatry*, *45*(12), 1393–1403.

Mayes, R., Bagwell, C., & Erkulwater, J. (2008). ADHD and the rise in stimulant use among children. *Harvard Review of Psychiatry*, *16*(3), 151–166.

McIntyre, R. S., & Jerrell, J. M. (2009). Polypharmacy in children and adolescents treated for major depressive disorder: A claims database study. *Journal of Clinical Psychiatry*, *70*(2), 240–246.

McKay, M. (2007). Forced drugging of children in foster care: Turning child abuse victims into involuntary psychiatric patients. *Journal of Orthomolecular Medicine*, *22*(2), 63–74.

Mehler-Wex, C., Kölch, M., Kirchheiner, J., Antony, G., Fegert, J. M., & Gerlach, M. (2009). Drug monitoring in child and adolescent psychiatry for improved efficacy and safety of psychopharmacotherapy. *Child and Adolescent Psychiatry and Mental Health, 3*(1), 14.

Mintz, D. L., & Flynn, D. F. (2012). How (not what) to prescribe: Nonpharmacologic aspects of psychopharmacology. *Psychiatric Clinics of North America, 35*(1), 143–163.

Najjar, F., Welch, C., Grapentine, W. L., Sachs, H., Siniscalchi, J., & Price, L. H. (2004). Trends in psychotropic drug use in a child psychiatric hospital from 1991–1998. *Journal of Child and Adolescent Psychopharmacology, 14*(1), 87–93.

Patel, N. C., Crismon, M. L., Hoagwood, K., Johnsrud, M. T., Rascati, K. L., Wilson, J. P., & Jensen, P. S. (2005). Trends in the use of typical and atypical antipsychotics in children and adolescents. *Journal of the American Academy of Child & Adolescent Psychiatry, 44*(6), 548–556.

Pathak, S., Arszman, S. P., Danielyan, A., Johns, E. S., Smirnov, A., & Kowatch, R. A. (2004). Psychotropic utilization and psychiatric presentation of hospitalized very young children. *Journal of Child & Adolescent Psychopharmacology, 14*(3), 433–442.

Pottick, K. J., Warner, L. A., & Yoder, K. A. (2005). Youths living away from families in the U.S. mental health system: Opportunities for targeted intervention. *Journal of Behavioral Health Services & Research, 32*(3), 264–281.

Rhoades, L. J. (1982). Psychosocial intervention: A way out for chronic patients. *Psychiatric Services, 33*(9), 709–710.

Roberts, R., Rodriguez, R., Murphy, D., & Crescenzi, T. (2003). Pediatric drug labeling: Improving the safety and efficacy of pediatric therapies. *JAMA, 290*, 905–911.

Ryan, J. B., Reid, R., Gallagher, K., & Ellis, C. (2008). Prevalence rates of psychotropic medications for students placed in residential facilities. *Behavioral Disorders, 33*(2), 99–107.

Safer, D. J., Zito, J. M., & dosReis, S. (2003). Concomitant psychotropic medication for youths. *American Journal of Psychiatry, 160*, 438–449.

Schachter, H. M., Pham, B., King, J., Langford, S., & Moher, D. (2001). How efficacious and safe is short-acting methylphenidate for the treatment of attention-deficit disorder in children and adolescents? A meta-analysis. *Canadian Medical Association Journal, 165*, 1475–1488.

Staller, J. A., Wade, M. J., & Baker, M. (2005). Current prescribing patterns in outpatient child and adolescent psychiatric practice in central New York. *Journal of Child and Adolescent Psychopharmacology, 15*(1), 57–61.

Stigler, K. A., & McDougle, C. J. (2008). Pharmacotherapy of irritability in pervasive developmental disorders. *Child and Adolescent Psychiatric Clinics of North America, 17*(4), 739–752.

Van Bellinghen, M., & De Troch, C. (2001). Risperidone in the treatment of behavioral disturbances in children and adolescents with borderline intellectual functioning: A double-blind, placebo-controlled pilot trial. *Journal of Child and Adolescent Psychopharmacology, 11*(1), 5–13.

Vitiello, B. (2005). Pharmacoepidemiology and pediatric psychopharmacology research. *Journal of Child and Adolescent Psychopharmacology, 15*(1), 10–11.

Vitiello, B. (2007). Research in child and adolescent psychopharmacology: Recent accomplishments and new challenges. *Psychopharmacology, 191*(1), 5–13.

Vitiello, B., Heiligenstein, J. H., Riddle, M. A., Greenhill, L. L., & Fegert, J. M. (2004). The interface between publicly funded and industry-funded research in pediatric psychopharmacology: Opportunities for integration and collaboration. *Biological Psychiatry, 56*(1), 3–9.

Vitiello, B., Rohde, P., Silva, S., Wells, K., Casat, C., Waslick, B., . . . TADS Team. (2006). Functioning and quality of life in the Treatment for Adolescents with Depression Study (TADS). *Journal of the American Academy of Child & Adolescent Psychiatry*, *45*(12), 1419–1426.

Walkup, J. T. (2003). Increasing use of psychotropic medications in children and adolescents: What does it mean? *Journal of Child and Adolescent Psychopharmacology*, *13*(1), 1–3.

Warner, L. A., Fontanella, C. A., & Pottick, K. J. (2007). Initiation and change of psychotropic medication regimens among adolescents in inpatient care. *Journal of Child and Adolescent Psychopharmacology*, *17*(5), 701–712.

Woolston, J. L. (1999). Combined pharmacotherapy: Pitfalls of treatment. *Journal of the American Academy of Child & Adolescent Psychiatry*, *38*(11), 1455–1457.

Zakriski, A. L., Wheeler, E., Burda, J., & Shields, A. (2005). Justifiable psychopharmacology or overzealous prescription? Examining parental reports of lifetime prescription histories of psychiatrically hospitalised children. *Child and Adolescent Mental Health*, *10*(1), 16–22.

Zito, J. M., & American Society of Clinical Psychopharmacology. (2007). Pharmacoepidemiology: Recent findings and challenges for child and adolescent psychopharmacology. *Journal of Clinical Psychiatry*, *68*(6), 966–967.

Zito, J. M., & Safer, D. J. (2005). Recent child pharmacoepidemiological findings. *Journal of Child and Adolescent Psychopharmacology*, *15*(1), 5–9.

Zito, J. M., Safer, D. J., & Craig, T. J. (2008). Pharmacoepidemiology of psychiatric disorders. In A. G. Hartzema, H. H. Tilson, & K. A. Chan (Eds.), *Pharmacoepidemiology and therapeutic risk management* (pp. 817–854). Cincinnati, OH: Harvey Whitney Books.

12 Initial Steps in the Culture Change Process

Beth Caldwell, Sue Beck, John Damon,
Joe Anne Hust, Jim Nyreen, and Raquel Montes

Culture change is very hard work! Transforming residential from a milieu-based program primarily focused on youth-improving behaviors to a short-term intervention that pragmatically supports youth and families in achieving sustained positive outcome postresidential requires significant culture change and sustained hard work by all levels of leaders in an organization. In recent years, residential leaders across the United States have become inspired to reevaluate how they provide services and have found guidance and support from the national Building Bridges Initiative (BBI). Many have embraced BBI principles (Blau, Caldwell, Fisher, Kuppinger, Levison-Johnson, & Lieberman, 2010), especially the principles of family-driven and youth-guided care, which, when operationalized, have evidence substantiating positive outcomes (Burns, Hoagwood & Mrazek, 1999; Courtney, Terao & Bost, 2004; Walters & Petr, 2008). When leaders attend BBI transformation events across the country, they often ask, "Where should we begin? What first steps are recommended? Is there a roadmap?" No, there is no step-by-step roadmap for residential transformation—yet; but frameworks do exist that can help leaders in the culture change process.

The Six Core Strategies, highlighted in Chapter 9, provide an evidence-based framework offering leaders specific strategies to change the way they deliver care in their programs (Substance Abuse and Mental Health Services Administration [SAMHSA], 2013). Many books and articles exist to educate leaders in how to approach culture change and recommend steps to take to realize successful transformations (Anthony & Huckshorn, 2008; Blau & Magrab, 2010); additionally, training programs abound in this area at the university level and through private businesses. This chapter adds to the available knowledge base by highlighting parts of the change process of individual programs that have a strong commitment to transformation that are specific towards long-term positive outcomes for youth and families touched by a residential intervention. It is intended that the strategies taken and lessons learned, shared from the perspective and in the voice of a family member, a youth advocate, and three executive leaders will provide some answers to the previous questions for residential leaders just starting their transformation process, and also provide valuable information for leaders already on their journeys.

Only five programs are highlighted in depth in this chapter; there are many more programs that have taken steps towards transformation whose stories could also provide valuable learning. For example, Youth Development Institute (YDI) leaders attended the Magellan Health Services, Inc., 2011 BBI kickoff in Maricopa County, Arizona. They were inspired to evaluate ways their program could transform, taking bold first steps:

- Creating a powerful youth advisory board that made substantial changes to rules, the environment, and long-term practices. Youth became part of both hiring panels for new employees and the orientation training team. New employees continually rate the youth training—including role-play sessions, created by youth, of real situations staff will face—as the most meaningful of the entire orientation.
- YDI leaders found that discharge plans that did not work (i.e., youth were hospitalized or returning to residential) began to fall apart within 6 months postdischarge. They decided to fund, on their own, clinical involvement in supporting youth and families in their homes and communities up to 6 months postdischarge. This work decreased readmissions—as clinical staff could help youth and families address challenges and find alternative resources and services when those identified on the discharge plan proved ineffective or not helpful. YDI's funding agency was so impressed that they now fund 3 months of aftercare.

Similar stories are told by leaders across the country who have taken part in BBI or other transformation initiatives. It is hoped that the five journeys discussed below will inspire others to share their successful strategies so that more youth and families realize sustained positive outcomes and ultimately lead better lives when touched by residential interventions, and that a step-by-step roadmap will evolve.

Joe Anne Hust, National Trainer, University of Maryland School of Social Work

A Parent's Perspective

The mission statement said, "*Dedicated* to healing abused, neglected and emotionally disturbed children and their families, *Committed* to building healthy relationships within the context of family, culture and community, *Providing* children the tools to lead productive, independent adult lives."[1] I was troubled by the words posted on the wall. "*Abused and emotionally disturbed children.*" Surely, they couldn't be talking about my child or my family! Having been hired as a parent partner to work in a wraparound program for a large agency that had historically provided both residential care and mental health services in Los Angeles County, California, I was told that my personal experience as a parent with a child who was struggling with mental health challenges could be used to support other parents. But my child was neither abused nor neglected, and I didn't think of her as emotionally disturbed. I wondered what these words meant for me and the work I had signed on to do. Even though I had misgivings, leaders within the organization who had sought me out to take the job convinced me that my "lived experience" could have benefit.

Through a Parent's Lens—Although leadership at Hathaway-Sycamores clearly embraced system-of-care values and made a special effort to welcome me as the first parent hired, it was not long before I learned not everyone was amicable to hiring parents. During employee orientation, I heard staff refer to families as "dysfunctional" or "the reason for the child's problem." I wondered if they would use that language if they knew I was a parent. My family's world was turned upside down when my child first started exhibiting signs of depression. Of course, my colleagues didn't understand what it was like for parents, and that was why I was hired—to help them understand. I figured their bias was learned—and if it could be learned, it could be unlearned. I realized then that my work was not only supporting other parents but also assisting professionals in preparing for change.

I noticed that children receiving services were often referred to by their diagnosis or symptoms (i.e., bipolar, runner, cutter) or as a "residential kid" rather than as a child that was part of a family. As I sat in meetings, I realized it was thought by some that children were better off growing up away from their families. I often heard, "This child has no parents" or "He is better off staying in residential until 18." Families were often not informed about their options for treatment. It seemed that decisions were predetermined by professionals, without family input. Having the advantage of being a "parent on the inside," I understood staffing and time constraints (i.e., contacting parents took up valuable time and could be "messy" because of family challenges). I perceived residential practices unwelcoming to families (e.g., waiting rooms with rules posted everywhere).

There were also discrepancies between what I was experiencing and what I was being trained to do in wraparound. Fortunately, agency leaders agreed and decided to move in the direction of transformational change, and this began by hiring more parents.

Parents as change agents—Hathaway-Sycamores found themselves at this crossroads a few years after implementing wraparound. The agency ran numerous community-based programs, but had long been a residential provider and the paradigm shift to system-of-care and wraparound values challenged this 100-year-old residential identity.

It was a conscious decision by agency leadership to hire large numbers of parents (38 in 2013) and redefine the way we did business. It became clear as more parents were hired that their presence put a face on "those parents" and language and conversations started to slowly change. Parent partners challenged the status quo by interrupting unintended bias and were able to create a sense of urgency for the right services and supports to families *now* rather than later. They used their lived experience with their own child to support other parents and to create learning opportunities for their professional partners about the challenges and barriers families faced.

My agency's leaders had change in mind, and contrary to the usual practice of placing parent partners in separate offices, they intermingled them throughout. It was common to find a therapist and a parent partner sharing a cubicle. A career ladder was developed to support retention, including parent-partner managers, directors, and an assistant vice president on the executive team. They were visible, and like a good, infectious virus were able to create change. It was groundbreaking.

My work initially involved parent partners and families. We educated staff on the parent partner role and added a section in new employee orientation on what to expect from and how to partner with parent partners. We modeled partnership at every level by pairing parent and professional cotrainers, even in clinical trainings.[2] We infused parent partners on workgroups and created strategic pairings of parents and professionals around common goals.

Primary to the paradigm shift was increasing the presence of families in all aspects of their child's care. It was much harder than we expected. Staff needed to be available evenings and weekends, providing transportation and child care. Other steps taken as part of transformation included the following:

- Developing an integrated plan of care for every child. If the child and family were being served in more than one program, there was still just one strength-based plan. Our mantra became "1 family, 1 plan."
- Using a wraparound-facilitated planning approach for all treatment meetings.
- Rewriting all training curriculum to include people-first language, current best practices, and ensure family inclusion.
- Revising all job descriptions, and incorporating family engagement skills.
- Creating new supervision models that included feedback from families.
- Becoming data driven—changing practice if not getting good outcomes.

It became clear that children served in residential were not that different from children served in community wraparound. One agency change initiative involved strategic pairing of directors from three programs: residential, wraparound, and parent partnerships in a county pilot using the wraparound process and parent partners to shorten lengths of stay in residential. The pilot, *Res/Wrap*, was so successful it eventually led to legislation known as the California Residentially-based Services Reform Initiative, and the agency's involvement in BBI's first national summit.

The Hathaway-Sycamores change transformation took several years. Among the lessons learned was that change is constant, and maintaining momentum requires constant attention. We acknowledged that implementing wraparound created the impetus for our change, but hiring parent partners made that change process real. Last, it is really hard work, and it takes visionary leadership to accomplish real change. The mission statement has changed, and now reads,

"Cultivating hope and resilience to enrich the well-being of children, adults, families, and communities."

Jim Nyreen, Assistant Executive Director, SCO Family of Services, New York

Every Day Counts

SCO Family of Services provides services to 60,000 children, youth, families, and adults, predominantly from New York City and Long Island. Our residential treatment facility (RTF) involved in transformation is a 56-bed program for males and females, ages 14 through 21 years, who have a primary psychiatric diagnosis and a cognitive deficit, with IQs in the Full Scale range of 50 through 79.

Transformation journey—The SCO RTF culture change journey began in June 2011, when a group of RTF leaders attended a BBI kickoff in New Hampshire. We returned with a renewed spirit and an increased level of hope for our older adolescents, some who had not been with families for years. The New York State Office of Mental Health started their own BBI in New York City later in 2011, providing multiple training and consultation opportunities.

We started our transformation by gathering information from surveys and discussions with families, youth, and staff. We used this information to develop an action plan and outcome measures focusing around three themes, increasing (1) contact between families and staff, (2) family and youth contact, and (3) family/youth connections in the community. With our hearts set on moving youth out of residential and back to their families, we created a mantra of "Every Day Counts." This phrase encapsulated what we wanted to do. Every day that a child is in residential, we needed to be working on moving him or her back to family. Every day away from family is 1 day too many. We also began pushing the theme that we were a community program that happened to be located on a residential campus. We began to view all of our staff as "community workers." With that in mind, we held kickoff meetings with all youth and staff, informed families of our plans, and then developed a transformation plan based on our three themes.

Our transformation process involved changes from the point of referral, when staff, youth, and families met to identify youth *and family* needs for the youth to return home. We also began to involve families in all aspects of residential program life (e.g., school, medical, clothing purchases, recreation), which strengthened positive working relationships between family, youth and staff. We emphasized staff education, involving nearly all staff in different training programs (e.g., Family Respect & Partnerships; Family Finding; Family Network Model). Our journey forced us to be open to change. This included reviewing staffing roles and needs. We decreased our number of psychologists and hired several social workers to work primarily in the community with families. We focused much more on trauma-informed care techniques (e.g., debriefing, safety plans, calming boxes, comfort rooms, eliminating points and levels, taking down observational cubicles/offices in the residential units that separated youth and staff).

We continue to focus on the three main theme areas, using data elements in each area:

1   *Increased contact between families and staff*—We started by tracking the amount of time our family advocate spent with families. We looked at where our families lived and found the majority were in two of five New York City boroughs. We focused on these two boroughs to hold family activities (e.g., bowling, trip to the aquarium, family dinners). Our goal over the coming year is to look at total contact with families by staff of all disciplines—including psychiatrists. Our thought is that more contact equals greater success in terms of shorter length of stay (LOS) and discharge to family. We developed a home stay questionnaire to create a platform to discuss issues such as medication, behaviors, sibling interactions, supervisory needs, and so forth. All staff are encouraged to communicate with families regarding "youth success" as opposed to having a primary problem focus. Finally, we utilize social work and direct-care staff to bring the residential intervention tools (e.g., skill building, safety plans, calming boxes) directly into the home.

2   *Increased family to youth contact*—Our goal here was to encourage as much contact per week between youth and family as possible, both in person and phone. Many youth now go home midweek, as well as weekends.

3   *Increased family/youth connections in the community*—Here, we tracked the number of families we connected to the family resource center in their local community. Despite serving youth with multiple challenges, we also approved a greater number of youth to have more "unescorted" time in the community. This improved youth confidence in their ability to function independently outside of residential. We track the number of youth who go off campus daily to be sure this process continues. A final change was to increase family/youth community activities by giving tickets to families for recreation and sports events so youth could attend with family rather than in a residential group.

Specific Challenges Encountered/Strategies Used:

- We had experienced ongoing AWOLs; youth were often running to family or just off grounds to get a soda or slice of pizza. We now encourage a much greater number of youth to go home midweek and to take trips into the community to promote independence and community engagement; this tested staff concerns regarding safety of residents leaving grounds unescorted.

- Eliminating the point and level system challenged this long-held structure and forced us to review the "why" behind behaviors and focus on individual needs for support.

- Securing services postdischarge (e.g., schools, clinics, after school settings) has been an ongoing challenge; social workers must continuously follow up on and advocate for services.
- Working with some state agencies has been a challenge. Many agencies still encourage longer residential stays. We continually remind them that youth and families do not need to reach perfection to be discharged home or to a less restrictive setting.

Data: Since our transformation journey began, there have been more youth being discharged (i.e., 31/FY2011 vs. 45/FY2012), more youth being discharged to less restrictive settings versus restrictive settings (i.e., 50% in FY2011 vs. 76% in FY2012), and there are larger numbers of youth returning to family (i.e., 25% in FY2011 vs. 56% in FY2012). We intend to increase our focus on using data to inform practice, especially long-term outcome data.

Recommendations for others starting their transformation process:

- Reset the program culture (for us it was from hopelessness to hope).
- Gain buy-in from all levels of staff—from direct care to the medical director.
- Change takes time—be patient.
- Never give up!
- Hire at least one full-time family advocate.
- Family/community connections are critical.
- It's not all about money—transformation during a fiscal crisis works, but you need to be creative.
- You cannot truly help youth without truly partnering with permanency resources.
- Always have a back-up plan.
- Viewing behavior through a trauma lens impacts how you respond and can help.
- Transformation is everyone's job.
- Every day counts!

Raquel Montes, Senior Youth Advocate, Casa Pacifica Centers for Children and Families, Camarillo, California

A Youth Advocate's Perspective

Casa Pacifica provides a range of in-home, community, emergency, and residential services for children and families throughout California's central coast. The 28-bed residential treatment program serves boys and girls ages 11 through 18 years. A strong belief of the agency that has emerged over recent years is that once young people have been part of the Casa Pacifica family, they will always be part of this family—even after they leave our care. This moral belief has shifted the agency culture in the way services are provided to families and youth. This change in practice emphasizes the BBI principle of family-driven and youth-guided care. Alumni services have been vital to ensure adherence to this moral commitment; we have established postresidential programs focused on individual strengths and needs, and coach youth towards independence.

Freeman's (2011) work influenced the "top to bottom approach" in which our CEO introduced new objectives for the agency, including increasing the service quality and respect for youth and families, reducing restrictive interventions, and empowering staff. These objectives triggered the shift in agency culture, including a refocus on values of respect, integrity, courage, and compassion. Staff signed a resolution of respect pledge, recognizing that the core values were especially relevant in our interaction with youth and families.

A culture compass was developed, serving as a framework for culture shift and support through the stages of change, and providing staff our agency mission and vision statement, core values, and workplace expectations. BBI became the catalyst for change that advanced our culture shift to the next level. Most importantly, youth advocates and parent partners were hired, becoming integral to the evolving change. Casa Pacifica signed the BBI joint resolution and committed to making changes and tracking outcomes based on BBI best practices and principles.

The residential leadership team, including a youth advocate and parent partner, used the results of the BBI self-assessment tool (SAT) as a quality improvement project. Targeted goals included engaging community partners and staff, and increasing youth-guided practices and family engagement. We used the SAT to interview all stakeholders and obtain data, creating an action plan with an 18-month timeline to realize goal completion.

Fear of the unknown made the changes challenging to staff, and continuous communication was essential to validate that change was occurring and provide staff with information about how these changes could benefit youth and families. After implementing improvements based on the SAT finding, we conducted a staff survey to assess how we were faring, specific to becoming youth-guided and family-driven. We found that staff had a difficult time with the concept of youth guided. They felt that youth were being allowed to just "run around" and do whatever they wanted, without consequences. Taking away the point and level system left frontline staff uneasy; a successful strategy to address this unease was training regarding natural and logical consequences and constant checking in at staff meetings.

Integrating youth advocates was also a challenge due to the difference in roles and expectations; this difference has taken a longer time for staff to accept. Youth advocate consistency and maturity has helped address this. Developing a youth and family advocacy training program for new hires, facilitated by youth advocates and parent partners, has also helped staff understand the value and importance of these positions.

Youth advocates now assist in facilitating resident councils, which focus on guaranteeing a youth voice; advocates also assist with follow-through on youth concerns. Allowing youth to have voice and choice over their care is vital as many have experienced many invalidating experiences with adults that could make being in residential without having a voice disempowering and over-whelming. An example of a change made was when youth shared with leader-ship the importance of informal peer-to-peer time; leadership responded by encouraging and making time for this type of informal support between youth.

Our culture shift has also supported significant reduction and duration of restraints and seclusion (e.g., from rates of 26 incidents of restraint per 1,000 resident days in 2006 to 6 in 2011; from an average of 30 minutes in 2006 to 4 minutes in 2011). All floor- and wall-assisted restraints have been eliminated. We are beginning to collect data on outcomes postdischarge, increased involve-ment of family members, and youth spending more time at home.

As a youth advocate, my recommendations for residential leaders include the following:

- Develop core values for your agency and get informed about best practices for residential, such as from BBI.
- Sign the BBI joint resolution and implement its self-assessment tool; create an action plan from the results of the SAT.
- Provide ongoing training programs for new hires informing them about BBI and its relevance to the agency's new culture and beliefs.
- Hire multiple youth and family advocates.
- Interview experienced youth advocates about ways that you can increase youth voice, choice, and empowerment in your residential program.

Sue Beck, Executive Director, Mount Prospect Academy/ Becket Family of Services, New Hampshire

Becket Family of Services offers a range of community-based, in-home, and residential services throughout the Northeast. Historically, Becket's treatment model for residential was client-centered, operating on the belief that by remov-ing a youth from a harmful home environment and providing a structured and disciplined routine, the youth would be successful upon return home. Today, Becket strives to partner with youth and families and to do *whatever it takes* to help them feel safe, respected, and ready to engage in a collaborative process towards long-term positive outcomes at home.

In 2010, we began to shift our perspective by opening in-home programs; these programs began to transform beliefs the agency had been founded on (i.e., youth treatment in the residence) to beliefs that focused primarily on the family system and community. In 2011, Mount Prospect Academy (MPA), our intensive residential treatment program, serving 101 males ages 11 to 21 years, was selected to participate in New Hampshire's Youth Transition to Permanency Project; through this project we formally adopted the BBI's principles, which became our new organizational mission. BBI provided us guidance in developing our strategic plan to ensure that we stayed focused on building and changing our services and culture to create a youth and family guided one. We took aggressive steps to change the culture within the residential program; for instance, we made the decision to merge our residential and community-based programs into one program under the same leadership. Our agency president, with the board of directors' support, sent a letter to all employees, youth, families, and stakeholders sharing that the organization would be transforming. An excerpt of his powerful and celebratory message reads as follows:

> Through our strategic planning efforts, MPA has been guided by the Building Bridges Initiative towards a youth and family guided model of care. . . . Given shorter lengths of stay, . . . we have had to address our traditional clinical "fix it" approach in favor of more realistic crisis stabilization and transition goals . . . we must accept that generally there will need to be ongoing clinical services following discharge and that the process of family preparation and transition must begin immediately and more earnestly. . . . MPA is beginning the process of requiring our clinical staff to spend more time in the home & community providing direct education, counseling and therapies.
>
> (J. Caron, personal communication, February 2012)

Steps taken included, but were not limited to

- leadership staff committing to culture change;
- developing an action plan, which prioritized data collection;
- utilizing the BBI self-assessment tool as well as focus groups and parent and youth report cards to provide us with information;
- responding to the data collected through these activities with open and honest discussions about where to focus our change efforts;
- eliminating our *dinosaur aged* behavior modification system, which included points and levels that contributed to dramatically reducing the number of physical restraints (i.e., by over 75% in a 2-year period; as Mohr, Martin, Olson, Pumariega, & Branca, 2009, illustrated, point and level systems do not allow for individualized treatment, are often too rigid, and do not translate very well into a home environment);
- through feedback from youth and families, creating a strength-based and skill-focused model that allows youth and family to have an active role and voice, easily translated to real life and home;
- adding a new leadership position, with responsibility for using data daily to be aware of and analyze what is going on in the milieu in a measurable way—helping leadership guide staff to improve the culture and to ensure extra supports for youth experiencing challenges;

- to support culture change, implementing a weekly 2-hour meeting between our residential director and all staff to focus on implementation of BBI practices and to address questions and challenges;
- establishing an active student council, which has been instrumental in building a youth-guided culture, including developing a school store, which took the place of our last time-out room, as well as a youth intake guide;
- supporting youth in their home communities by assigning youth at least one permanency team member who is community based, focusing on family and community work (i.e., family therapy in homes) and by scheduling treatment meetings more frequently in the client's natural community with a resultant increase in attendance as it is more convenient for families, referral sources, school districts, and others;
- creating the *Family Intake Guide for Residential Program*, which provides program information geared toward families/guardians and includes a magnet with a toll free 24 hour/7 day a week family support line and contact numbers;
- disconnecting trips and programming from behaviors (i.e., a rough school day does not prevent a youth from going to the community after school);
- increasing the number and variety of community activities, which are offered 7 days a week; and
- providing transportation to all youth 7 days a week, anywhere in New England, with a mindset that transportation will not be a barrier.

Unintended consequences/words of wisdom—We wouldn't be honest if we said we did not have any setbacks or barriers along our journey. The key is to identify the barriers and offer solutions; a few most notable barriers included issues related to lack of information or education, poor planning, rigid thinking, and comfort zones:

- Some key stakeholders were just not working towards a common goal. For example, it is critical that all stakeholders are all working towards youth- and family-guided care. We offered more information and advocated for additional trainings to be provided to our referral sources.
- One unintended consequence we endured was a higher fiscal increase related to an increase in transportation. To solve this, we focused on shifting costs elsewhere in the budget. It is critical not to panic and decrease travel that is vital to supporting home time and family work.
- Rigid thinking and old school mindsets of staff can result in minimal change. Due to different perspectives and expectations on workers, some workers resigned from their roles. This was not the end of the world; it was best that they moved on. Focusing on recruitment strategies and finding new workers who believe in the mission brought positive energy into the program. Leadership is key, should be outcome focused, and should send the message to the organization that we are changing and they can be part

of this or not—but the change is going to happen. Change in general can be hard on people, but staying true to the course, being firm but supportive, has been effective.

Moving towards our goals—Beckett has accomplished a great deal. We have decreased length of stay from 15 months in 2010 to 5 months in 2012. We now offer a range of residential programs, including very short-term stabilization, comprehensive assessment and support, and our intensive residential. We have evolved significantly in the past few years, but we still have a long road ahead.

Culture change is a long process, and it must be guided by core beliefs and values. We have established these through this process. Becket believes wholeheartedly that through a continuity of care model with an intensive permanency and strength-based focus, families can become stable, self-sufficient, and successful if they are treated with respect, feel safe, and they have a voice in the process. We believe that with the right combination of supports, all youth, regardless of their presenting issues, can remain safely in their home and community without long-term residential placement. We will constantly challenge ourselves to be open and honest about where we are in providing a youth- and family-guided culture. It will be an ongoing process that will be driven by data, action planning, and endless opportunities that will echo the voices of the many youth and families whom we work with.

John Damon, Chief Executive Officer, Mississippi Children's Home Services

Our Journey Beyond the Box

Founded in 1912, Mississippi Children's Home Services (MCHS) provides a state-wide continuum of behavioral health, educational, and social services for children and families. MCHS has embraced four core values that are consistent with the BBI principles: (1) The VOICE of our children and families always comes first; (2) RELATIONSHIPS matter; (3) we take great JOY in service to others; and (4) our families and our communities deserve our VERY BEST. The transformation of our organization began with the end in mind . . . privileging the voice of children and families.

MCHS began the journey in the mid-1990s, viewing the family primarily through a child-advocate lens in which the family was viewed as the source of many of the youth's problems—problems requiring intensive residential intervention. Care at that time was organized with families on the periphery. Recognizing the need to align with the emerging systems of care model, MCHS embarked on a sequence of shifts in understanding and embracing the critical role of families. The advent of BBI in 2005 served as an additional catalyst in moving MCHS further towards recognizing the pivotal and central role of families. This organizational evolution from peripheral to partner to family-guided has focused MCHS on the belief that the families of youth need support, they know their child best, and MCHS' role is to come alongside the family sufficiently to instill hope and facilitate change.

Within complex organizations, research suggests a period of 3 to 7 years is to be expected for any sustained enterprise-level change effort. Inherent in the cultural shift at MCHS have been both transactional and transformative changes. The first of the transformational efforts was the creation of a full-time family partner position in 2009. She brings the perspective of having a child with emotional challenges and of having been served within MCHS. The family partner is often the first face that families see in the admissions process; she coaches families on their involvement in the care planning process and on their central role in assuring optimal services. The family partner is instrumental in quality improvement, reviewing every policy to assure policies are sensitive to and inclusive of families.

MCHS has also engaged in transactional changes to privilege the voice of families and children. The "treatment team" model was abandoned in favor of a Child and Family Team process modeled after elements of BBI work. Families are provided an opportunity to tour the campus and unpack their child's belongings in their room before finishing the admissions processes. "Family time" has replaced "family visits," and Child and Family Teams are flexible to accommodate family schedules.

MCHS maintains a robust student council with youth, meeting periodically with residential leaders and discussing topics such as safety and well-being. Leaders regularly engage our youth through "front porch" meetings scheduled by and for youth issues. The first person new staff meet during orientation is the family partner followed by a small group of youth who share their experiences and observations, and often have quite pointed pieces of advice for new staff. The family partner sits in on hiring interviews for new staff, with youth joining the interview process for some candidates. One youth asked a candidate, "This is a pretty stressful place at times. What do you do to take care of yourself?" What a great question—one that also told MCHS that this youth had absorbed some of the trauma-informed care information.

As with every journey, there have been lessons learned that have helped inform the transformation:

1   *Clarify organization values*—An organization needs to be absolutely clear in what it believes and use that clarity to anchor and drive the change process. Over a 2-year process, MCHS has moved from an assortment of well-intentioned values through an exhausting list of 10 values to its current four values. The difference today is that MCHS has willed itself to align fully with these values, and constancy with these values is the single litmus test for everything from policy development, to program design, to performance reviews.
2   *Minimize confusion*—There is a large difference between surface compliance and any change in approach developing deep roots within an organization. While the transactional changes have helped position MCHS, the real process of transformation has only begun firmly to take hold with the development of and alignment with the four values. Alignment of

performance reviews and behavioral expectations have both driven personal change and created an effective measurement template for supervision. The family partner role needs to be clearly defined and supported with adequate resources. They need to truly be "at the table" at all levels within the organization, because the danger is a default position of just becoming a customer service representative who handles family concerns and complaints. Board buy-in has been nurtured with alignment of values forming the basis for board agendas, discussions, and decision making.

3   *Minimize politics and drama*—Change is messy. It is a constant struggle to assure that there is consonance between the formal and informal dialogue within the organization. The change from viewing families as the problem to being a "partner" to those who truly drive the care and treatment process has been marked by some successes and occasional backslides. Operationalization of the continuing change process has become easier with the presentation, alignment, and public discussion of the four core values. Work with youth and their families creates all types of learning opportunities, and the concurrent "stories" need to be shared throughout the organization. Learn from mistakes; celebrate and replicate successes.

4   *Assure that residential is truly seen as an intervention, not as a placement*—Persistent advocacy and education has been necessary at the state and national level to assure that residential levels of care are neither vilified nor misconstrued as "bad." Residential needs to be an integral part of a continuum and be seen as an effective intervention for youth in need of a short-term, highly structured treatment approach within a context of timely return to their community. MCHS has been highly active in providing education and information for both state and federal legislators on what constitutes a robust and properly designed continuum of care, provided either by a single organization or through collaboration with other providers. It utilizes its postgraduate fellows to conduct research focused on the efficacy of care within residential, publishing seven articles in peer-reviewed journals in the past 6 years.

5   *Adopt a trauma-informed approach*—Integrating trauma-informed care into the organizational culture was initiated in the early 2000s. This effort fell short of leadership expectations and failed to capture the imaginations of staff. MCHS recently initiated another effort to focus on a more comprehensive approach.

There are specific challenges ahead. Opportunities for growth, either organically or through acquisition, will require a robust process to integrate the new with the current so that there is a minimal amount of time and effort spent on working multiple cultures. New models of service delivery will be in all of our futures. The MCHS response has been to view new practices and models within the context of our core values and within the context of the BBI principles to "preserve the core, stimulate progress." In keeping with the end in mind, the "core" we will preserve will be privileging the voice of our children and families.

Contact Information:

Susan Beck, MSW
Executive Director
Mount Prospect Academy
(603)726-1552
Susan.Beck@Mountprospectacademy.org

David & Trish Cocoros
Co-Executive Directors
Youth Development Institute
(602) 256-5300
david.cocoros@ydi.org; trish.cocoros@ydi.org

John D. Damon, PhD
Chief Executive Officer
Mississippi Children's Home Services
(601) 352-7784
john.damon@mchscares.org

Steve Elson, PhD
Chief Advancement Officer
selson@casapacifica.org
&
Raquel Montes, BA
Senior Youth Advocate
rmontes@casapacifica.org
Casa Pacifica Centers for Children and Families
(805) 366-4100

Joe Anne Hust
Peer Support & System of Care Implementation Manager
The Institute for Innovation and Implementation—University of Maryland,
School of Social Work
(443) 610-6853
jhust@ssw.umaryland.edu

William P. Martone, MS
President/CEO
williammartone@hathaway-sycamores.org
&
Debbie Manners, MSW
Senior Executive Vice President
debbiemanners@hathaway-sycamores.org
Hathaway-Sycamores Child & Family Services
(626) 395-7100

Jim Nyreen, MSW
Assistant Executive Director
SCO Family of Services
(718) 523-2227
jnyreen@sco.org

Notes

1   This reflects the mission statement of Hathaway-Sycamores in 2000, when I was hired. It was changed in 2002 and again adapted in 2006, reflecting the agency's institutional commitment to deep culture change through all levels of the organization.
2   An example of a clinical training on bipolar might include clinicians training on symptoms of bipolar and parent partners describing what a child with bipolar might look like at home.

References

Anthony, W. A., & Huckshorn, K. A. (2008). *Principled leadership in mental health systems and programs.* Boston, MA: Center for Psychiatric Rehabilitation, Trustees of Boston University.

Blau, G. M., Caldwell, B., Fisher, S., Kuppinger, A., Levison-Johnson, J., & Lieberman, R. (2010). The Building Bridges Initiative: Residential and community-based providers, families and youth coming together to improve outcomes. *Child Welfare, 89*(2), 21–38.

Blau, G. M., & Magrab, P. R. (Eds.). (2010). *The leadership equation: Strategies for individuals who are champions for children, youth and families.* Baltimore, MD: Brookes.

Burns, B. J., Hoagwood, K., & Mrazek, P. J. (1999). Effective treatment for mental disorders in children and adolescents. *Clinical Child and Family Psychology Review, 2*(4), 199–254.

Courtney, M. E., Terao, M. E., & Bost, N. (2004). *Midwest evaluation of the adult functioning of former foster youth: Conditions of youth preparing to leave state care.* Chicago, IL: Chapin Hall Center for Children at the University of Chicago.

Freeman, J. (2011). From coercion to connection: Shifting an organizational culture. *Relational Child & Youth Care Practice, 24,* 128–132.

Mohr, W. K., Martin, A., Olson, J. N., Pumariega, A. J., & Branca, N. (2009). Beyond point and level systems: Moving toward child-centered programming. *American Journal of Orthopsychiatry, 79*(1), 8–18.

Substance Abuse and Mental Health Services Administration. (2013). Six core strategies to prevent conflict and violence: Reducing the use of seclusion and restraint. *National Registry of Evidence-based Programs and Practice.* Retrieved July 12, 2013, from www.nrepp.samhsa.gov/ViewIntervention.aspx?id = 278

Walters, U. M., & Petr, C. G. (2008). Family-centered residential treatment: Knowledge, research, and values converge. *Residential Treatment for Children & Youth, 25*(1), 1–16.

13 Creating Organizational Culture Change

One Agency's Transformation Towards Long-Term Positive Outcomes

Jim L. Dalton

Introduction

The effectiveness of residential programs for children and adolescents (hereafter referred to as "youth") has been scrutinized and questioned for decades. The financial and emotional costs of removing a youth from their homes and communities has been, and will continue to be, a significant concern, and it is critical that residential agencies demonstrate efficiency and positive outcomes.

To develop a focus on service effectiveness—including the creation of a family-driven, youth-guided, and culturally and linguistically competent philosophy; an emphasis on evidence-informed and evidence-based practices and data; and a commitment to high-quality care—it is often necessary to create real and sustained organizational culture change. Culture change across the entire organization includes defining and implementing a core set of values and operating principles, expanding leadership skills, providing consistent internal staff training and supervision, and moving the organization to focus on outcomes that extend beyond the time spent in a residential program. This chapter will provide information about the culture change process and illustrate one agency's commitment and journey to demonstrate successful long-term positive outcomes.

Each year, thousands of youth enter residential programs across the country. These youth are typically separated from their families and communities for months, and in some cases years, as they receive various therapies and interventions aimed at reducing maladaptive behaviors and increasing prosocial, healthy choices, and interactions. Residential programs tend to vary in scope, size, and specialty, and range from large institutional settings to small, community-based group-living settings, with many offering a wide continuum of less restrictive options. For most residential programs, the goal is for young people to return to their families, homes, and communities as soon as possible (Lyons, McCulloch, & Hamilton, 2006).

Most industry leaders would agree that the profile of the young person referred to residential has changed over the years, with residential programs increasingly reserved for youth with the most complex and intensive needs. Today, the majority of youth admitted to residential are assessed by professionals to be significantly impaired in their ability to control impulsive, aggressive, and self-destructive actions and have previously participated in some form of community-based services without significant reduction in risk behaviors. Many residential programs have modified services over the years to accommodate such high levels of risk by adding staff members, by increasing psychiatric services, and by providing more secure and safe living settings, among other steps.

There is some evidence of positive outcomes in the literature associated with participation in residential interventions for youth and families (Butler & McPherson, 2007; Child Welfare League of America, Inc., 2005). In addition, anecdotal reports from some youth have indicated a sense of belonging, safety, and relationship building during residential interventions as well as some treatment gains in the areas of trauma resolution, educational progress, skill building, and family engagement and conflict reduction. While there remains a strong need to further evaluate the effectiveness of residential interventions, what we do know is that when high-quality, family-driven, and youth-guided interventions are deployed, residential programs can serve as an important component of a system of care for youth and families.

However, critics of residential programs for young people with severe behavioral and psychiatric challenges have long noted the limitations and risks of congregate care settings. These risks include deviance training; injuries associated with the use of seclusion and restraint; the use of chemical restraint; lack of evidence-informed and evidence-based interventions; and high rates of recidivism postdischarge (*Mental Health*, 1999). They also cite the lack of family engagement, the lack of community exposure, and the lack of association with prosocial peers as significant limitations in residential programs, noting that in many programs youth discharged from residential interventions return to residential or similar levels of care at high rates. In some programs, recidivism rates have run as high as 60% to 80% in the first 12 months postdischarge. Studies have established that treatments that are found efficacious in rigorous, controlled environments often fail to show effectiveness in the real world (Holstead et al., 2010).

The recent, rapid advances in the study of residential interventions should inform and strengthen the importance of long-term, positive outcomes for youth and families touched by residential interventions. To achieve long-term positive outcomes for youth and families served, residential leaders will need to consider the culture change that is necessary—at all levels of the organization. The remaining sections of this chapter attempt to identify common barriers to change and provide a real world example of one agency's transformation toward long-term positive outcomes.

Change and Transformation in Residential Programs

If Nothing Changes, Nothing Changes

Change in organizations and agencies is typically preceded by significant external events or forces, such as funding cuts, changes in market opportunity, or community or media responses to incidents or events associated with the organization. Residential programs tend to be vulnerable to these external events, and as a result, they change often. These changes commonly include staff and personnel changes, program changes, management and supervision processes changes, and changes to risk management and risk prevention programs. These changes tend to be reactive rather than proactive.

Internal Initiatives

Change in agencies can also occur as the result of planned initiatives that are internally motivated. Internally motivated opportunities are typically the result of a strong commitment to improved outcomes for youth and families that are both immediately achieved and likely to be sustained over long periods of time (e.g., greater than 2 years). Indeed, one of the biggest criticisms of residential programs—and one that cannot be overlooked—is the lack of long-term sustained progress and stability in the home and community postdischarge. Youth and family service agencies that commit to measure success as evidenced by sustained permanency with the identified caregiver in the home and community over a period of years (not simply 30 or 60 days postdischarge), and collect data at aggressive time intervals to assess their results, undertake significant change, and transformation to implement the key steps that will improve treatment and support practices, improve youth and family experience, and reach the goal of long-term positive outcomes.

Defining Outcomes

Focusing on long-term outcomes requires defining "success" associated with residential interventions, an area of concern and controversy for years. Many residential programs do not collect postdischarge functional outcome data and lack systematic information regarding the impact of their interventions in the short or long term for youth and families (see Chapter 14). Some programs define success as "graduating" from a predetermined program module. Others claim success if the youth is transitioned to a community-based service provider from residential. If long-term positive outcomes are the goals of the residential program, the definition and threshold of success should reflect these values and intentions.

Outcome statements serve to direct and refine our practices towards the desired end result. When an agency defines success as related to long-term, positive outcomes for youth and families, the definition has a direct impact on practices deployed. Imagine how programs are designed and interventions conducted if the successful outcome is simply "complete the program." In that same program, imagine how different practices emerge when successful outcome is evidenced by not only program completion but by safe and healthy interactions over months or years postdischarge. It is the latter that will truly change the way an organization is structured and how the organization interacts with communities, youth, and families.

Leadership

Such significant change is rarely accomplished without the influence, direction, involvement, and encouragement of the top leaders of the agency—including the CEO/president and the board of directors. While these leaders often do endorse and encourage change and transformation—and believe in the need— they may underestimate or misunderstand their role in engineering significant change. The involvement of top leadership is key in implementing transformation, and organizations falter in their change processes when the leaders are perceived to be removed or distant from the process.

Internal Staff Leadership

Leadership is also key throughout the staff group. While an ideal and carefully selected single change agent or idea champion can have dramatic impact on transformation success and buy-in from others, several authors have endorsed that a "guiding coalition" is the most important variable available to induce agency stakeholders towards positive change. This selected group of individuals lends legitimacy to change efforts and facilitates the acceptance and encouragement of resources and emotional support energy towards change and transformation. This legitimizing group can subtly influence disparate employees and overcome obstacles by the leveraging of personal ties and other informal avenues of influence. Indeed, "Whenever some minimum mass is not achieved early in the process, nothing much worthwhile happens" (Kotter, 1999, p. 87).

Throughout experiences with change and transformation in organizations, it is not uncommon that the longer term and most influential employees have the most difficulty with change and transformation toward improved outcomes. This is most often the result of the ingrained investment and the hard work put forth by these employees in establishing the current state of affairs at the organization. The employee who has always been the biggest advocate of the agency and the processes, who has made significant contributions, and who is very well known inside and outside of the agency, can become one of the biggest obstacles and barriers to internal change. The most successful organizations place value on the youth and families served and the vision to improve outcomes at a higher level than the value of their commitment to long-term employees whose personal visions may no longer match with the new vision (Nadler & Nadler, 1998).

Family and Youth Leadership

For nearly 100 years, residential programs have struggled with how to effectively integrate and involve families into their care systems. Historically, residential programs have been predominantly youth centered, with the family being one of many ancillary treatment targets. Programs have focused on "fixing" the youth so that an improved and more stable child can be reintegrated into the family and community. Despite significant research that consistently demonstrates that positive processes and outcomes in residential programs correlates with the degree of family involvement, family presence in residential programs for youth tends to vary—ranging from none at all to more active participation.

It is critical in the transformation process for organizational leaders to ensure that families impacted by decisions are involved in those decisions. Families and youth have valuable insights into how to improve outcomes, based on lived experience, and it is not only fair but also more effective to include them as partners and leaders in decisions that will impact them or their peers. Agencies that employ family members/parents, that have family members/parents and youth on the board of directors, that have family members/parents serve as quality officers, and that require parents/family members and youth on all committees within the agency have greater ability to make well-thought-out decisions to improve outcomes. In the change and transformation process, having youth and family voices and perspectives at all times is a critical best practice to ensure success.

Regulatory Barriers

A common barrier to agency transformation to support long-term positive outcomes for youth and families that is communicated by agency leaders across the country is licensing/regulatory limitations on practices. Governmental regulation and oversight, accreditation standards, and Medicaid requirements, while well intentioned, can at times run counter to needed practices that promote long-term positive outcomes from residential programs. For example, despite evidence that small community-based living settings that mimic the family's home limit the risks and limitations of larger congregate care settings (Holstead et al., 2010), such community-based practice settings are often unsupported by state financing and policy due to lack of information, lack of understanding of the research, or institutional inertia. These realities are significant barriers and do impact agency transformation initiatives—even when there is strong commitment to positive change.

Despite these limitations, residential programs have found some success in the face of these challenges. For example, in Indiana, one organization partnered with a local governmental agency to pilot small residential sites in family communities as the primary out-of-home placement setting. The results of the pilot were described in a research article that compared the outcomes of institutional-based residential interventions versus those occurring primarily in small, community-based settings. The results were overwhelming in favor of the small community and family-focused settings as evidenced by shorter lengths of stay, reduced critical incidents, increases in prosocial peer associations, and increases in school attendance as compared to institutional setting controls (Holstead et al., 2010). In 1-year follow-up, discharged youth who were treated in their own communities and who were highly engaged with the families on a daily basis had significantly lower recidivism rates when compared to discharged controls. In this situation, a clear and present positive result was yielded through a strategy that involved educating and engaging oversight bodies in partnership towards better outcomes. These type of relationships and arrangements between providers and regulators need to be made a priority by all parties, with the creation of fiscal and policy improvements to achieve long-term positive outcomes.

Real World Examples of Specific Change and Transformation Towards Improved Long-Term Outcomes

When agencies and individuals are motivated by internal or external factors to improve long-term outcomes associated with the residential interventions they provide, changes are inevitable. Some of these changes can be immediate and others will require more planning, resources, and coordination. The following are examples of practical strategies that are utilized in one residential organization and that have had impacts on long-term positive outcomes.

Damar Services, Inc.—Indiana

Since Damar was founded in 1967, the organization has regularly initiated changes in response to the evolving needs of the community—including the modification of the name of the organization to Damar Services, Inc., in the late 1990s—to better reflect the practices and goals of the agency. In 2004, after many years of successful operations and cautious growth, the Board of Directors was introduced to the residential outcomes literature. Concerned by these findings and Damar's own history of practices that reinforced them, the board approved and funded an internal department to address best practice initiatives, first known as "Damar Best." In 2005, the agency became involved with the National Building Bridges Initiative (BBI), and endorsed the BBI principles. With both top leadership and internally motivated excitement toward improving outcomes for youth and families served, Damar embarked on a mission of change and transformation, embracing BBI core values and principles as drivers of the change process. This process of change and transformation has been ongoing and requires constant attention and strengthening of the work force and work culture, but has yielded significant positive results.

Change and Transformation Quick Wins and Tools

After considering and vetting the overall goals and process of needed change, some "quick wins" to jumpstart the transformation process are important to achieve. Quick wins are designed to engage staff members, youth, and families at the beginning levels as examples of needed change and transformation. Damar found that these quick wins need to be practical and easily associated with its new vision towards improved long-term outcomes for youth and families served in residential settings. The following identifies 10 examples of strategies and practices Damar implemented that became quick and enduring wins.

Training—Damar found that for stakeholders to be engaged in change towards more family-driven and youth-guided interventions, they must first understand which, how, and why current practices are ineffective and then be provided with evidence-informed and evidence-based practice alternatives. Damar leadership decided that the identification of outcome data for individual agencies and the residential intervention industry as a whole was a good place to start. It found that positive outcomes for youth are associated with high degrees of family involvement and implemented training opportunities that teach and promote family engagement practices, the development of positive family interactions among members, the importance of culturally relevant practices with families, and the importance of youth spending time with family in the context of interventions. A major change in practice was the deployment of well-trained and well-prepared direct care staff into the homes and communities of youth placed in residential care settings. Staff members were trained to specialize in families instead of units or programs, and their schedules were designed to match the needs of the families instead of the needs of the agency. A training curriculum was devised and rolled out to highly motivated and engaged direct-care employees. Damar quickly discovered that this change in philosophy, approach, and behavior of direct-care staff to support families in need was one of the most potent changes in the process to support long-term outcomes.

Clearly defining outcome targets—There is an increasing amount of research focused on residential interventions for youth. However while outcome definitions are converging and practices are changing across the country, there remains disparity among residential programs as to how to define and measure long-term program effectiveness. Believing that our philosophy and understanding guides our interventions, Damar engaged significant family and staff participation in the establishment of clearly defined outcome goals and measures. These definitions both impacted and were impacted by agency practices and experience, and evolved over time.

A good definition of success (2005):

> Success is achieved when the youth or family's functioning does not result in re-admission or other out-of-home placement in a similar or higher level of care during the 12-months post discharge from the residential program.

A better definition of success (2007):

> A successful outcome from our program is achieved with the youth and family remain together in the home and community, avoiding any out-of-home placement, for a period of no less than 24-months after discharge from the residential program.

An even better definition of success (2009):

> Youth and families are supported at levels needed well after discharge from the residential program with "success" being achieved only when the family remains together in a safe and healthy environment at 1-year, 3-years, and 5-years post discharge.

Use of language—Language has strong impact on the way staff, youth, and families think and behave in and around residential programs. Damar believes working with family members to develop language and communications that are respectful and empowering to youth and families promote family involvement and engagement. For instance, through training and support and through consultation with family members, Damar eliminated the use of the term *home visit*. We learned from families that youth do not "visit" their homes or families. Rather, they spend time with families in communities. Damar found that simply replacing the term *home visit* with *family time* in all discussions and policies could have significant impact on staff, youth, and families towards improved outcomes for youth and families touched by residential interventions.

Associated with the use of the term *visit*, which so often accompanies residential program interventions, are agency policies on *visitation*. We were concerned that restrictive visitation policies, as has often been common in residential programs, were not sensitive to the needs of families and youth. Through intensive family engagement and parent consultation, Damar discovered that these restrictive practices tend to undervalue the role of the parent in the youth's support services and progress. We realized that parents should not have to be invited to the organization or check a schedule to ensure that their presence will be accepted. Rather, programs should be flexible and adapt to the schedule and needs of the family, and encourage family time at the organization and in the family home as much as possible. We decided that family time should never be contingent on behavioral progress or compliance, unless there is imminent concern for safety. Even then, the family should be the primary decision maker in terms of family time.

Treatment plans and community integration—Research in the child welfare and correctional literature has identified risk and recidivism variables associated with long-term outcomes. Surprisingly, review of residential program treatment plans finds few of these variables included as treatment plan targets—even though the correlation with long-term outcomes has been established (Holstead et al., 2010). Treatment-plan format and content is often dictated by state licensing agencies and/or governmental payers (e.g., Medicaid). Because these mandated requirements are not likely to change, many agencies have found ways to meet licensing and governing body requirements while still addressing important variables associated with long-term outcomes. For example, Damar adjusted treatment plan requirements to always include the known variables associated with long-term outcomes.

Multiple family roles—Regardless of their level of functioning or situation, all families and parents have strengths and can positively influence and help guide the intervention process. As is clear in the work summarized previously, Damar believes that embracing the family's expertise and integrating their knowledge and involvement in interventions promotes long-term outcome practices. At Damar, a primary part of the change and transformation process has been to ensure that families and parents serve important roles within residential programs, with their participation continually invited and valued. Below are some of the important roles that family members and parents have come to serve at Damar.

Co-expert—As an expert contributor in treatment planning, case formulation, interventions, and data collection for their own children.

Employee—As a paid staff member who works with their own child to implement the family-based intervention plan or works with other youth and families with similar challenges.

Staff trainer—As a provider of content training and/or training responses from a family/parent perspective.

Interviewer—As a member of the agency interview team to help select qualified applicants to work with their children and the children of other parents.

Board member—As a voting member of the governing board of the agency and by offering critical input into planning, strategies, policy changes, and resource needs and allocations.

Committee member—As a member of agency committees to ensure that parent and family perspectives are included in all policies, procedures, data collection, as well as changes and strategies to improve outcomes. Damar forbids any committees to meet without a parent and/or youth participation.

Advocate—As a voice on intra- and interagency initiatives, on advisory committees, and in policy-making decisions.

Performance and quality improvement officer—As a representative, evaluator, and data collector to inform the performance and quality improvement (PQI) process at the agency.

Parent liaison—As an available resource to other parents who have youth in care—especially those who have little experience with complex residential program systems.

Close to home—Damar believes that residential programs that make commitments to family-driven and youth-guided care towards positive and sustained outcomes should not accept residential referrals who reside in distant communities. This is based on experience that families who reside more than 30 miles from the residential program have great difficulty with appropriate family and community involvement and engagement in care. The distance can be daunting, and logistics and transportation issues are challenging. Damar has found that providing services to youth and families that reside close to the residential program has promoted greater likelihood of family engagement and long-term outcomes.

Generalization of gains—The generalization of skills training from the residential program to the youth and family's real-world setting is of vital importance. Damar's review of the data found that the degree of gains made within the residential program do not necessarily correlate with long-term sustained outcomes. As such, it decided that engaging families from the beginning to support and inform interventions, responses to negative behaviors, and crisis-intervention steps would be critical towards long-term sustained improvements, and that if interventions or programs would be difficult to implement in the youth and family's real-world setting, the interventions should not be used in the residential program. For example, Damar elected to stop using point and level systems based on realizing at the time that these approaches are often not available for use in the youth's natural environment and, when available, are typically not used to the level of fidelity required for effective generalization of gains.

Primary incident of concern—Agencies typically rank critical incidents that occur within the residential program in order of concern or impact, with aggressive, self-injury, elopement, and sexual acting-out incidents often seen as most critical. Damar changed the way it considers, defines, and categorizes "critical incidents" to be more consistent with its definition of long-term outcomes. For example, Damar considers lack of family and community involvement to be a critical incident variable, including a youth's lack of face-to-face contact with his or her family and/or community; if a 24-hour period passes without family or community engagement, this is considered a critical incident—required to be recorded, documented, and addressed through agency protocols for critical incident review. Because significant critical incidents must be documented, reviewed, and corrected, significant effort is made to avoid such incidents—attempting to promote family engagement towards long-term outcomes.

Prosocial peers—There is strong evidence that adolescent problem behavior is strongly embedded in peer groups. In fact, hundreds of controlled studies have indicated relatively high rates of negative effects when interventions are provided within the context of a negative peer group (Dishion, McCord, & Poulin, 1999). There is also significant research that suggests that exposure to prosocial and positive peer influences has positive effects on outcomes. In response, Damar has attempted to increase positive prosocial modeling and engagement, increasing the amount of prosocial peer associations for youth during the course of residential interventions—and especially during postresidential services. Damar has discovered that prosocial peers can be available to those served in residential programs through volunteers, paid programs, local community groups, and public schools.

Set standards and hold others accountable—New practices require lots of support, communication, and supervision to maintain—especially those that may run counter to traditional residential program practices. Examples of vehicles and tools used at Damar to promote changes toward transformation include

- a strong performance and quality improvement process with designated indicators aimed at long-term outcome practice compliance;
- visual reminders through posters, events, and celebrations;
- parent and youth testimonials;
- frequent direct-care service trainings;

- frequent communications through e-mail and mobile applications of the importance of achieving long-term outcomes for youth and families served;
- strong and active supervision of employees; and
- sharing improved outcome data with all stakeholders, among others.

The Results of Transformation

Through engaging parents, youth, and staff in the development of a full continuum of care, Damar has become the largest provider of children's residential interventions in the state of Indiana. Five-year outcomes ending in 2012 demonstrated 83% of youth touched by residential services were provided services by residential direct-care and clinical staff in their homes and communities. With a focus on family-driven and youth-guided care, community and home generalization of interventions, and ongoing support of families continued by residential staff well beyond discharge, Damar measures the effectiveness of residential interventions postdischarge at 1-, 3-, and 5-year intervals, with recidivism rates of less than 10%.

Final Remarks

While there is significant research to support program changes that are underway towards improved outcomes for youth and families served through residential interventions, transformation of residential programs is still quite new and evolving. Attempts and efforts to achieve long-term outcomes for youth and families as the primary measure of success still remains incompatible with many traditional residential program practices. Today's residential programs need leadership staff who embrace the revised practices associated with sustained long-term outcomes and who encourage and support the engagement of youth and families at high levels by listening and learning. Change and transformation is difficult work and can be hard to sustain. However, it is necessary as we continue to improve the outcomes associated with residential interventions.

Contact Information:

Jim Dalton, PsyD, HSPP, CSAYC
President and CEO
Damar Services, Inc.
jimd@damar.org
(317) 856-5201

References

Butler, L. S., & McPherson, P. M. (2007). Is residential treatment misunderstood? *Journal of Child and Family Studies, 16*(4), 465–472.

Child Welfare League of America, Inc. (2005). *Position statement on residential services.* Available from www.cwla.org/programs/groupcare/rgcqpostionstatement.pdf

Dishion, T. J., McCord, J., & Poulin, F. (1999). When interventions harm: Peer groups and problem behavior. *American Psychologist, 54*(9), 755–764.

Holstead, J., Dalton, J., Horne, A. & Lamond, D. (2010). Modernizing residential treatment centers for children and youth—an informed approach to improve long-term outcomes: The Damar pilot. *Child Welfare, 89*(2), 115–129.

Kotter, J. (1999). *What leaders really do.* Boston, MA: Harvard Business School Press.

Lyons, J. S., McCulloch, J. R., & Hamilton, J. (2006). Monitoring and managing outcomes in residential treatment: Practice-based evidence in search of evidence-based practice. *Journal of the American Academy of Child and Adolescent Psychiatry, 45*(2), 247–251.

Mental health: A report of the Surgeon General (1999). Washington, DC: United States Public Health Services, Center for Mental Health Services, National Institute of Mental Health.

Nadler, D., & Nadler, M. B. (1998). *Champions of change: How CEOs and their companies are mastering the skill of radical change.* San Francisco, CA: Jossey-Bass.

14   Tracking Long-Term Strength-Based Outcomes

Richard Dougherty, Deborah Strod, Sylvia Fisher, Samantha Broderick, and Robert E. Lieberman

Introduction: The Need for Long-Term, Strength-Based Outcomes

Achieving sustained positive outcomes for children and adolescents (hereafter referred to as "youth") and their families who have received residential interventions is critically important. Defining and measuring those outcomes ultimately serves all constituencies, beginning with the youth and families themselves who deserve outcome information to make informed choices about their care. Providers need outcome information not only to improve practices but also to articulate their role and value in systems adapting to health-care reform. The payers and overall systems that serve youth and families also need outcome information to manage and improve care. The key questions include 'Which outcomes should be measured for these different levels of oversight?' and 'How and when should those outcomes best be tracked?' This chapter addresses these questions, first discussing the needs for and uses of outcomes information, then the selection of measures and, finally, describing the ways a practice-based research approach can maintain a focus on outcomes tracking.

While there is consensus that residential interventions can produce positive gains in behavioral, social, and family functioning (Bettman & Jasperson, 2009), such gains often deteriorate after discharge (Leichtman, Leichtman, Barber, & Neese, 2001). The challenge for our youth and family serving systems is to identify what can be done to improve the postdischarge outcomes. For instance, increasing family involvement during care and residential stability and youth/family engagement in services after discharge have been shown to improve outcomes (Frensch & Cameron, 2002). With different perspectives and sources of data, providers and health plans should measure not only short-term outcomes of care but also long-term outcomes, over at least a 2- to 3-year period.

The burden of collecting and analyzing these measures should not fall exclusively on providers. Providers must measure performance and be accountable, but at the same time the ultimate responsibility for making changes to improve long-term outcomes lies with the overall system comprised of payers, policy makers, residential providers, their community partners, and others. By focusing on postdischarge outcomes, residential providers generate data to inform continuous quality improvement efforts and focus attention on coordination of services with other youth and family-serving organizations. Similarly, payers and human service systems need performance and outcome information to optimize decisions about the number and capacity of residential programs in the system of care and, with youth and families, to select appropriate levels of care for individual youth.

Residential programs that take responsibility for measuring long-term outcomes are better prepared to assess how changes in their own practices can improve outcomes postdischarge. They are also better positioned to articulate their value in a system of care and respond to changes in the health-care and youth and family serving systems. As a result of increased health insurance coverage under health-care reform, insurers and managed-care organizations will increasingly be responsible for funding alternatives to inpatient levels of care. Data demonstrating the long-term effectiveness of residential services will support decisions to incorporate these services into insurance coverage.

Most residential services, however, are in the early stages of using data to demonstrate their efficiency and effectiveness (Center for Health Care Strategies [CHCS], 2010). With some notable exceptions, most programs have not devoted resources to routine, long-term follow-up data collection of any kind. Few programs are looking at 6-month or 1-year outcomes, and even fewer currently track outcomes over multiple years. This must change if programs are going to be able to justify their effectiveness, and deliver interventions that improve the capabilities, skills, and well-being of youth with serious emotional conditions once they return to the community. Well-known examples of successful use of long-term outcomes data include Children's Village's (New York) focus on ensuring that graduates are in school soon after discharge (within 2 weeks) and stay there long term (Levison-Johnson et al., 2012). Damar Services (Indiana) seeks to decrease recidivism through community-based residential care (Dalton, 2010). Pressley Ridge (Ohio, Pennsylvania, West Virginia, Delaware, and Maryland), a pioneer in collecting outcomes data for 25 years, has focused on work/school preparedness in response to graduates' low employment. These and other programs provide illustrations of specific strategies for the collection and use of outcomes data to drive effective change, which can be combined and adapted for different providers and systems.

Selecting Strength-Based Outcomes Important to Youth and Families, Payers, and Systems

Three major categories of measures address critical aspects of the experience of youth and families during and after residential services:

- *Process indicators* measure key program activities (e.g., youth and family participation in treatment planning/child and family team meetings, use of home-based support, postdischarge follow-up, use of seclusion and restraint).

- *Experience of care measures* reflect the lived experience of youth and family during the residential intervention (e.g., degree of youth and family voice in treatment planning and program oversight, responsiveness of staff, perceptions about quality).
- *Functional outcomes* assess the functioning of youth and family in a variety of arenas (e.g., school participation/attendance; family problem-solving abilities and communication; youth self-management of behavior).

Administrative process measures collected routinely by programs often include length of stay, discharge destination, medication usage/delivery/adherence, restraint and seclusion rates, critical incident rates, and discharge type. Programs should also collect information on the level of restrictiveness of the discharge destination (e.g. using the Restrictiveness of Living Environment Scales or a similar tool).

Many youth, families, providers and insurers have recognized that delivery systems must incorporate key system-of-care values, such as youth-guided, family-driven, community-based and culturally/linguistically competent services and supports (CHCS, 2010). Studies stress that these are important components of long-term success after residential interventions in part because they empower youth and families and ensure that the care provided is relevant to them (Hair, 2005; Levison-Johnson et al., 2012; Walter & Petr, 2008). Experience-of-care measures should reflect youth-guided and family-driven practice, providing key data about youth and family perceptions of their involvement in decision making and care.

The set of functional outcomes deemed by youth and families to be most relevant and important tend to cluster across four domains (Building Bridges Initiative, 2012):

- *Home*—Safe, stable, and supportive living environment.
- *Purpose*—Meaningful daily activities, such as a job, school, volunteerism, and the independence, income, and resources to participate in society.
- *Community*—Relationships and social networks that provide support, friendship, and love.
- *Health*—Sustained basic physical and behavioral health/well-being, and overcoming or managing health challenges.

Youth and families consider specific developmental skills and strength-based outcomes to be important, particularly those supporting certain functional life domains that overlap with the four areas listed above. These include self- and somatic regulation, executive functioning, communication skills, and school- and work-readiness skills, among others (Bellonci et al., 2012). Families also want to develop the skills and competencies needed to sustain youth successfully in the home (Bettmann & Jasperson, 2009).

When the ultimate goals of residential interventions are framed as building strengths and developmental skills for the youth and families, and the capacity to support families after discharge, this leads naturally to a focus on skills and quality of life, experience of care, and long-term postdischarge success. Integrating measures of these outcomes into residential operations will make the measures more relevant for youth and families and dovetail with priorities of boards, funders, and other constituencies.

Measures and Tools for Assessing Outcomes[1]

Outcome tools must be valid and reliable, providing meaningful during-treatment and postdischarge information. Many organizations and a growing number of state systems are using the Child and Adolescent Needs and Strengths (CANS; Lyons, Griffin, & Fazio, 2013), which was developed as a strength-based (not symptom-based) tool. Other widely used instruments include the Child Behavior Checklist (CBCL; Achenbach, 2013), the Child and Adolescent Functional Assessment Scale (CAFAS; Hodges, n.d.), and the Ohio Scales (Ogles, 2013). IARCCA, an Association of Children and Family Services, is testing a new strength-based screening tool used in Canada—the Child and Youth Resilience Measure (Liebenberg, Ungar, & Van de Vijver, 2013). Some use the Youth Outcomes family of questionnaires (Burlingame & Lambert, 2013).

Other specialized instruments can supplement these measures of family functioning or parental stress. InnerChange uses a program-specific tool through which youth and adults provide feedback to each other about goals they set in a master treatment plan. For example, at 1 year, 62% of youth reported their mother doing well on her goals (New Haven, 2013).

Programs also use a variety of experience-of-care tools, developed in-house or available publicly, such as the Youth Services Survey (YSS) and YSS-Family Survey (Brunk, Koch, & McCall, 2013). Experience-of-care surveys should be done while the youth is in residential care as well as shortly after discharge. Feedback during care may provide guidance that allows responsive treatment, but some researchers and advocates argue that surveys done while the youth is in care may not include negative feedback due to fear of reprisal. While some programs and researchers have concerns about the validity and reliability of such measures, experience-of-care surveys ensure that the voices of those served by the program are heard routinely. In addition, the Affordable Care Act sets a clear standard that patient reported outcomes are valid measures of health service effectiveness (Bellonci et al., 2012).

Programs must weigh cost, clinician/youth time, clinical usefulness, and payer documentation requirements. Costs may need to be built into daily rates, and time to administer tools must be built into clinical and standard operations, including admissions and discharge routines and treatment plan reviews. A growing movement among policy makers seeks the widespread adoption of outcomes measurement avoiding use of proprietary tools due to cost, or to effect change in federal policies governing public support of proprietary tools (Hoagwood, 2013). Programs may consider an independent consultant for during- and postresidential assessments; while this can be costly, it saves staff time and can increase objectivity and consistency in pre- and postdischarge measurements. Another alternative would be to develop relationships with professors from local colleges/universities who might be interested in collaborating and engaging students or interns in evaluation projects.

Tracking Outcomes Through Practice-Based Research

Establishing a practice-based research infrastructure within the organization can provide a framework for the use of long-term outcomes measurement. A framework should start by identifying indicators of success that are important to the organization and key constituencies, for example, by convening a group planning and prioritization exercise. As a part of this process, organizations must specify the measures and tools, and identify ways to incorporate data collection into routine clinical practice and operations. This kind of process builds consensus in the organization around a measurement strategy. Care must be exercised to ensure that the measurement strategy meets several important criteria, particularly simplicity, ease of data collection, and focus on outcomes that correlate to long-term success of youth.

In addition to routine collection of administrative and tool-based data, practice-based research can embed data collection in clinical interactions. Youth and/or family members can assess their experience and functional progress using participatory research methods or during collaborative therapeutic conversations with individuals from the treatment team who are well trained in family-driven, youth-guided care. Program-wide implementation should include a structured approach to data collection from the youth or family, a process to initiate the conversations, and methods for analyzing results. Another approach is a more structured survey, reviewed with, and interpreted, by youth and families. These implementation strategies are affordable and utilize existing capacity.

Practical Considerations in Long-Term Outcomes Tracking

As long-term outcomes tracking becomes more routine and a national norm, much can be learned from those who have already implemented such systems. Each program, association, or system should adapt outcome-tracking efforts to its own history, environment, and available resources. Some individual providers begin by conducting point-in-time studies of postdischarge outcomes, and then establish ongoing tracking. Some have also participated in ongoing projects supported by provider associations or payers. Some systems share administrative data with each other and between programs. Sometimes this is done in collaboration with university partners. Though investments of time and money for initiating long-term outcomes measurement need to be addressed, one program has noted, "our investment in outcomes is returned to us at least 100 fold" (D. Tibbits, personal communication, October 15, 2013).

A few exemplary organizations or programs track their own long-term outcomes using data collected through routine operations. For instance, Boys

Town, in Nebraska, conducts more than 4,000 short follow-up interviews each year at 6, 12, and 24 months after discharge. Children's Village, in New York, collects data on stability at home, progress at school, work, and recidivism 12 months postdischarge (Blau, Hueberger, Caldwell, Lieberman, & Lim, 2012). Damar Services, participating in Indiana's Reform Initiative, tracks number of days out of home, treatment in [youth's] own home/community, recidivism (up to 5 years postdischarge), number of closed cases, and cost (Dalton, 2010). All of these programs routinely report their results publicly, and use these data in program improvement efforts.

IARCCA, an Association of Children and Family Services (formerly the Indiana Association of Residential Child Caring Agencies) and the Minnesota Coalition of Child Caring Agencies (MCCCA) are two ongoing examples of voluntary, collaborative efforts by associations. Since 1985, through MCCCA, Volunteers of America has been collecting 6-month postdischarge outcomes along with 34 other organizations. They share these data so that their colleagues have benchmarks. For the past 15 years, IARCCA has provided a data-collection framework and aggregated benchmarking for residential programs, primarily in Indiana, but also in some other states. Robust online data systems provide key support to such collaborative efforts; one caveat is that low participation rates can limit the benchmarking value of the data.

In Illinois, most of the youth in residential care are in the child welfare system, which has developed system-wide outcome metrics. Illinois also uses a risk-adjustment formula in its aggregated benchmarking so that programs can have more relevant comparison data. The child welfare system tracks ongoing information on where youth are living and analyzes the levels of restrictiveness associated with those placements/living arrangements. The California Residentially-Based Services Reform (CARBSI) effort has brought together data from Juvenile Justice, Education and Child Welfare to provide robust tracking of long-term residential outcomes (Martone, 2010).

From these and other efforts, a number of implementation strategies emerge:

- *Establish permission for contact*—Most programs with successful follow-up initiatives routinely obtain permission for future contact in initial admission paperwork. Most try to reach all families and youth postdischarge, not just a sample, with varying success rates.
- *Develop effective techniques for finding youth and families postdischarge*—During follow up, Boys Town confirms contact information and asks who would know where the youth is, if the contact information fails in the future. Search services are also used, when necessary to find current addresses.
- *Adequately staff postdischarge tracking*—Some programs simply ask existing staff to make phone calls to follow up on youth and families with whom they have worked; some may have administrative staff make calls. Others fund a dedicated staff position(s) for outcomes work through quality improvement departments, and some have dedicated research staff. Some programs keep a simple spreadsheet suggesting when calls should be made;

others utilize a full-scale reminder system incorporating the use of ticklers. Boys Town noted that it takes an average of seven calls to secure a response.

- *Select from different follow-up approaches*—Follow-up methods include phone, mail, e-mail, and online. Follow-up interviews vary from open, unscripted conversation (Children's Village, Utah Youth Village) to standardized questions (Boys Town).
- *Develop efficient data collection and analysis methods*—An association, payer, or system-level project can supply data collection software and analysis services, through which multiple programs can achieve economies of scale. However, many programs have invested in this basic infrastructure of their own accord.

Measuring Outcomes at Multiple Levels

Although data collected at the individual program level is of great value to both the program and the youth and families served, payer/service-system data should be aggregated across programs and at the payer/service-system level. This approach allows for provider benchmarking (i.e., comparisons to average scores). It also facilitates monitoring, performance management, and increased accountability of the youth and family and payer systems. Health and service systems need information about how residential services are functioning as a component of a wider array of community and other out-of-home interventions a youth and family may receive. This could include several potential measures, such as postdischarge follow up. At all levels, the relative costs of services and supports received by youth and families who have received residential interventions must also be assessed, and the consolidation of these data sources can enhance decision making across all constituencies.

While many confounding factors impede the interpretation of results, outcomes data should ultimately help to determine where services are best delivered. A residential intervention may be necessary to provide intensive services and supports to help youth and families learn the skills to manage symptoms, face challenges, and set sustainable goals. Optimally, these interventions are short term. There is a clear preference among youth and families to have care delivered in the home or in the community to the extent possible; there is also evidence indicating that some interventions provided in residential can successfully be implemented using intensive home services (Magellan Health Services, 2011). With increased levels of insurance and managed-care coverage under health reform, there will also be strong incentives for effective services to be provided in the least costly way. All of these factors necessitate that data are available to assess fidelity of practice implementation, and what the long-term outcomes and cost are.

Residential providers are the best source of administrative data for the residential episode; this should include postresidential follow up with youth and family members. It is often necessary for community providers to supply data about progress after discharge, though a number of states, like the Massachusetts

Caring Together Initiative, are increasingly purchasing postdischarge, follow-up, and support services. Since payers and health plans have access to claims-based tools and system-level measures, the administrative measures they use may complement, but will differ from, those that providers can implement. For instance, claims-based data are the best source of reliable information from services provided by multiple providers. Claims-based measures may include service access, penetration rates and utilization, average length of stay, readmission, days in out-of-home placement, postdischarge follow-up, and cost of services. While payers have access to claims records after residential discharge, providers will have to implement a follow-up survey to collect important information not available in claims records (e.g., school attendance and risk factors like drug use and social relationships).

Ultimately, an effective service system needs to collect and analyze performance and outcome data at multiple system levels—individuals, providers, and across the system. System-level administrative data is essential to understanding issues about geographic access to, and utilization of, services for youth. Provider-level data from clinical assessments, experience of care, and follow-up on functional outcomes and well-being can also be aggregated to a system-wide level, particularly if common or comparable tools are used. Data at an individual level should be used to monitor treatment progress and goal attainment. The state of New Jersey, in collaboration with PerformCare, utilizes a universal assessment tool (which includes the CANS and other data elements) administered at 6-month intervals across all system of care providers with which a youth and family are engaged. This extends data collection across system of care services both before and after a residential episode, and the data can be stratified by individual, provider, region, and system.

Summary

The adoption of practice-based research strategies by individual programs collecting outcome-related data before and during residential and after discharge should be a minimum expectation of youth and family serving systems across the country. Progress for individual youth and families should be assessed with a standard set of outcome measures. Programs should track their performance through a system of measurement that monitors the same outcomes across different services at multiple points in time. At a program level, data and comparative analyses are essential for quality improvement. Associations and states can take steps to support residential programs with greater economies of scale, providing benchmarking capabilities, and an industry-wide approach for monitoring quality.

Programs providing residential interventions need to engage in routine collection, analysis, and dissemination of long-term outcome data for the youth and families they serve to provide the most efficient and effective care possible and, ultimately, remain in business. To achieve this goal, programs should begin by being more transparent and accountable to youth, families, and payers and by collaborating with providers, payers, and state/federal agencies. Individual programs must share the commitment to accountability that is implicit in a large-scale outcome measurement effort.

Comparable system-level action is also necessary to manage spending, build the capacity of the service system, and set new expectations and standards for performance and quality. Programs, payers, and state/federal agencies must connect with community providers, care-management entities, and other education, health, and human services organizations that serve the same population to coordinate efforts with appropriate data-sharing arrangements. Advocates, providers, provider associations, payers, and regulators must also be involved in this process to ensure its success. Creating the capacity to track long-term outcomes and collect, analyze, and disseminate data on multiple levels will ultimately benefit youth, their families, and the complex systems that serve them.

Contact Information for Individual Programs:

Samantha Jo Broderick, LSW, DRCC
Provider/Member Communications Manager
PerformCare—An AmeriHealth Caritas Company
300 Horizon Drive-Suite 306
Robbinsville, NJ 08691-1919
Phone: (609) 689-5400

Linda S. Butler PhD, LCSW
Director of Research & Special Projects
Spurwink
899 Riverside Street
Portland, ME 04103
Phone: (207) 871-1200
www.spurwink.org

Jim Dalton, PsyD, HSPP, CSAYC
President and COO
Damar Services, Inc.
6067 Decatur Blvd.
Indianapolis, IN 46241
Phone: (317) 856-5201
jimd@damar.org

Cathleen Graham, MSW, LCSW
Executive Director
IARCCA, an Association of Children & Family Services
5519 E. 82nd St, Suite A
Indianapolis, IN 46250
Phone: (317) 849-8497
www.IARCCA.org
www.EvaluateOutcomesNow.org

John Hall, MS, MMFT
Clinical Director of Research and Development
Telos
870 West Center Street
Orem, UT 84057
john@telosrtc.com

Jacob Z. Hess, Ph.D.
Research Director
Utah Youth Village
5800 S. Highland Drive
Salt Lake City, UT 84121
Phone: (801) 712-1346
jhess@youthvillage.org

Jonathan Huefner, PhD, Research Scientist
Mary Beth Chmelka, Senior Research Analyst
National Research Institute for Child and Family Studies
Father Flanagan's Boys' Home
Boys Town, NE 68010
Phone: (402) 498-1257
Fax: (402) 498-1315
jonathan.huefner@boystown.org
Mary.Chmelka@boystown.org

Jeremy Christopher Kohomban, PhD
President and Chief Executive Officer
The Children's Village and Harlem Dowling
125th Street Harlem
New York, NY 10027
Phone: (212) 932-2200
JKohomban@childrensvillage.org

William Martone, MS
President & CEO
Hathaway-Sycamores Child and Family Services
210 South De Lacey Avenue, Suite 110
Pasadena, CA 91105
Phone: (626) 395-7100
Fax: (626) 395-7270
williammartone@hathaway-sycamores.org

Alan Morris, PsyD
Associate Director, CARTS Program
University of Illinois at Chicago
1747 W. Roosevelt Road

Chicago, IL 60608
Phone: (312) 413-4599

Kristine Parkins MSW, LCSW, SAC
Clinicare
Chief Clinical Officer
550 North Dewey Street
P.O. Box 1168
Eau Claire, WI 54702-1168
Phone: (715) 834-6681
Fax: (715) 834-9954
parkins@clinicarecorp.com

Terry Thompson
Director, Volunteers of America Residential Services
22426 St. Francis Blvd
Anoka, MN 55303
Phone: (763) 753-2500
tthompson@voamn.org

Dustin Tibbits
President & Chief Clinical Officer
InnerChange
661 East Technology Avenue, Building B
Orem, UT 84607
Phone: (801) 380-4367
dustinet@innerchange.com

Annette Trunzo, PhD
Director of Organizational Performance
Pressley Ridge
530 Marshall Avenue
Pittsburgh, PA 15214
Phone: (412) 992-5625
ATrunzo@pressleyridge.org

Note

1 Authors and current sources for tools mentioned in this section are provided in the References.

References

Achenbach, T. (2013). *Child Behavior Checklist (CBCL)*. Retrieved November 21, 2013, from www.aseba.org
Bellonci, C., Jordan, P., Massey, O. T., Lieberman, R., Zubritsky, C., & Edwall, G. (2012, September). Reframing mental health practice for children, youth and families: In

search of developmental competencies to improve functioning across life domains [Issue brief]. *Outcomes Roundtable for Children and Families.*

Bettmann, J. E., & Jasperson, R. A. (2009). Adolescents in residential and inpatient treatment: A review of the outcome literature. *Child & Youth Care Forum, 38*(4), 161–183.

Blau, G., Hueberger, J., Caldwell, B., Lieberman, R., & Lim, A. (2012). *The Building Bridges Initiative.* Retrieved October 10, 2013, from www.tapartnership.org/docs/Building%20Bridges%20Initiative%20(Blau%20Caldwell%20Leiberman%20et%20al%20%202012).pdf

Building Bridges Initiative. (2012). *A Building Bridges Initiative tip sheet: Evaluating and improving outcomes for youth who have received residential services.* Retrieved July 22, 2013, from www.buildingbridges4youth.org/sites/default/files/Outcomes%20Tipsheet%20-%20Final.pdf

Brunk, M., Koch, J. R., & McCall, D. (2013). *Youth Services Survey and Youth Services Survey-Family.* Retrieved November 21, 2013, from www.nri-inc.org/projects/SDICC/urs_forms.cfm

Burlingame, G., & Lambert, M. (2013). *Youth Outcome Questionnaire.* Retrieved November 21, 2013, from www.oqmeasures.com/

Center for Health Care Strategies. (2010). *System of care approaches in residential treatment facilities serving children with serious behavioral health needs.* Retrieved August 13, 2013, from www.chcs.org/usr_doc/System_of_Care_Approaches_in_RTFs.pdf

Dalton, J. (2010, October 29). *Modernizing residential care.* Presentation at the Massachusetts Interagency Residential Provider forum. Retrieved October 21, 2013, from www.mass.gov/eohhs/docs/eohhs/chapter257/youth-intermediate-5.pdf

Frensch, K. M., & Cameron, G. (2002). Treatment of choice or a last resort? A review of residential mental health placements for children and youth. *Child & Youth Care Forum, 31*(5), 313–345.

Hair, H. J. (2005). Outcomes for children and adolescents after residential treatment: A review of research from 1993 to 2003. *Journal of Child and Family Studies, 14*(4), 551–575.

Hoagwood, K. (2013, April 8). *TED Talk: Kimberly Hoagwood: The fourth quadrant: Giving it away.* National Council for Behavioral Health Conference, Las Vegas, NV.

Hodges, K. (n.d.). *Child and Adolescent Functional Assessment Scale (CAFAS).* Retrieved November 21, 2013, from www.fasoutcomes.com/Content.aspx?ContentID=12

Leichtman, M., Leichtman, M. L., Barber, C. C., & Neese, D. T. (2001). Effectiveness of intensive short-term residential treatment with severely disturbed adolescents. *American Journal of Orthopsychiatry, 71*(2), 227–235.

Levison-Johnson, J., Kohomban, J., Blau, G., Caldwell B., Dougherty, R., & Warder, R. (2012, Spring). Keep your eyes on the prize: Defining and tracking what is important in residential care. *Teaching-Family Association Newsletter, 38*(1): 1, 5–8.

Liebenberg, L., Ungar, M., & Van de Vijver, F. R. R. (2013). *The Child and Youth Resilience Measure.* Retrieved November 21, 2013 from http://resilienceresearch.org/research-and-evaluation/research-tools/134

Lyons, J. S., Griffin, E., & Fazio, M. (2013). *Child and Adolescent Needs and Strengths (CANS).* Retrieved November 21, 2013 from www.praedfoundation.org/About%20the%20CANS.html#Here

Magellan Health Services. (2011). *Intensive residential treatment facility (RTF) program two-year outcomes report.* Retrieved July 22, 2013, from www.magellanofpa.com/media/168454/pa_intensive_rtf_2-year_report_final_sm.pdf

Martone, W. P. (2010, October 29). *California Residentially-based Services Reform Initiative.* Presented at Massachusetts Interagency Residential Provider Forum. Retrieved July 23, 2013, from www.mass.gov/eohhs/docs/eohhs/chapter257/youth-intermediate-3c.pdf

New Haven Residential Treatment Center. (2013). *Treatment outcome data.* Retrieved October 13, 2013, from www.newhavenrtc.com/treatment-outcomedata.php

Ogles, B. M. (2013). *Ohio Scales.* Retrieved from https://sites.google.com/site/ohioscales/home

Walter, U. M., & Petr, C. G. (2008). Family-centered residential treatment: Knowledge, research, and values converge. *Residential Treatment for Children & Youth,* 25(1), 1–16.

Interviews

Butler, Linda S., Director of Research & Special Projects, Spurwink, Portland, ME. August, 2013.

Graham, Cathy, Executive Director, IARCCA, an Association of Children & Family Services. August 7, 2013.

Hall, John, Clinical Director of Research and Development, Telos Residential Treatment, Orem, UT. July 31, 2013.

Hess, Jacob Z., PhD, Research Director, Utah Youth Village, Salt Lake City, UT. August 5, 2013.

Huefner, Jonathan, PhD, Research Scientist, and Mary B. (Beth) Chmelka, Senior Research Analyst, National Research Institute for Child and Family Studies, Father Flanagan's Boys' Home, Boys Town, NE. July 30, 2013.

Morris, Alan, Associate Director, CARTS Program, University of Illinois at Chicago. July 31, 2013.

Parkins, Kristine, Chief Clinical Officer, Clinicare. July 31 and August 1, 2013.

Thompson, Terry, Director, Volunteers of America Residential Services, Volunteers of America Minnesota, MN. August 6, 2013.

Tibbits, Dustin, President & Chief Clinical Officer, InnerChange, Orem, UT. October 8 and 15, 2013.

Trunzo, Annette, Pressley Ridge. September 26, 2013.

15 Fiscal Strategies

Federal, State, and County Examples of Transformation[1]

Julie Collins, William Mclaughlin, Sherry Peters, and Michael Rauso

Introduction

With the growing interest by states, counties, and local providers to operationalize best practices overall, and specifically Building Bridges Initiative (BBI) principles and best practices in residential transformation efforts, there has been a corresponding interest for information about funding options to facilitate this development.

This chapter provides information about different federal, state, county, and local funding options that are currently used or could be used in transforming residential interventions and a range of best practices as identified in Table 15.1. It also includes methodologies for payment and contracting along with strategies for engaging providers in the transition. These are critical approaches to consider, regardless which funding option(s) might be used. The five examples (at state, county, and local levels) included illustrate how these options, methodologies, and strategies have been used to fund best practices in residential intervention transformation.

Table 15.1 identifies the potential funding options to promote transformation efforts. They are primarily federal/state partnerships paired with the system that has responsibility for decision making and oversight. These options may be helpful either alone or in combination. Funding options can be used for residential interventions, home and community-based programs, or both. Some are more flexible than others and some have specific advantages to consider, such as an enhanced federal match or expanded eligibility for specific situations.

To gain sufficient flexibility, states, counties, and local entities also had to find the right methodology(ies) and strategy(ies) to disperse the funds and work together. Table 15.2 shows the most common methodologies and strategies used by states, counties, and providers. Each has its own benefits and limitations, and, often, more than one is used. For example, multiple funding options are braided, and a case rate is used along with a reinvestment strategy for any savings, as in the Massachusetts example. Usually, the state/county will start small, as a pilot program or using a simple methodology. As the level of sophistication

Table 15.1 Funding options for residential transformation[2]

Funding Resources		Services		BBI Best Practices					
Category	Selected Funding Within Categories of Funding Resources	Residential (24-Hour) With Shorter LOS	Home and Community-Based Interventions	Respite Including 24-Hour Residential	Child & Family Team Wraparound with Fidelity	Parent and Youth Support Partners	Crisis Services—Mobile and Residential	Flexible Funding Supports	Wide Array of Services
Medicaid Authorities and Demonstrations	Rehab Option	x	x		x	x	x		x
	Psych Under 21*	x				x			
	1915(c) waiver and 1915(c) PRTF bridge waiver		x	x	x	x	x	x	x
	1915 (b) waiver	x	x	x	x	x	x	x	x
	1115 waiver	x	x	x	x	x	x	x	x
	Money Follows the Person (MFP)*,**		x	x	x	x	x	x	x
	1915(i)		x	x	x	x	x	x	x
	Section 2703 Health Home**				x	x			
	EPSDT (mandated benefit)		x		x	x	x		x
Child Welfare	Title IV-E	x		x			x		
	Title IV-E Waivers		x	x	x	x	x	x	
	Child Welfare Demonstration Projects		x	x	x	x		x	x

Mental Health	SAMHSA Block Grants	x	x	x	x	x	x	x
	Children's Mental Health Initiative Grant (System of Care)		x	x	x	x	x	x
Substance Abuse	SAMHSA Block Grants	x	x	x	x	x	x	x
Education	Individuals with Disabilities Education Act (IDEA)	x	x	x	x		x	x
Juvenile Justice	Title II B. Formula Grants		x	x	x	x		x
	Justice Assistance Grants		x	x	x	x		x
State General Funds	Legislative or Executive Allocations	x	x	x	x	x	x	x
Private	Foundations, Private Insurance, Others	x	x	x	x	x	x	X

* Institutional Eligibility (sometimes referred to as "Family of One") for Medicaid may be a resource for families with incomes that would not qualify for Medicaid.
** Enhanced Federal Match

Table 15.2 Common funding approaches

Methodology	Benefits	Limitations
A. Realignment of Existing Funds • Blended/pooled—Use funds from different systems/programs put together for specific program/approach. • Braided—Funds from different sources remain in the same pots but are used to support a combined initiative that allows flexibility but are also as integrated as possible. • Flex funding—Allows funds earmarked for one purpose to be used for another, such as concrete supports for families in crisis.	• Increase dollars to fund transformation. • Better use of limited funds. • Better use of current dollars. • When funds are blended, it is much easier for provider; same expectations. • No need to make significant policy changes. • Provides greater flexibly for funder as well as provider around spectrum of services provided. • Easier to use different payment methodologies. • When flex, funding is used to cover services to support the family and youth to remain at home.	• Requires partnering/collaboration. • May require some regulation changes. • If funds braided, provider will be accountable to each funding stream.
B. Payment • Per diem rate—Initially increase, and then provide a lower when LOS extends beyond acceptable limit. • Case rate—Daily, monthly, or yearly. • Can include risk sharing with built-in protections as well as performance requirements.	• Flexibility to increase intensive part of service & decrease LOS. • Great flexibility for provider to invest in creating/providing other services while remaining whole. • Case rates help provider be able to provide the intensive services when they are really needed/maintain children in their home/community. • Service plan can be very individualized. • Case rate—Can use existing funding sources; no need to obtain waivers.	• Limited by what is paid for through the per diem rate. • Develop and implement case rate approach is complicated/significant workload. • Case rates are risky when the payor and providers do not have the level of sophistication needed.
C. Contracting • Performance based—Contract for results; can include incentives or penalties.	• Funder able to contract for results vs. services. • Providers incentivized to get good outcomes. • Can improve use of existing dollars.	• When contracting, focuses only on penalties. • When not enough time is given for providers to be able to change the way they are serving children so that they can reach successful outcomes. • Does not necessarily mean it is less expensive.

Strategies	Benefits	Limitations
A. Reinvestment of savings—Money not spent; can take place at provider level, county/state level.	• Incentivizes providers to make necessary changes.	• When savings don't go back into the community to increase continuum of services.
B. Measure improvement over time—Reward if improvements and penalize if not.	• Ensure gains made are transferable into the home/community. • Hold providers accountable.	• Expense of tracking outcomes over time, data sharing, keeping track of the children and families.
C. Other—Wide variety of approaches (e.g., shift change over time/give period of time for provider(s) to change, use data, develop baseline and provide TA, and collaborate with the providers to create the approach/get buy-in).	• Providers feel supported, respected, that it is achievable, and are given the tools to help them.	• It takes much more time to do it this way but contributes to success.

grows, by both the contracting entity and their provider(s), the use of multiple methodologies and strategies also evolves. The examples included in this chapter illustrate this process.

More recent initiatives have included a number of BBI recommended best practices (several are identified in Table 15.1) in the request for proposals and contracts with providers. Provider-led initiatives have also reflected these and their outcomes have been used to encourage funders to assist in leveraging additional funding options and/or making the contractual, regulatory, or legislative changes needed to more broadly fund them—leading to improved outcomes for children, youth, and families served.

Los Angeles County, California

The Los Angeles County, California (LAC), example incorporates the work of private provider innovators (see EMQ FamiliesFirst below), which the state and county's early efforts built upon; the state's Residentially-Based Services (RBS) reform initiative; and, AB 1453 legislation passed in 2007. AB 1453 authorizes California counties to transform their residential interventions using alternative program and funding models while shifting residential interventions from long-term *placements* to planned, short-term, and individualized *interventions,* with integrated "follow along community-based services" that reconnect youth with their families, schools, and communities. AB 1453 includes principles aligned with BBI and provides the opportunity to explore a new program model and a funding redesign, offering the financial flexibility to support creative, individualized services.

The LAC RBS model draws from its successful, provider-driven, two-year Res/Wrap pilot project, which combined wraparound with residential interventions for shorter length of stay (LOS) and reduced recidivism.

The LAC RBS model focuses on children and youth involved with the Department of Children and Family Services who are currently in or identified for high-level residential interventions. The model is a 22-month arc of care that allocates up to 10 months of enhanced residential interventions and 12 months of wraparound services when the youth returns to the community. While the contracted providers are funded up to 10 months of enhanced residential interventions, they actually strive for a much shorter length of stay. The funding model supports transition from more traditional residential interventions to development of critical services (care coordination via the Child and Family Team [CFT], parent partner involvement, family finding, bridge care,[3] and respite care) within residential interventions to support youth returning to their home and community much sooner.

These changes were possible due to AB 1453, which allowed pilot counties to explore alternate funding streams and methods. More importantly, it allowed the program model to influence the funding model. In addition, there was a strong commitment from the California Department of Social Services (CDSS) to allow flexibility around funding. The Memorandum of Understanding between CDSS and LAC defines the funding model and provides financial opportunities to allow the county the ability to tailor it to fit their needs. LAC's RBS program included flexibility to waive certain fiscal requirements while ensuring cost neutrality.[4]

The case-rate funding methodology used was intended to support contracted providers' development of the required services and capacity to serve children and youth with short-term residential intervention. It also included the additional supports needed for their return home and maintenance in the community.

The funding to support the model is "front-loaded," meaning the contracted RBS provider is paid above the regular residential interventions rate up to 10 months. After 10 months, the monthly rate drops to the "wraparound service rate." Table 15.3 shows the breakdown of the case rate for the specific services.

All the four CA pilot counties' RBS providers must track the following outcomes:

1   *Safety*—In placement and in home-based services.
2   *Permanency*—Shortened timelines to the family being engaged, to permanency for the youth, and for LOS in residential, along with stability in home-based settings.
3   *Well-being*—Family/youth satisfaction with RBS, family connection, culturally and linguistically sensitive family involvement and services, educational improvement, and sociobehavioral improvement.[5]

The initial data collected from 2010–2012 indicate that the pilot achieved some success. The average LOS for the 40 youth exiting the program during that time was well below prior LOS rates. Compared to the average LOS in residential interventions for 2007–2008, where the *total residential services* average equaled 32.4 months, there was a significant decrease in LOS during RBS residential intervention (8.46 months). There were a number of other positive outcomes realized from the LAC RBS, such as an increased number of youth realizing permanency and increased support of family members in their homes and communities.

The original design of the RBS demonstration pilot focused too narrowly on transforming residential interventions and not the total system of care, including family foster care and community-based services. This unfortunately sometimes resulted in the LOS in residential being prolonged because there were not enough foster homes available or willing to take youth coming directly from residential.

Table 15.3 Funding of LAC RBS model[6]

Component of Care	Planned LOS in Months	Cost of Care per Month	Source of Funds	Notes
1. Residential Care				
a. Residential Care and Treatment	≤ 10 mos (9 mos is the planned avg. stay)	$10,194	Title IV-E Maint. & Admin. and State AFDC-FC & Admin.	
b. CFT				
c. Family Finding, Engagement, Placement and Support (FFEPS)				• Tier 1 costs used for planning purposes throughout
d. Flexible Services				• Maximum ITFC rate used for planning purposes
2. Community Care	≤ 12 mos			• Respite included in Wrap
a. Tier 1 Wraparound	—	$4,184	Title IV-E Maint. & Admin.	• Flexible Services are part of the appropriate Comm. Care rate
b. Tier 2 Wraparound	—	$1,250	And	• Crisis Stabilization is included in the Open Doors residential rate
c. ITFC	—	$4,476	State AFDC-FC & Admin.	
d. Respite	≤ 30 days			
e. Bridge Care	—			
f. Flexible Services	—	≤ $4,476		
g. Crisis Stabilization	≤ 7 days			
3. Mental Health Services				
a. Residential Care	≤ 10 mos	$5,000	EPSDT	
b. Community Care	≤ 12 mos	$2,246	EPSDT	

Massachusetts

Massachusetts is a state example in which the Departments of Children and Families (DCF) and Mental Health (DMH) jointly created and manage a system redesign for residential interventions, called Caring Together. Caring Together ultimately resulted from provider advocacy for payment equity and parity, which lead to the promulgation of new state law (Chapter 257) that established new rates for all residential service being procured by DCF and DMH, and bound the new rates in regulation. The rate-setting process gave both agencies the unique opportunity to create new program specifications and standards, adopting the BBI framework as its platform. The process began in 2010. It took 2 years to develop the new specifications and standards, and educate all residential providers on BBI through multiple training opportunities. Full implementation of Caring Together is expected to take place during late 2013 or early 2014.

Under Caring Together, families affiliated with DCF or DMH receive continuity of services and providers throughout the life of the family's involvement, regardless of whether they receive residential interventions or family/community-based services. This is the result of the prior input from children and families receiving traditional congregate care who requested programmatic and systemic changes, such as continuity and consistency in assigned staff. The departments responded by reviewing case practice models and minimizing the number of staff assignments during the life of a family's involvement. They also embraced the BBI's key values and emphasized the creation of new youth-graduate and family roles, and strong partnerships between families, youth, community and residential service providers, advocates, and policy makers and embedded them in the Caring Together program design.

Caring Together asserts that policy and practice changes integrating residential and family-driven, youth-guided, and trauma-informed community services, while emphasizing quality management, a new governance structure, and flexible funding will result in better outcomes for children, youth, and families.

All providers are required to develop and maintain a plan and process for quality management and improvement utilizing mechanisms to gather and evaluate data regarding the quality and effectiveness of programmatic and administrative operations of its services.

The new governance structure relies on an interagency board of senior executives of the purchasing agencies as well as family and youth-graduate representatives with lived experience. This holds the system accountable to the top executives and the youth and families it serves, provides assurance for sustainability through changes in administration, and provides a structure to support further system integration across other child and family serving agencies reimbursed by Medicaid.

Caring Together is funded with Medicaid and federal IV-E waiver dollars, and uses a rate-setting approach designed to incentivize key practices and outcomes. The waiver allows the spending of savings derived from reductions in the use of residential intervention for community-based services. It provides immediate financing flexibility and the expansion of community-based services.

Massachusetts is committed to a rate-setting approach that enhances outcomes by providing greater flexibility to providers. It draws on the lessons learned from previous reform efforts. In a prior initiative, during the first 18 months there was a shadow rate used followed by a reconciliation process. This effectively limited the potential losses the government or agencies could experience while at the same time providing all parties with experience associated with a case rate. It also fostered an environment of collaborative problem solving and group learning.

Under Caring Together, three rates have been developed for implementation: an in-care rate, a rate for community-based services, and an overlap rate. These rates were carefully developed with providers using actual costs while considering staffing requirements and intensity. The intent is to use cost-based rates for the initial phase. Over time, as experience builds, incentives will be added to the rates that will reward achievement of outcomes.

Desired outcomes include reduced recidivism, increased tenure in the community, improved child well-being, increased high school graduation rates, and improved parental capacity. These have not yet been fully defined in operational and measureable terms. This will be done collaboratively with providers and will be used as the basis for the next phase of rate setting, which will build upon a public–private stakeholder partnership.

Historically, Massachusetts relied heavily on residential interventions, and there was little reason to change, as doing so created risk. Over the past 6 or 7 years, there has been a 40% reduction in the use of residential interventions resulting from a system-wide emphasis on family engagement, family empowerment, and integration of trauma-informed services. These changes also better aligned risks with policy and have yielded a surplus of residential resources that helped set the stage for this next transformation.

Westchester County, New York

Westchester County, New York (WC NY), is a county example that illustrates the value of what can be accomplished through collaborative efforts. A clear focus on transformation has been maintained for over 20 years and multiple changes in administrations. New reforms were built directly on the foundation of earlier initiatives. WC NY was motivated by the desire to serve youth in family and family-like settings within the community, to develop a rich community-based service network, and to reduce reliance on residential interventions. WC NY has strategically employed initiatives to advance the vision and has achieved remarkable changes in the service system and outcomes.

In 1993, WC was chosen as a Phase I Coordinated Children's Services Initiative (CCSI) by NY State. CCSI is a multi-agency effort promoting community-based alternatives supporting the care of children in family and family-like settings for children with emotional, social, or behavioral disabilities. CCSI was planned by state administrators and local providers. CCSI supports CASSP values and practices, creating structures promoting coordination and collaboration of planning efforts. CCSI has a three-tiered structure that emphasizes partnership at each level. Tier I, the community level, develops individual strength-based wraparound plans for children at risk of placement and their families. Tier II, the county level interagency leadership team, consists of local government, service-system partners, community members, and family representatives. It promotes improved coordination, actively supports Tier I teams, and resolves barriers. Tier III is a state-level team of agency, family, and youth representatives that identify and address systems-level solutions identified by Tier II teams from across the state. Additionally, CCSI strengthened partnerships between major child-serving systems, developed a parent and youth movement, enhanced coordination through best practice models, and built a foundation for future reforms.

In 1999, WC received a Systems of Care (SOC) grant for children with complex needs that built upon CCSI and yielded a community-based system of care. It further strengthened collaboration and was mirrored throughout the entire service system, from frontline workers and families to department heads and agency executives.

In 2008, WC Tier II formally endorsed BBI. Led by the child welfare agency and representatives of county child-serving system leadership, the committee reconsidered WC's use of residential interventions. The WC Tier II established a formal blueprint for reducing the use of residential interventions, expanding community capacity for supporting and strengthening families, engaging residential providers as full partners, and reducing racial disparities. Previously, residential providers participated in CCSI and SOC efforts, but not as full partners.

The resulting changes include modifying contract language to incorporate CCSI and SOC language; developing residential planning subcommittees to plan wraparound services and targeted interventions for all children referred for residential interventions; utilizing a data-driven approach for decision making, program evaluation, and analysis; and developing an aftercare program for children discharged from care. Other reforms include redesigning residential programming to promote family engagement, offering workforce development and training for children and families, and creating and enhancing trauma-informed practices.

WC's fiscal strategies include reinvestment of savings and braiding of various funds. The cross-systems planning structure evolved into a county cabinet that continuously evaluates funding. It maximizes existing resources using traditional funding streams, considers changes in funding, and identifies and pursues time-limited grants. The planning group explores new funding opportunities and reinvests many of the savings into community-based, lower level of care resources.

The funding includes child welfare Title IVE funds, Preventive Services, NY State Office for Children and Services Community Optional Preventive, Bridges to Health Waiver, and tax levy funds. The mental health funds include New York State Office of Mental Health resources, such as intensive case management, Home and Community-Based Waiver, Crisis Prevention Funding, and block grant funding. WC has braided funding to support critical services such as the cross-systems unit, respite programs for children with serious emotional, social, and behavioral challenges, early childhood crisis response program, and family and peer youth support groups.

Better outcomes for families, children, and youth are achieved at higher rates and dramatic changes occurred in the service system. Residential interventions decreased while lower level of care and aftercare services provided in closer proximity to the youth's home and community grew. From 2009 to 2012, the total in-care population decreased by 25% and residential interventions dropped by 43%. The annual rate of discharges from care exceeded the rate of admissions at a yearly average of 38.5%. There was a 34% decrease in Persons in Need of Supervision and Juvenile Delinquent placements/admissions from 2008 to 2012. Investments in community-based services grew significantly and demonstrated positive results. WC also noted a 38% reduction in recidivism rates (a child returning to out-of-home placement within 1 year of discharge) from 2004 to 2012.

A consistent vision, strong leadership, and an inclusive approach where the value of partnership and collaboration is clear and demonstrated at every level of interaction are necessary for success. WC NY changes were built on a commitment to collaboration, and it remains the strongest influence in sustaining positive changes.

EMQ FamiliesFirst (California) and The Children's Village (New York)

EMQ FamiliesFirst (EMQ FF) and the Children's Village are both good examples of private providers who recognized the need to change not only their residential interventions but also their organizations. Both agencies serve communities with prior Substance Abuse and Mental Health Services Administration (SAMHSA) SOC grants. While residential interventions were not an included service in early grant requirements, these communities embraced principles consistent with BBI. Although Chapter XII details the transformation process for both agencies, this chapter highlights the creative ways both have financed incorporation of best practices consistent with BBI best practices.

EMQ FF, with its board's support, closed 100 of its residential intervention beds, while it worked with Santa Clara County to redirect the resulting saved $10 million into community-based wraparound services. The agency ran at a deficit for 4 years, while it worked with the county to secure the state's share of cost for the new wraparound services. This was accomplished through passage of new legislation, AB 2297. The resulting 5-year demonstration project allowed the 40% state share of funding for children placed in or at risk of placement in high-level group homes to be served through wraparound. Simultaneously, EMQ FF initiated discussions with Santa Clara County social services and mental health agencies to make Title XIX mental health funding available through a "certification of match," in which county-group home dollars funding wraparound were utilized as match for Federal Title XIX dollars.[7] Several years later, California implemented Early Periodic Screening, Diagnosis and Treatment (EPSDT) in which the state paid the required match for federal Title XIX dollars, and the certification of match was no longer necessary. There were five subsequent legislative changes that supported making wraparound permanent in the California Welfare and Institution Code.

The funding structure today is a braided combination of child welfare Title IV-E dollars that would have otherwise covered placement in high-level residential interventions and MediCal-EPSDT. The success of this transformation has allowed EMQ FF to incorporate wraparound/BBI best practices (e.g., EMQ FF has hired 40 parent partners and 5 youth partners) and several evidence-based practices throughout the agency's programming, both residential and community-based. All agency programs utilize the Child and Adolescent Needs and Strength (CANS) and a set of questions regarding living situation, juvenile justice involvement, and educational attainment to assess outcomes over time. Furthermore, wraparound programs utilize the Wraparound Fidelity Index 4 (WFI) to assess fidelity to wraparound implementation stages and principles. The successes and learning from their early transformative work and best practices informed the early implementation of the changes.

Children's Village (CV), on the other hand, went outside of its payment funding structure to obtain private funding of costs for targeted new initiatives. They obtained $100,000 in foundation dollars that covered start-up costs for two parent advocates and a youth development program, and expansion over a 2-year period. The program has become self-sufficient through rate-based funding from New York City Administration for Children Services and private dollars. It expanded the number of parent advocates, added parent council leaders, created a youth leadership council and funds youth participation. As part of CV's efforts to ensure family involvement in decision making and shorten the amount of time a youth might be placed outside of the home, CV obtained private funds to purchase a mobile van. The Family Team Conferencing Van travels to families/neighborhoods and provides a convenient location for families to become involved in team meetings. Recent data show a 90% level of family participation in these.

CV incorporates all of the best practices listed in Table 15.1 It uses private dollars to address flexible funding for supports to family/youth in the community. These private dollars fund an aftercare program (a minimum of 1 year of support and services) for youth that leave residential, called WAY Home. This evidence-informed promising practice program developed by CV more than 30 years ago has shortened the LOS for youth and dramatically improved their outcomes. The program began with private funding, and in the last 2 years has received 50% in public financing and costs $3,500.00 per child/youth. The initial 8 to 9 months are more intensive, with services reduced over time. The outcomes are tracked and led to the addition of Multi-Systemic Therapy (MST) interventions for the 15% considered "high-risk" that were using about 80% of the resources. With the support of private funding, the addition of MST has yielded significant positive outcomes for the youth successfully remaining in the home (80% vs. 20% of the comparison group) and in school (76% vs. 43% of the comparison group). CV has continued to obtain private funds to expand use of EBPs including MST-PSB (problematic sexual behavior) to children in the adjudicated sexual offender programs. In time, CV acquired MST-SA (substance abuse), and then invested in Positive Behavioral Interventions and Support and Trauma System Therapy for their residential interventions. Most recently, private funding has helped CV acquire training in Functional Family Therapy and Multidimensional Treatment Foster Care.

CV continues to look for additional funding to continue the transformation of residential interventions and is currently working on obtaining a Social Impact Bond, with the financing coming from Goldman Sachs. The effort is being facilitated by the New York City Mayor's Office. A Social Impact Bond is a contract with the public sector in which it commits to pay for improved social outcomes.[8] This contract is used to raise investment from socially motivated investors to pay for a range of interventions to improve social outcomes. The financial returns investors receive are dependent on the degree to which outcomes improve. CV will be implementing MST-FIT (Family Integrated Transitions), which is an adaptation of MST specifically designed for aftercare and their WAY Home program.

Psychiatric Residential Treatment Facilities

The Community Alternatives to Psychiatric Residential Treatment Facilities (PRTF) Demonstration Grant Program exemplifies a federally funded effort to provide information on the potential effectiveness of home and community-based alternatives to residential interventions. The states and providers used many of the same principles and best practices as BBI. Section 6063 of the Deficit Reduction Act of 2005 authorized up to $218 million to develop a 5-year demonstration program providing home and community-based services to children and youth as alternatives to PRTF's in up to 10 states using 1915(c) waiver authority. Nine states implemented these projects designed to test the cost effectiveness of providing services in a home or community-based setting rather than in a PRTF, and to test whether the services improve or maintain the child's and youth's functioning.

The demonstration has successfully enabled enrolled children and youth to either maintain or improve their functioning at less than a third of the cost of serving them in a PRTF. The demonstration served children and youth who were either *diverted* from being served in a PRTF altogether or were *transitioned* from a PRTF into the community, often earlier than would have been possible without the waiver.

Although the demonstration ended on September 30, 2012, seven states (Montana, Mississippi, Indiana, Virginia, South Carolina, Maryland, Georgia) all approved through 1915(c) waiver authority to continue to serve those enrolled on the last day of the demonstration using a bridge 1915(c) waiver. No new enrollees are permitted beyond the demonstration waiver period unless federal legislation is enacted to allow PRTF to be considered one of the institutions of comparison for calculating the cost neutrality required in a 1915(c) waiver. In addition, Montana, Indiana, Georgia, Maryland, and South Carolina will use 1915(i) state plan amendments for diverting new children and youth (those who would have been eligible for the waiver) from PRTFs, Money Follows the Person (MFP) Demonstration grants to transition children and youth out of PRTFs or psychiatric hospitals after 90 days, or a combination of both. Kansas has transitioned children and youth in the program into its Home and Community-Based Services (HCBS) Serious Emotional Disturbance (SED) 1915(c) waiver (using the hospital as the institution of comparison rather than the PRTF). Mississippi has added intensive outpatient services that include the wraparound practice model to their Medicaid State Plan, and Alaska has been able to serve the individuals with a combination of Medicaid State Plan services and other state funding to serve individuals with a fetal alcohol spectrum disorder (FASD), or a suspected FASD. Indiana was able to develop similar services as those offered in the demonstration for children and youth in the child welfare system who may not have been eligible for the waiver or who are not eligible for Medicaid through the state's IV-E waiver.

All of these states have demonstrated a commitment to child, youth, and family voice and choice in their approach to serving those covered by the waiver. Most had family partners at both the policy level (state and local) and in their practice model at the child, youth, and family level. All nine embraced the wraparound philosophy; most utilized a SOC framework that mirrored BBI values and principles; and Maryland, Georgia, Mississippi, and Montana were actively engaged in training and coaching during the demonstration years to ensure a wraparound practice model implemented with fidelity. Indiana, Virginia, and South Carolina requested more training and coaching in the wraparound practice model following the last year of the demonstration to either develop or improve the fidelity. Maryland and Georgia developed Care Management Entities to support the wraparound practice model and served not only Medicaid-eligible children and youth but also children and youth funded through other child- and youth-serving systems.

Each state measured the child, youth, and family outcomes using one of three instruments: the CANS, the Child and Family Assessment Scale, or the Child Behavior Checklist. All states discovered that most of the children and youth did well with the benefit package offered through the waiver. While each state developed a benefit package independently, common threads wove through most. The services included intensive care coordination (often called "wraparound facilitation"), respite (both in-home and residential), intensive in-home services (therapy as well as supportive services such as mentoring), parent and youth support partners, crisis response services (mobile and residential), nonmedical transportation, and nontraditional therapies, such as equine, art, music, movement, and horticulture. In Alaska, since the population being served was composed of children and youth who not only met the PRTF level of care but also had a suspected FASD, the focus was primarily on mentoring with an emphasis on provider training. This was to ensure providers increased their awareness of not only the impact of FASD but also on the strategies that are most helpful to the children and youth who are being served.

As each of the nine states moved through the process of implementation over 5 years, many successes were realized, as well as some challenges that needed to be addressed. Many successes were related not only to the wraparound practice model, intensive care coordination, and a wide array of intensive services, but also to the strong partnerships between all the child-serving agencies at the state level along with the partnerships between the state agencies and the local providers, or even between providers who were serving the children, youth, and families.

Some of the challenges experienced by many of the states were difficulty with recruitment and retention of providers; limited training opportunities for EBPs and approaches for children and youth with co-occurring mental health and developmental disabilities or substance use disorders; consistency across providers, especially with understanding the importance of fidelity to the wraparound process (if using wrap facilitation); difficulty with identifying and addressing cultural and linguistic challenges; and difficulty with involving children, youth, and families at all levels.

One of the major lessons learned over the 5 years was that most of the children and youth who met the criteria to be served in a PRTF, regardless of the diagnosis, had experienced multiple traumatic experiences that had not necessarily been identified or addressed, even if identified. All the states not only recognized the importance of addressing the needs of children and youth affected by trauma through developing policies and practices for a trauma-informed system of care so as not to retraumatize the children and youth, but they also recognized the importance of training clinicians in residential and community-based services in specific EBPs.

Summary of Recommendations and Lessons Learned

While the previous examples provide good information for replication or new transformational ideas, there are a number of key recommendations that emerge from the lessons learned that the authors would like to put forth. Although there might be jurisdiction, specific considerations the recommendations listed here are relevant across all jurisdictions.

Address funding complexity—Consider adaptations or modifications to current legislation to ensure the model works. It is important to be creative using nontraditional funding sources such as foundation grants, waivers, or private funding, or the creation of new law(s) in order to finance the transformation. These can take significant time to develop but will provide the flexibility needed to make the shift. The funding structure also should be realistic and support the start-up costs and the significant investment required for training/coaching of staff.

Share financial risk—Government entities and providers must be willing to share financial risk to make the significant shift being required: for providers, one-time funding presents a risk for staffing, infrastructure, and ongoing fiscal

Contact Information for Examples:

Los Angeles County, CA	Dr. Michael J. Rauso Department of Children and Family Services	(213) 763-1528	rausom@dcfs.lacounty.gov
Massachusetts	Robert Wentworth Department of Children and Families	(617) 748-2379	robert.wentworth@state.ma us
	Janice Lebel Department of Mental Health	(617) 626-8085	Janice.lebel@state.ma us
Westchester County, NY	Michael Orth Department of Community Mental Health	(914) 995-5225	mmo6@westchestergov.com
	Kevin McGuire Department of Social Services	(914) 995-5501	kmm9@westchestergov.com
EMQ FamiliesFirst	Darryl Evora	(408) 364-4027	devora@emqff.org
Children's Village	Jeremy Kohomban	(212) 932-2200 – Ext 1201	jkohomban@childrensvillage.org
PRTF	Sherry Peters National Technical Assistance Center for Children's Mental Health, Georgetown University	(202) 687-7157	slp45@georgetown.edu

viability; for government entities, the time to contract, amend, implement, and sustain is very time-consuming and carries fiscal risk. A partnership between the public and private sector is critical. Acknowledgement of the risks of one-time funding, the need to work closely together to ensure immediate needs and outcomes are being met, and a plan for a long-term solutions are also critical.

Collaboration is essential—Transformation requires much give and take by the government entity and providers and requires both partners to work together. Although the previous jurisdictions were strong examples of collaboration and partnership, they still experienced struggles, such as implementation, fidelity, and sustainability of the programs they were creating. Ongoing collaboration and discussion in an open, trusting, and data-informed environment focused on learning is essential. Early and ongoing collaboration and partnership among local, state, and federal entities is essential.

Notes

1   Special acknowledgement: Special thanks go to the individuals and/or teams who gave so generously of their time to ensure we had the information needed.
2   For more details about the funding options go to www.medicaid.gov/Federal-Pol icy-Guidance/Downloads/CIB-05-07-2013.pdf, www.acf.hhs.gov/programs/cb/news/ title-iv-e-waiver-demonstration-projects, www.samhsa.gov/grants/blockgrant/, http:// idea.ed.gov/, www.ojjdp.gov/grants/solicitations/FY2013/TitleII.pdf, www.bja.gov/ ProgramDetails.aspx?Program_ID=59
3   Bridge care is a previously planned lower level of care (most likely a foster home within the demonstration provider's service umbrella) concurrently prepared to receive a youth from RBS should the family not be ready to safely reunify.
4   For more information, see www.RBSreform.org
5   As measured by the Child and Adolescent Needs and Strengths (CANS) tool.
6   This is modified from the CDSS/Los Angeles County Department of Children and Family Services Memorandum of Understanding. For further information, go to www.childsworld.ca.gov/res/pdf/LA_RBS_MOU_10-6020.pdf
7   For more information, see www.cms.hhs.gov/home/medicaid.asp
8   For further information, go to www.rockefellerfoundation.org/uploads/files/655fab01- 83b9-49eb-b856-a1f61bc9e6ca-small.pdf.

Resources

Medicaid financing for family and youth peer support: A scan of state programs. (2012, May). Hamilton, NJ: Center for Health Care Strategies.
Stroul, B. A., Pires, S. A., Armstrong, M. I., McCarthy, J., Pizzigati, K., & Wood, G. M., (2008). *Effective financing strategies for systems of care: Examples from the field—A resource compendium for developing a comprehensive financing plan* (RTC study 3: Financing structures and strategies to support effective systems of care, FMHI pub. # 235–02). Tampa, FL: University of South Florida, Louis de la Parte Florida Mental Health Institute (FMHI), Research and Training Center for Children's Mental Health.
Stroul, B. A., & Friedman, R. M. (2011). *Effective strategies for expanding the system of care approach. A report on the study of strategies for expanding systems of care.* Atlanta, GA: ICF Macro.

16 International Approaches to Residential Interventions

John S. Lyons and Thahn Ly

Providing services for children and adolescents (hereafter referred to as "youth") in residential settings is a practice that extends around the world. Most countries have some type of strategy that combines living arrangements with active interventions in an effort to help vulnerable or high-need youth. In many ways, there are more similarities internationally than differences. Despite the commonality of residential interventions, there are also considerable variations in how these types of intervention strategies are used in an overall approach to supporting children, adolescents, and families. Sometimes these variations are related to historical considerations, sometimes to poverty, sometimes to healthcare financing, and sometimes to varying cultural beliefs about raising children and adolescents. Given these variations, there are experiences and insights elsewhere around the globe that might inform the evolution of residential interventions in the United States. It is in this spirit that we approach an effort to develop a general understanding of international strategies in residential interventions for youth. We do not call these strategies *innovations* because this term refers to "new ideas" and therefore must always be culture bound. An innovation in one context is not necessarily an innovation in another.

An International Perspective on Residential Interventions

As we begin, we should start with a few disclaimers. First, the world is a very large place, with a lot of activity. Some of that activity gets communicated globally and some of it does not. We could only include practices that we could discover. We used multiple strategies to identify current practices. We reviewed existing clinical and scientific literature; we did a wide Internet search for so-called gray literature from other counties. And, we solicited input from identified experts in different countries who might be more familiar with local or national approaches. Second, we restricted our review to literature written in English. While English is often considered the international language of science, there is assuredly important information published in other languages.

Of course, our approach has an enormous likelihood of missing some important things. We give our sincerest apologies to the creators and purveyors of creative strategies around the world that we failed to mention. If you believe we have missed something important, we ask that you contact us so we can share the information more broadly in the future. We see this effort as the beginning of an integrated international understanding rather than as a full expression of such understanding.

There are a number of different ways to organize current practices. For our purposes, we have chosen to discuss current practices in residential interventions around the world by continent. We recognize that continents are large, and this approach creates some arbitrary distinctions; however, the world is large, and we have to have some organizing principles.

Africa and the Middle East

For most of Africa and the Middle East, we did not find published work in English regarding residential interventions. We did find that many of these states have refugee camps and programs where large numbers of youth live in one place. We also found that the level of need in many of these settings is quite basic and not specifically focused on addressing the specialized needs of youth with behavioral and/or emotional challenges.

For published works in English, what we did find came from Israel, and it turns out that the traditions of kibbutzim are quite consistent with congregate-care approaches. In some ways, we might argue, regarding the current practices in residential interventions in Israel, that this system has not strayed as far from the theoretical underpinnings of the originators of the approach. For example, residential interventions in Israel remain far more consistent with psychoanalytic traditions than its American counterparts (e.g., Dvir, Weiner, & Kupermintz, 2012). That being said, the family-oriented movement has come to Israel as well (Elizur, 2012; Grupper & Mero-Jaffe, 2008). Community residential care and day residential care represent interesting practices and are consistent with some of the evolving practices in the United States, such as focusing on the need to create a smooth transition between residential and community-based interventions (Elizur, 2012). Dvir and colleagues emphasized that for the small percentage of youth in residential care with absolutely no family, efforts should be made to find a "lifelong trustee" to establish a secure, long-term relationship with the child as that is a clear indicator of adult success.

Israeli residential providers emphasize the importance of academic improvement as a key outcome of residential interventions (Attar-Schwartz, 2009). Perhaps in this model residential is best conceptualized as a boarding school for youth with complex needs that interfere with the education—the priority remains successful education. Treatment and support are used to potentiate academic success rather than being seen as separate or having the reverse relationship.

There has also been some interesting work on the nature of the roles of childcare workers who work in residential settings. Concepts of secondary trauma and compassion fatigue are well described (Dvir et al., 2012; Zerach, 2013), and strategies to assist staff are encouraged. In addition, residential interventions in Israel are based on the tradition of the *madrich*, which is the term for a group leader in congregate who serves multiple roles, including a mentoring role (Gottesman, 1993). This role is nonprofessional and may require more of a personal commitment and interpersonal skills than specific technical training. There may be some parallels in the United States with the use of mentors and the development of natural supports.

In South Africa, Oprah Winfrey has funded the development of a residential school for girls. Although this school was originally designed to support the educational achievement and attainment of gifted young women, it became clear that the level of traumatic stress in this population was sufficiently high to require a trauma-informed approach to potentiate the successful education of these girls, who often come from difficult circumstances. The school has worked with Bruce Perry, MD, and the Child Trauma Institute to develop trauma-informed care throughout this residential school as a defining characteristic. Creating a truly trauma-informed residential environment is an important practice evolution (see Chapter 7) from which many others can learn. This type of environment is quite different from those using token economies or similar environments based on behavior management.

Asia, Australia, and New Zealand

In some ways, Australia and New Zealand fit geographically with their Asian neighbors; however, in other ways, there are significant cultural differences that impact the delivery of residential interventions. As former colonies and current members of the British Commonwealth, both Australia and New Zealand borrow a great deal from England, and to a lesser extent Europe, the United States, and Canada. Asia is an enormous and diverse region. In Australia and New Zealand, residential interventions have been struggling with the challenges of family integration, cultural sensitivity, service coordination and collaboration, and infusing effective practices into residential settings in a fashion comparable to North America (Bauer & Nay, 2011; Bell, 2006; Churven & Cintio, 1983; Hunt, 2010; McNamara, 2010).

McLean, Price-Robertson, and Robinson (2011) wrote an important report on the evolution of residential treatment in Australia that was away from a housing strategy for "hard cases" focused on community safety and into a treatment strategy focused on identifying and addressing complex needs, such as trauma and severe mental illness.

Of course, no discussion about adolescent mental health work in Australia would be complete without mention of the work of Patrick McGorry, who was named Australian of the Year in 2010 (cf. McGorry, 2011). His pioneering work with early onset psychosis is an important innovation that should inform residential-based programs facing these challenges (McGorry, Nelson, & Goldstone, 2012). The relevance to residential interventions has to do with his work to improve treatment of early onset psychosis and help smooth the transitions of young adults from the child-serving system to the adult mental health system; sometimes this effort starts during initial episodes of residential care.

Unfortunately, for the purposes of this chapter, large parts of Asia do not communicate in English, so it is likely that interesting residential approaches are occurring in places such as Japan, South Korea, or China but cannot be represented here. Singapore is an exception and provides a bit of a window into Eastern Asian culture. In Singapore, which is multiethnic but majority Chinese, taking another family's child into your home is not really a widely accepted cultural practice. Families open their homes to other family members who have experienced challenging times, but nonfamily children living in a home is far less common. As such, it is very difficult to recruit foster parents. For this reason, residential programs are often designed for youth who are otherwise doing quite well—more like what we would describe as the traditional orphanage model in the United States.

Canada

As a close neighbor of the United States, Canada shares much in common with the U.S. in terms of its basic approaches to residential interventions. However, understanding residential interventions in Canada requires appreciation of a cultural and historical consideration—the impact of residential schools on Aboriginal peoples (cf. Miller, 1996). In the 1950s and 1960s, it was a national policy to force children of First Nations, Inuit, and Métis heritage to acculturate to mainstream Canadian culture (essentially Western European culture in the New World). For many children and youth this was accomplished by literally rounding them up (called the 60's scoop among Aboriginal peoples) and placing them in residential schools. This horribly misguided effort had catastrophic consequences for an entire generation of aboriginal families that still resonates in the culture today. The secondary effect of this policy was to severely damage the reputation of legitimate approaches to residential interventions, particularly with disadvantaged children and youth. It should be noted that a similar history has impact on the understanding of residential care in Australia.

Damaging history aside, there are a number of residential centers operating in Canada and new ones continue to open. The geography of the country (like Australia and rural parts of the United States; Anderson, & Estle, 2001) can make community-based interventions challenging for very high-need youth, so the efficiency of residentially based interventions are a powerful draw. Ranch Erlo in Saskatchewan has a program where families can live for a period of time on the campus of the residential center. This allows for a greater integration of family work with the treatment of the child given the limitations of geography on maintaining family connections.

Newfoundland/Labrador funded a comprehensive review of residential treatment (Lyons, Bornstein, Navarro, Rowe, & Vasiliadis, 2010) which resulted in the design and implementation of that province's first residential programs. This design incorporates current thinking about culturally effective practices, with efforts made to provide culturally specific treatment to First Nations, Métis, and Inuit youth while in residence and to support ongoing connections to these youths' culture.

An interesting practice in Canada has been the successful embedding of research measurement strategies into ongoing residential interventions. Several groups have successfully established ongoing data collection that informs an understanding of both clinical and systems outcomes for youth served. Because of these successful efforts, there are several research teams with large, real world datasets that can provide significant practice-based evidence about the outcomes and impact of residential interventions for youth with varying challenges (e.g., Preyde, Adams, Cameron, & Frensch, 2009; Preyde, Frensch, Cameron, Hazineh, & Riosa, 2010).

Europe and Russia

In Denmark, Egelund and Jaakobsen (2011) reported on a strategy to individualize services within residential programs. The authors aptly describe the challenge of residential treatment models that standardize the milieu and the treatment so that there is little room to adjust the interventions to match the child or youth (with the exception of different psychotropic medications). Their approach to individualization represents a strategy for managing the program tension of "uniform individuality," that is, running a program model efficiently while personalizing care (Lyons, 2004). It begins with a thorough understanding of the youth followed by the ability to adjust the intervention based on this understanding.

In England, Arcelus, Bellerby, and Vostanis (1999) reported on a direct access model for mental health treatment for youth in residential and foster care programs. Youth are able to directly access community mental health care, creating an opportunity for a more continuity of mental health treatment as compared to a system that bundles the treatment within the residential stay. As such, this approach improves ongoing access to mental health care for a population at high risk for mental health challenges. Such a model is a bit different than providing care in the treatment facility; rather, facilitating access to care by mental health specialists who are better positioned to continue to provide supports and services regardless of the child's living situation (provided geographic accessibility). Golding (2010) has reported on strategies to create specialty mental health care that is equipped to address complex needs of the most challenging children and youth (including trauma). This work represents an important contribution to facilitating improved continuity of care in high-risk populations. The approach is congruent with efforts in the United States to incorporate evidence-based treatments into residential interventions and linking them to treatment in community settings while the child is still living in the residential program (Levison-Johnson & Kohomban, this volume) so that the most effective interventions are used during the stay.

In Scotland, the government has recently expanded secure care for youth offenders as one of a series of efforts to address crime and delinquency. This represents a shift from the traditional Scottish approach of locating care within existing community structures, such as school (Smith & Milligan, 2004). This expansion, of course, is controversial; however, it has stimulated efforts to determine effective practices within these settings, which not surprisingly emphasize the importance of healthy relationships (Batchelor & McNeill, 2004).

In the Netherlands, in one of the longest term follow-along studies of residential interventions, Scholte and Van der Ploeg (2000) reported that the 2-year outcomes of youth who completed residential treatment were comparable to those of the same age youth in the general population over the same period of time, which is notable given the high level of need at the initiation of services. Unfortunately, only 42% of youth completed treatment, which reduces the ability to generalize results. However, this study does provide some indication that, for some youth and families, residential may support positive outcomes.

In Spain, residential programming is organized somewhat differently when compared to the United States. First, residential centers are primarily alternative living arrangements for youth without anyone to care for them. Second, the majority of residential programs would be comparable to group homes in that they are located in small houses or apartment building and house only about 6 to 10 youth. It is less common for large facilities (80 or more) to exist, although several do (Bravo & Del Valle, 2009). In a study of the mental health needs of children in these settings, Sainero, Bravo, & del Valle (2013) reported that 26% of children had received or were receiving any mental health care, even though about 44% of children had a documented level of symptoms (using the Child Behavioral Checklist [CBCL]) that would suggest a potential benefit from mental health treatment.

South America

It was difficult to identify and describe residential interventions on the continent given the language constraint of the present chapter to English, since the entire continent speaks either Spanish or Portuguese. That said, it is clear from the existing literature that in South America many of the same considerations of integrating residential interventions into community treatment are a priority (Vidal, Bandeira, & Gontijo, 2008). As reported elsewhere in the world, success in the community requires both resources and supports, as well as integration with more intensive residential interventions.

Perhaps in counterpoint, the treatment of young children in residential centers appears to be somewhat more common in some areas of South America than in the United States (Rosa, Santos, Melo, & Souza, 2010). However, similar to the recent efforts in the United States, there is a focus on involvement of family and caregivers from the community even when a child is placed in an institution.

Summary

While the present chapter by no means represents an exhaustive tour of all the important work around the world, this review of residential interventions from an international perspective demonstrates that despite the vast differences across geographies and cultures there are many similar challenges for designing and implementing effective strategies to serve children and adolescents with both housing and treatment needs, and their families. In many countries outside of North America, residential programming for youth continues to be part of the fabric of the child-serving system. Further, it is common outside of the United States for residential episodes to extend for longer durations than are currently supported in the United States.

Despite these differences, there appears to be close to universal agreement on the following:

- Family and relationship ties are important for children even if they are not living with the family.
- Matching effective interventions to meet the individual needs of children and youth is a priority challenge in organized settings.
- Trauma-informed approaches are indicated in places where very high-need children and youth reside.
- Linking episodes of residential care to community-based care to create more seamless approaches to working with youth and their families is important for maximum effectiveness.

It is also clear from the international efforts that there are many intelligent and committed people around the world seeking to improve the lives of youth and families. Developing strategies to organize these amazing human resources in a fashion that builds on each other's work would be a significant contribution to the overall well-being of our children and families wherever they might live.

References

Anderson, R. L., & Estle, G. (2001). Predicting level of mental health care among children served in a delivery system in a rural state. *Journal of Rural Health, 17*(3), 259–265.

Arcelus, J., Bellerby, T., & Vostanis, P. (1999). A mental-health service for young people in the care of the local authority. *Clinical Child Psychology and Psychiatry, 4*(2), 233–245.

Attar-Schwartz, S. (2009). School functioning of children in residential care: The contributions of multilevel correlates. *Child Abuse & Neglect, 33*(7), 429–440.

Batchelor, S., & McNeill, F. (2004). The young person-worker relationship. In T. Bateman & J. Pitts (Eds.), *The Russel House companion to youth justice* (pp.). London, England: Russell House.

Bauer, M., & Nay, R. (2011). Improving family–staff relationships in assisted living facilities: The views of family. *Journal of Advanced Nursing, 67*(6), 1232–1241.

Bell, E. (2006). Self, meaning, and culture in service design: Using a hermeneutic technique to design a residential service for adolescents with drug issues. *International Journal of Drug Policy, 17*(5), 425–435.

Bravo, A., & Del Valle, J. (2009). Crisis and review of residential care: Its role in child protection. *Papeles del Psicologo, 30,* 42–52.

Brodaty, H., Fleming, R., Low, L. F., Casey, A. N., Spitzer, P., Bell, J. P., … Goodenough, B. (2012). *Study protocol for a randomized controlled trial of humor therapy in residential care: The Sydney Multisite Intervention of LaughterBosses and ElderClowns (SMILE).*

Churven, P., & Cintio, B. (1983). An application of strategic family therapy to a residential child and family psychiatry service: Redbank House. *Australian and New Zealand Journal of Psychiatry, 17*(2), 191–195.

Dvir, O., Weiner, A., & Kupermintz, H. (2012). Children in residential group care with no family ties: Facing existential aloneness. *Residential Treatment for Children & Youth, 29*(4), 282–304.

Elizur, Y. (2012). Development and dissemination of collaborative family-oriented services: The case of community/day residential care in Israel. *Family Process, 51*(1), 140–156.

Golding, K. S. (2010). Multi-agency and specialist working to meet the mental health needs of children in care and adopted. *Clinical Child Psychology and Psychiatry, 15*(4), 573–587.

Gottesmann, M. (1993, April). Professionalization of the residential youth care worker—Or a possible alternative in Israel. *Child and Youth Care Forum, 22*(2), 159–163.

Grupper, E., & Mero-Jaffe, I. (2008, February). Residential staff's changing attitudes toward parents of children in their care: Rationale and healing effects on children, parents, and staff. *Child & Youth Care Forum, 37*(1), 43–56.

Hunt, K. F. (2010). The impact of brief play therapy training on the emotional awareness of care workers in a young children's residential care setting in Australia. *British Journal of Guidance & Counselling, 38*(3), 287–299.

Lyons, J. S. (2004). *Redressing the emperor: Improving our children's public mental health system.* Westport: CT: Greenwood.

Lyons, J. S., Bornstein, S., Navarro, P., Rowe, B., & Vasiliadis, H. M. (2010). Youth residential treatment options in Newfoundland & Labrador.

McGorry, P. (2011). 21st century mental health care: What it looks like and how to achieve it. *Australian Psychiatry, 19*(1), 5–11.

McGorry, P. D., Nelson, B., & Goldstone, S. (2012). Providing care to young people with emerging risk of psychosis: Balancing potential risks and benefits. *Neuropsychiatry, 2*(4), 345–353.

McLean, S., Price-Robertson, R., & Robinson, E. (2011). Therapeutic residential care in Australia: Taking stock and looking forward. *National Child Protection Clearinghouse Issues, 35,* 1–24.

McNamara, P. M. (2010). Staff support and supervision in residential youth justice: An Australian model. *Residential Treatment for Children & Youth, 27*(3), 214–240.

Miller, J. R. (1996). *Shingwauk's vision: A history of Native residential schools.* Toronto, Canada: University of Toronto Press.

Preyde, M., Adams, G., Cameron, G., & Frensch, K. (2009). Outcomes of children participating in mental health residential and intensive family services: Preliminary findings. *Residential Treatment for Children & Youth, 26*(1), 1–20.

Preyde, M., Frensch, K., Cameron, G., Hazineh, L., & Riosa, P. B. (2010). Mental health outcomes of children and youth accessing residential programs or a home-based alternative. *Social Work in Mental Health, 9*(1), 1–21.

Rosa, E. M., Santos, A. P. D., Melo, C. R. D. S., & Souza, M. R. D. (2010). Ecological contexts in a host institution for children. *Estudos de Psicologia (Natal), 15*(3), 233–241.

Sainero, A., Bravo, A., & del Valle, J. F. (2013). Examining needs and referrals to mental health services for children in residential care in Spain: An empirical study in an autonomous community. *Journal of Emotional and Behavioral Disorders, 35*(9), 1393–1399.

Scholte, E. M., & Van der Ploeg, J. D. (2000). Exploring factors governing successful residential treatment of youngsters with serious behavioural difficulties findings from a longitudinal study in Holland. *Childhood, 7*(2), 129–153.

Smith, M., & Milligan, I. (2004). The expansion of secure accommodation in Scotland: In the best interests of the child? *Youth Justice, 4*(3), 178–190.

Vidal, C. E. L., Bandeira, M., & Gontijo, E. D. (2008). Psychiatric reform and assisted residential services. *Jornal Brasileiro de Psiquiatria, 57*(1), 70–79.

Zerach, G. (2013). Compassion fatigue and compassion satisfaction among residential child care workers: The role of personality resources. *Residential Treatment for Children & Youth, 30*(1), 72–91.

17 Best Practices in Residential

The Road Ahead

Gary M. Blau, Beth Caldwell, and Robert E. Lieberman

This book was designed to provide an objective look at what is emerging as best residential practice and to provide concrete, practical strategies to improve services and systems. The focus was to review what has been learned from the literature, research, evidence-informed practices, and evidence-informed opinion leaders as well as from the actual experiences and outcomes of youth and family members and a large number of residential providers. What we hope emerged from this comprehensive effort is a coherent picture about how to make residential interventions more effective, including how to better engage youth and families, how to link residential and community providers, how to implement promising and best practices, how to use and incorporate evidence-informed and evidence-based approaches, how to improve the measurement of quality and long-term outcomes, and how organizations can address critical issues, such as trauma and cultural competency.

The editors of this volume share a collective belief that children and adolescents should grow up with a family and in a community, and that out-of-home placements should be prevented if possible. We also believe that if such a placement is required and does occur, the interventions provided should be high quality, and the length of the residential intervention as short as possible. The ultimate goal has been to assist residential providers and their system partners, inclusive of youth and families, to create the services, supports, environments, and policies necessary to improve the lives of children, adolescents, and families. We hope this volume succeeded and met those expectations.

This book's comprehensive look at current residential best practices, and the developing state-of-the-art practices for when children and families require residential interventions, has produced a number of important themes and specific strategies that have proven successful in locations across the country in reducing lengths of stay and supporting youth and families in living together successfully in the community. These clearly demonstrate that agencies and communities have a vested interest in successful outcomes—meaning, outcomes that endure postdischarge and beyond. Finding ways to implement these best practice approaches will help actualize a shared vision that the services provided will result in improved functioning and better lives. Best practice themes that emerged from this book include the following:

- *Residential is an intervention not a placement or a specific treatment*—The research has consistently found that gains developed in residential are only maintained postdischarge in the presence of the active and integral involvement of the family throughout the treatment process, and continuity of support in the community. This has to be a take-home message. And, these data highlight the importance of viewing residential as a specialized intervention for a specific purpose, individualized to the youth and their family. It is simply erroneous to believe that residential will work if it is considered a placement or a treatment. Treating the youth in isolation from family and their community of reference disrupts continuity of experience and compromises outcomes.
    - It is for this reason that the language of this book intentionally referred to *residential interventions*, as opposed to residential treatment or residential care, or other such terminology. Changing the mindset in the field changes the point of focus to the intervention(s) that are provided and to the youth and families being served and supported. Regarding the work of residential as an intervention creates more precise thinking about what specific actions will be effective. This approach also leads to a more productive engagement with staff, community partners, advocates, and the youth and families to define long-term positive outcomes and what steps will be needed to achieve and sustain functional improvements. There are successes highlighted throughout this book that are demonstrated by agencies that have accomplished successful transformations (both initial and long term) to change their residential mindset. These examples show how the process of changing mindsets and practices can yield long-term positive outcomes.
- *Create and sustain partnerships*—Establishing partnerships that link efforts between all providers, inclusive of residential and community, while collaborating as equals with the youth and family, helps create a shared vision of what success should look like and creates a shared responsibility to achieve positive long-term outcomes. This is quite complicated as it involves dialogue, compromise, and sharing of power and responsibility to create coordinated approaches that will support the youth and families to develop the skills and assets to make changes that are meaningful in their own lives.
    - This book has described many strategies for developing partnerships between residential and community providers, along with youth, families, advocates, policy makers, and payers to make system changes that support best practices and improved outcomes. The effectiveness of these practices highlights the importance of these partnerships as a general principle and underscores the importance of the mission of the national Building Bridges Initiative (BBI), which is to encourage this work across the country. As stated in the BBI mission statement, the intent of this effort is to

- identify and promote practice and policy initiatives that will create strong and closely coordinated *partnerships and collaborations* between families, youth, community, and residentially-based treatment and service providers, advocates and policy makers to ensure that comprehensive services and supports are family-driven, youth-guided, strength-based, culturally and linguistically competent, individualized, evidence- and practice-informed, and *consistent with the research on sustained positive outcomes.*

- *Ensure that youth and families have voice and choice*—Practices in residential or community services that minimize meaningful voice and choice are unacceptable. Such practices convey a level of disregard and disrespect that none of us would want to accept in our own lives, especially if the practices impacted our own children. We must constantly demonstrate respect at all levels of service delivery and system development. That is why Chapters 3, 4, and 5 identify specific ways that youth and family voice and choice can be incorporated into the service philosophy and approach, for example, by hiring youth and family advocates and then training them to co-lead transformational strategic planning.
  - In residential interventions in which the placement setting creates a power differential, it is even more critical to systematically embed strategies that engage youth and families to collaboratively identify and address immediate and long-term goals as well as to influence the policies and practices of the program. Youth- and family-driven strategies interwoven throughout this book offer many opportunities to elicit and empower youth and family voice and choice, for example, hiring family and peer support to help youth and families during planning meetings and establishing youth leadership groups that can impact policies and procedures within the residential program and also develop the ability to participate in a variety of community forums that can influence the public and professionals alike.

- *Implement universal trauma sensitive practices*—The public health maxim of acting as if every young person served in a residential program has suffered overwhelming stress and trauma is a critical approach. The inherent characteristics of a residential intervention are rife with elements of loss and powerlessness, and thus inherently retraumatizing. Overcoming this potential impact requires extensive careful work by the organization—from the overall philosophy; to how staff are trained; staff are expected to respond to and interact with youth, families, advocates, and community partners; and the setting is designed, all of which must reflect an approach that ensures that best practices are being used and monitored.
  - Approaches and practices identified throughout the book come together to define and describe a trauma-informed approach, building on the core strategies presented in the chapters on trauma-informed care and

preventing seclusion and restraint. Strategically and tactically, organizing the transformational change process to create trauma-informed organizations is daunting, but as can be seen by the many examples, is quite doable, especially when organizations work to engage everyone in the process—from youth and families served to advocates, direct-care, food-service, and maintenance staff to the CEO and board. The result for those many programs that have taken on this challenge is inescapable: greater engagement, better residential intervention experiences, fewer traumatizing incidences, and better long-term outcomes.

- *Define and measure long-term outcomes*—Defining desired long-term outcomes provides the benchmarks against which progress and long-term success can be measured. Generating a shared vision with the youth and family as well as with community partners facilitates this process and establishes an environment in which any disagreements can be addressed and resolved, with the needs of youth and family served always central, whether at an individual or systemic level.
  - Establishing outcome measurement systems that reflect this considerable hard work fosters engagement and shared responsibility, as well as accountability. More importantly, they lead to greater effectiveness and improvements in the services and supports being provided. Policy and regulatory mandates aside, outcome measurement done thoughtfully and carefully generates the ongoing reflection, dialogue, and learning that residential programs need to achieve success, and it is critical for the ongoing dissemination of best practices. For example, several organizations, such as Damar and Pressley Ridge, along with many others described in this volume, have been able to use post-discharge outcome data as part of a change process to generate transformation in their programs.

Embedded throughout these themes is the importance of cultural and linguistic competence. A progressive residential intervention will carefully consider the cultural beliefs and practices of the child and family, and ask for their voice in expressing the needs and strengths of their cultural experience. As articulated in Chapter 10, outcomes improve when an organization is culturally competent, and all organizations will benefit from ongoing self-assessment about how diversity can inform and enrich the work. In addition, engaging youth, families, and advocates, representing all cultures, as part of developing a shared vision for outcomes measurement ensures that cultural considerations will be included in the indicators of success to be measured.

As reported by several chapter authors, there are many agencies throughout the country that have embarked on the challenge to improve their practice by implementing these themes and related strategies to one degree or another. As is also evident, these have yet to lead to a comprehensive and consistent best practice model; programs continue to implement disparate practices, or sets of practices. While the notable progress, achieved in the last 10 years or so, serves as an important first step for the field, there remains a significant need to define and expand upon these best practice interventions through ongoing research.

Making these changes is hard. If it were easy to understand and implement the five general themes described above, the field would be further along. Reframing residential as an intervention, establishing collaborative partnerships with youth, families, and community, empowering youth and family voice, creating trauma-informed programs and systems, and measuring long-term outcomes, each individually and collectively require significant change—change in mindset, change in culture, change in old habits, change in practice, change in cultural responsiveness, change in ways of thinking. The reality that change is hard, however, is not an excuse to avoid making change. That is what this book has tried to do—provide a starting point so that no matter where an organization is on the transformation continuum, there is a place to begin, or continue, or evolve. As the Chinese philosopher Lao-Tzu once said, "A journey of a thousand miles begins with one step."

The many organizations highlighted in this book have embraced the change process. Sustaining the change is also difficult; in fact, most of those organizations have encountered challenges in sustaining the change. The effort is not a one-time event—the cultural and organizational change strategies highlighted in this book must be renewed and refreshed regularly for the best practice mindset and specific practices to become embedded, nurtured, and sustained in the organization and the community.

For this process to occur, it is critical that the policy and financing environment shift to support the change. This has begun to occur increasingly, with many strategies having emerged, and more to come, for example the extension of the Home and Community-Based Services waiver to PRTF programs, the demonstration of which is described in Chapter 15. Helping the populace broadly understand the stakes as well as the long-term data-supported outcomes that result from best practices can help shift the overall societal mindset and culture. While some may say this is overly optimistic, the evidence in this book from an increasing number of locations is that it can be done, and it is not unreasonable to hope that as the evidence mounts the overall cultural and political mindset will continue to shift to support practices that yield long-term, positive outcomes.

The road ahead in the big picture is to some degree dependent on how well the field does in moving in this direction in the years to come. With healthcare reform a prominent agenda, and an increased focus on accountability for outcomes in the policy arena, there is an opportunity to galvanize support for implementation of best practice changes. This needs to be informed by research, in particular, practice-based measurement and research that can be embedded in residential organizations and lead to identification of best practice models, more robust synthesis of the best practice strategies that have begun to proliferate, and development of new tools to support the ongoing improvements in achieving results. For individual organizations, we hope that the immediate road ahead has been identified in this book. There is much an individual organization can do to respond more sensitively, respectfully, and effectively to the needs and the strengths of the youth and families they serve and support. Each chapter has also identified resources—individuals and organizations that can be contacted—to help on this journey. In addition, each chapter describes specific actions an organization can take, and strategies from which organizations can build a foundation to help children and families recover from serious adversity and life challenges.

The work has started, and the urgency to move beyond the current state of the field is high. In addition to implementing multiple practices identified throughout this book, the editors recommend that all residential stakeholders commit to a number of areas to support improvement on the program, local, state, and national level. Suggestions for additional focus follow:

- Endorse the BBI joint resolution, join a BBI workgroup to support the field in moving forward, and/or download BBI documents to support your own program/city/state (www.buildingbridges4youth.org).
- Become an active member of one of the national or state associations dedicated to supporting residential programs and their community counterparts in moving to the best practice arena.
- Start your own community transformation/improvement partnership workgroup to identify challenges/barriers and develop strategies to address.
- Work with your state to embrace transformation and develop a range of flexible policies and fiscal practices for residential interventions.
- Support efforts at the state and national levels to improve fiscal policies that support better outcomes and best practices.
- Support efforts for licensing agencies and accrediting bodies to raise the bar—to include, within their expectations, a full array of practices consistent with sustained positive outcomes.
- Become part of taking the field to the next steps. Perhaps the next book on residential best practices will have the evidence, practice, policy, and financing data needed to provide information on
  - more extensive evaluations of different fiscal models to support flexibility and long-term positive outcomes;
  - more extensive evaluations of different practices that support engagement, successful work with families, and successful community support networks;
  - development and evaluation of practices to successfully address a range of specialized needs and populations, for example:
    - successfully supporting families and reunification in rural areas, where programs may be multiple hours away from the residential program;
    - successfully working with community schools and identifying creative educational approaches to support youth who have experienced multiple educational failures, often contributing to out-of-home placements;

- • successfully supporting siblings of youth receiving residential interventions;
- • successfully supporting adoptive youth and their adoptive and biological families, and preventing failed adoptions;
- • successfully supporting youth with unique and/or multiple challenges, such as substance abuse, intellectual disabilities, a variety of physical challenges (i.e., speech and language issues), autism spectrum disorders, and complex trauma, and their families; and
- • successfully supporting youth based on specialty areas, such as gender, ethnicities, developmental stages, sexual identification, and/or age, and their families;
- • research on best, evidence-informed, and evidence-based practices used in collaboration with and/or as part of residential interventions (e.g., mentoring; Assertive Community Treatment; Collaborative Problem Solving, Multisystemic Therapy; Trauma Systems Therapy) to ensure they are implemented in a manner that is family-driven and youth-guided, and to assess impact on long-term (i.e., 2 to 3 years postresidential intervention) sustained outcomes;
- • tools, templates, sample documents, and others that support the field in doing its work effectively (e.g., tracking long-term outcomes efficiently; working successfully with families in their homes; implementing wraparound/child and family teams that are successfully integrated between residential and community; surveying best practices in operationalizing cultural and linguistic competence, and developing findings into a fact sheet).

Are you ready to tackle such a book? If that sounds like a challenge, it is. To successfully address all of these areas and move services and systems forward, we believe that it will take a new generation of dedicated residential leaders; a generation willing to embrace and implement the current best practices and to take these challenges head on—a generation of passionate and hardworking residential leaders committed to best practice principles and practices and committed to tracking long-term outcome data and using those data to change and improve everyday residential practice. This generation of leaders must be willing to "do whatever it takes" to build a new model for residential—one that is steeped in family-driven and youth-guided care, cultural and linguistic competence, and trauma-informed approaches versus the traditional focus on "correcting youth behaviors in a milieu" or maintaining a point and level system. This new model must include strong community partnerships and be supported by a variety of flexible fiscal practices and policies.

Please share this challenge with your colleagues and with the youth and families you serve. Please redefine the residential work as interventions, develop robust partnerships in all directions, empower youth and families, implement universal trauma-sensitive practices, and measure and be accountable for your long-term positive outcomes. Doing so will improve the experience of youth and families you serve and support and improve your experience and that of your staff, improve the experience of the communities with which you work, improve your business, actualize your mission, and—most importantly— ensure sustained, positive outcomes for youth and families. The youth and families we are here to serve deserve no less.

Index

Page numbers in italic format indicate figures and tables.

Community Resource Assessment
(CRA) 66
community services 5, 64, 96, 105, 203
core beliefs 41, 165
corporal punishment 110, 121
critical incidents, defining 179
cultural and linguistic competence
(CLC): description of 5; elements of
62–8; how to move agenda for 68–70;
improving 22–3; introduction to 61;
reason for addressing 61–2; resources
for 71; self-assessment checklist for
72–5; summary of 70–1
culture change process: Becket Family of
Services and 162–5; challenges related
to 159–60, 164; Every Day Counts
concept for 158–60; introduction
to 154–5; Mississippi Children's
Home Services and 165–7; parent's
perspective for 155–8; staff hiring
process and 164; strategies for 155–67;
youth advocate's perspective 160–2

Damar Services 100, 175–80
data collection and analysis 114–15, 183,
186, 188
deaths from restraint 111, 121
demographics 62, 142
DePelchin Children's Center 64
dialectical behavior therapy (DBT) 136
direct care staff 83, 88, 100, 101
discharge planning: CLC and 64;
for LGBTQ youth 67; medication
interventions and 147–8; residential
programs and 49
diverse workforce 64, 66

Early Periodic Screening, Diagnosis and
Treatment (EPSDT) 207
education and career development 134–5
EMQ Families First 18, 30, 206–7, *211*
*Engage Us: A Guide Written by Families
for Residential Providers* 37
engaging families: description of 5;
introduction to 34; psychotropic
medications and 144–5; *see also* clinical
engagement strategies; residential
programs
environmental considerations 88–91,
117, 118
environmental distress 82
Europe and Russia, residential programs
in 217–18
Every Day Counts concept 158–60

evidence-based design (EBD) 88, 89
evidence-based practices (EBP) 2, 65,
112–13, 228
evidence-informed best practices 2, 149,
170, 171, 228

families: with adolescents *129*; building
alliance with 39, 41; communication
with 20; creating cultural identities
of 63; focusing on 39–41; including,
in all activities 118–19; matching
engagements to 43; as nonnegotiable
requirement 96; partnership with
19–20; relationships 20, 129, 136–7;
role of 20–1, 177–8; understanding
needs of 36–7
Family Acceptance Project (FAP) 67
Family Advocacy Stabilization and
Support Team (FASST) 101–2
family advocates 159, 160, 162, 224
family-driven care: administrative
practices for 24–6; admission process
for 18–19; children's families and
17–24; consistent approach for 29–30;
defined 4–5, 15–16; overview of
15–17; principles of *16*; research and
impact and 17; resources for 30–1
family life cycle stages 129–30
family partners: culture change process
and 166; different titles of 26;
establishing direct phone line with
24; family-driven care and 18–19;
hiring of 25; organizational change
and 28–30; role of 27–8; successfully
working with 26–9
Family Search and Engagement (FSE) 17,
24, 100
family support: benefits of 29; family
relationships and 136–7; posttransition
success through 17
family therapy 11–12
family time 21–2, 177
family voice and choice 44, 98–9, 209, 224
Federation of Families for Children's
Mental Health ix, 16
female gender considerations 84–6
fetal alcohol spectrum disorder (FASD)
209, 210
fiscal and policy strategies: Children's
Village 207–8; CLC and 67; EMQ
Families First 206–7; funding
approaches *198–9*; funding options
196–7; introduction to 195, 200;
lessons learned from 210, 212; Los

Warwick House program 102–3
WAY Home Program 103–4
wellness and self-care 135–6
wellness recovery action plans (WRAPs)
    51
Westchester County 204–6
workforce accountability 67
workforce development 115–17
workforce diversity 64, 66
wraparound program 155–7, 200–2,
    205–7, 209–10

young adults: addressing policy for 139;
    development of 126–8; family life cycle
    and 129–30; residential interventions
    for 131–9; understanding needs of
    126–31; *see also* transition
youth: building alliance with 39;
    community forums for 57–8; creating
    cultural identities of

63; focusing on concerns of
    39; including, in all activities 118–19;
    leadership training for 56–7;
    physical effects of trauma on 83–4;
    self-advocacy skills for 57; *see also*
    psychotropic medications
youth-adult partnerships 46, 47, 53–4, 58
youth advocates: administrative process
    and 19, 23; culture change process and
    160–2; for youth-guided care 48
Youth Development Institute 119, 155
youth engagement: embracing 52;
    organizational levels of 47–8
youth-guided care: barriers to embracing
    47–58; clinical practices for 50–1;
    description of 5, 46; implementation
    considerations 58–9; resources for 59
Youth MOVE 54, 55
youth peer support 52–3
youth voice and choice 44, 98–9, 162, 209